The Americas That Might Have Been

I A
Generational
Fa Mo
Sn Boo
So Da
China

I B
Descript
Fa Si So So

Scandinavia

II N
Lineal
Narrow
celld (ssated) culd

II N
Lineal
Broad
(lateral)
celth | cale

III
skewed merging

skewed merging

The Americas That Might Have Been

Native American Social Systems Through Time

Julian Granberry

THE UNIVERSITY OF ALABAMA PRESS
Tuscaloosa

Typeface: AGaramond and Triplex Condensed Serif

∞

The paper on which this book is printed meets the minimum requirements of American
National Standard for Information Science—Permanence of Paper for Printed Library
Materials, ANSI Z39.48-1984.

Library of Congress Cataloging-in-Publication Data

Granberry, Julian.
The Americas that might have been : Native American social systems
through time / Julian Granberry.
p. cm.
Includes bibliographical references and index.
ISBN 0-8173-1457-1 (cloth : alk. paper) — ISBN 0-8173-5182-5 (pbk. : alk. paper)
1. Indians—First contact with Europeans. 2. Indians—Transatlantic influences. 3. Indians—
Colonization. 4. America—Discovery and exploration. 5. America—Colonization.
6. Europe—Colonies—America. I. Title.
E59.F53G73 2005
303.48′2′08997—dc22

2004019072

Cover photo: K'inich Janaab' Pakal I, King of the Maya Kingdom of B'aakal (Palenque),
b. 23 March 603–d. 28 August 683, reigned 615–683. Photo by Irmgard Groth-Kimball
(Thames & Hudson). Courtesy of Thames & Hudson Ltd.

OVERTURE

Dreaming alone of yet uncharted seas
Beyond the western curve,
Where, in the womb of the ocean,
Lay continents undreamed and consequence
Past all imagining:
Dreaming alone, Cristóforo Colombo
Struck forth his vision.
The dream becomes the act: *with* signal vigor
This first Conquistador
Ripped from the western sea the riotous wealth
And squalor of the future centuries
And showed, in his myopic prescience,
The shape of our modern world.

—*Columbus: Dream and Act*
A Tragic Suite, by Foster Provost

Contents

Figures

Preface

This book owes its ultimate genesis to four individuals. Franz Boas set me on the direction my professional life has taken, and Mary Haas, Charles Hockett, and Ben Rouse kept me steadfastly on that path over more than fifty years. Without their views of social phenomena, I am sure this book would never have been written.

Though I did not have the pleasure of being taught by Papa Franz, as his students called him, over a number of years toward the end of his life I had the pleasure, as a child of ten or so, of encountering him at family Christmas gatherings. When he discovered that I was interested in other peoples, places, times, and languages, he told me that what I was interested in was called *anthropology*. He also told me that if I wanted to become an anthropologist, which I did, that I must learn *everything* about any people that I studied—their language, their customs, their history and distant past, what they did, and what they thought and talked about. Otherwise, he said, I wouldn't really understand them, and I wouldn't really be an anthropologist. I later learned, when I went on to college, that this holistic approach was the trademark of Franz Boas's philosophy, and I followed his advice—something for which I have never been sorry. It's that holistic approach, fostered as well by my college professors, that led through the years toward its expression in my work and in this particular book.

I am equally indebted to the late Mary Haas, of the Department of Linguistics at the University of California at Berkeley. At the age of sixteen, my interest in native American languages—I have Mississippi Choctaw forebears—led me to write Mary. This kind lady, who had been one of Boas's students and who was the acknowledged dean of Southeastern Indian language studies, not only answered my letter but also sent me a copy of everything she had published on the topic, especially the Muskogean languages, of which Choc-

taw is one, and she became my lifelong friend and mentor until her death in
1996. During a period of more than fifty years, Mary answered my every
question, steering me in the right direction, and encouraging me to keep up
my interest and work on the Southeastern peoples.

Charles F. Hockett of the Departments of Linguistics and Anthropology at
Cornell University—Chaz, as he liked to be called—was, like Mary, teacher,
colleague, correspondent, and staunch friend from my teenage years until his
death in 2000. Like Papa Franz and Mary, he, too, was an old-fashioned holistic thinker—F. S. C. Northrup of Yale once told me that he considered
Chaz one of America's foremost twentieth-century philosophers.

Ben Rouse, of the Department of Anthropology at Yale University, trained
me as an undergraduate student in the niceties of the methods of both archaeological fieldwork and analysis and prehistory. Like Mary and Chaz, his
advice and helpfulness did not cease when I left Yale but have continued un-
interrupted at any time I needed advice on things archaeological right up to
the present.

It is particularly the input of these four individuals, along with guidance
from George Murdock, Ralph Linton, Marvin Opler, Leonard Bloomfield,
George Trager, Henry Lee Smith, Jr., John Goggin, Chuck Fairbanks, and Bill
Sears, my college professors, that ultimately prompted me to address the
student-generated question "What would the New World be like today—
politically, economically, and culturally—if Columbus and the Europeans
had never found it, and how would American peoples interact with the
world's other societies?"

As the 500th anniversary of Columbus's discovery of the New World grew
near in the late 1980s and early 1990s, the same kind of "what if" questions
increasingly arose among scholars. At that time I was privileged to work with
The Phileas Society of Detroit and Ft. Lauderdale in the preparation of a
series of television lectures and discussions on Columbus, his voyages, and the
impact of his discoveries on native America and on Europe. The erudition of
the men and women who participated in this project heightened my feeling
that the native American "what if" questions had to be addressed. The insights
of my colleagues in that venture—Fred Ruffner, Robert Tolf, Consuelo Varela,
Mike Gannon, Foster Provost, Kathy Deagan, and many others—are grate-
fully acknowledged.

I am also indebted to Norman Thrower of the University of California at
Los Angeles, who heard my initial presentation of *The Americas That Might
Have Been* at The Phileas Society meeting in Ft. Lauderdale in November of
1989 and invited me to amplify the theme at a conference the following year

in Los Angeles. His encouragement was greatly appreciated at a time when even many of his own colleagues were vociferously rejecting the hypothesis out-of-hand. In similar vein George Scheper and Florence Hesler of Essex Community College in Baltimore allowed me to present the materials of this study at two National Endowment for the Humanities Summer Institutes on *Texts of the Pre-Columbian/Spanish Encounters: 1492–1650,* one at Johns Hopkins in Baltimore, the other in Mexico City. Those two memorable workshops provided significantly helpful feedback from both faculty and students, and I am most grateful to Florence and George for their kind invitation to work with them.

The end result is *The Americas That Might Have Been.* It is a book I expect practically everyone to find some fault with. Students of the individual native American peoples and cultures I discuss may feel that I have left out some important points in their own areas of expertise. Historians, anthropological theorists, and archaeologists are likely to feel the same way and, almost certainly, to feel that I have taken an alien theoretical bent. The nonspecialist reader, on the other hand, will probably consider parts of the book overly technical or overly compact. Based on what I have to say in these pages, I am sure that many will also feel that I occasionally sound quite anti-European, anti-Spanish, anti-Christian, and, at times, even anti-American. I hasten to let you know that I am none of the above. I am simply reporting and describing, not rendering moral judgments on my own or any other society. My hope, in any case, is that everyone will also find a great deal that is new, interesting, and useful, for the individual societies and cultures, often studied as separate subjects, did not exist in isolation. They were and still are part of a larger whole, and I hope that this book gives some idea of that more unified view.

The University of Alabama Press found two perceptive readers for the manuscript, and these anonymous individuals provided critiques that enabled me to bring my coverage up-to-date and to explain a number of important theoretical points in a manner understandable, I hope, to both the general reader and the occasional professional anthropologist who may stumble across the book. Without the positive input from the staff, the book would not have become reality. To these readers and editors, to The Phileas Society, to my students over the past many decades, to Drs. Boas, Haas, and Hockett, and to my teachers at Yale, the University of Florida, and the University of Buffalo I give my many thanks for all they have contributed to my approach to understanding human nature in general and native American peoples in particular. Needless to say, the "blame" for whatever I have to say and the manner in which I say it falls exclusively at my own feet.

The Americas That Might Have Been

Introduction
The Whys and Wherefores

Setting the Scene

The arrival of Christopher Columbus on the Bahamian island of Guanahaní in 1492, followed by the large-scale European settlement in the Americas, was one of the most profound and momentous events in world history. The impact of the settlers who followed in Columbus's footsteps was of a magnitude beyond description, and, half a millennium later, it is still being felt.

Suppose, however, that Columbus had *not* arrived and that no European settlement, Spanish or otherwise, had taken place in the New World. What if the glories of Aztec Mexico, Maya Middle America, and Inca Peru had survived intact? What part would an Iroquois Confederacy in the American Northeast, powerful city-states all along the Mississippi River in the American Midwest and Southeast, a Navajo Nation and Pueblo city-states in the Southwest, an Eskimo Nation in the Far North, or a Taíno Arawak state in the Caribbean play in American and world politics in the twenty-first century? Would such native American states tip the present balance of power? Would we even recognize a world in which native America played a role?

This kind of fantasy conjecture has rightly been called "the fallacy of historical questions" (Fischer 1970:15–21), and our supposition is certainly a fine example, inasmuch as the Europeans *did* come to our shores; they *did* largely displace the native population of the New World, and most North, Central, and South Americans of today *are* primarily the product of a European rather than a native American cultural background. This particular "what if" question, however, has been asked so often that—hypothetical though it surely is—it is worthy of consideration. Not too long ago, though, it would never have been asked, or it would have been laughed at and considered less than superfluous if it had been. In the unique decade between 1982 and 1992, however, just that question became startlingly common, almost routine.

Why? The governments of most of the New World nations, and some of the Old, were beginning to prepare for a 1992 celebration of the 500th anniversary of Columbus's arrival in the Americas, and many native American peoples were, understandably, preparing for what might be called a counter-celebration of that same event. Many countries formed national quincentenary commissions specifically to make such plans, and conferences and publications on Columbus, his voyages, and the Old and New Worlds of the time proliferated at a staggering rate. Even the national news magazines and media deemed the topic worthy of occasional coverage. Columbus and Columbus specialists found themselves suddenly in an unaccustomed limelight.

Our attention at the beginning of the decade of the 1990s was understandably focused on Columbus the man and his European heritage, in an attempt to explain why the discoveries took place when they did and why and how Columbus became the specific catalyst. As we approached the anniversary year itself, however, questions about the "other end" of Columbus's voyages— the places and peoples Columbus and the Europeans encountered—were not only increasingly common but took the fore.

Not that New World peoples and places were given short shrift before: from the outset of its formation, two of the five themes defined by the United States Columbus Jubilee Commission related to native America, but only later did interest in the Found become as great as interest in the Finder, and now, with the official designation of 2004 as the Year of the American Indian, that interest has become a major focus.

For the man in the street, which includes everyone except the dyed-in-the-wool Columbus scholar and American Indian specialist, the heart of the matter is centered around the changes that European occupation of the Americas wrought. Were those changes "good" or were they "bad"? The popular press would have us take sides and leap on the bandwagon of one extreme or the other. We were asked to look at Columbus and the European settlers either as saints bringing culture and civilization or as evil incarnate, bringing, often with malice aforethought, disease, enslavement, exploitation, and, in many cases, ultimate cultural and physical extinction.

It should go without saying, however, that history and life aren't that simple. Reality is infinitely more complex, for the most noble of motives can spawn devastation beyond imagination and repair, while the most malevolent exploitation can eventually lead to good. Humans prove surprisingly resilient, and they usually, though not always, seem to survive even the most adverse circumstances.

While the native American bore the brunt of social change and became the inevitable underdog, the job of the historian and social commentator is not to lay blame on one party or the other but simply to record. There is both evil and good to report. Whether one considers the results of the voyages of Columbus and those who came after him as the *Beginning of the End* or the *End of the Beginning* remains a subjective and individual decision. "Reality" probably lies somewhere in between, and if there is a "truth," that is where we are most likely to find it.

The average person's questions about the Discovery inevitably boil down to "What have we missed? What would the Americas be like today, if Columbus had never arrived, if *no* European had *ever* come to the New World?" Or, to put it another way, "What would the world be like today, if the native American societies of 1492 still existed, in modern form, of course, without the intrusion of alien lifeways—if they were discovered in 1992 instead of 1492, or, at least, if known to the rest of the world, had been left to their own devices during the past five centuries?" These are mind-bending but not particularly surprising questions. They are those wonderments that must, sooner or later, somehow come up in any discussion of Columbus's voyages and their aftermath, part of those imponderables that eventually occur to most listeners.

The Overall View

There has been some rather good fiction written on this topic—Gary Jennings's 1980 novel *Aztec* and its two sequels, for example—but there has never been an attempt to answer the questions factually except from the viewpoint of the either/or polemics of the dedicated and well-meaning European-American scholar or the equally dedicated and vocal native American activist. There has certainly been no attempt to answer those questions from a critical examination of the data of empirical archaeology, linguistics, and ethnohistory combined. For the general reader, such an attempt is what this volume tries to do, in as understandable a manner as possible—to provide at least one reasoned scenario for such a revision of history, a scenario that avoids taking sides as much as possible yet one in which we hope to have the courage to call a spade a spade.

I attempt to do so without dragging in fictional people or events—other than the initial assumption of a New World without Columbus or Europeans —and without presuming to do any cultural mind reading with regard to what capricious and unforetold events might have happened in a native America untrammeled by foreign influence between 1492 and today. I try to define those societies at that time and extrapolate to the present with the smallest number of assumptions possible. To make such a picture understandable to the general reader, one must draw heavily on comparisons with more familiar regions of the world, those covered in the daily headlines and television newscasts, and we have not hesitated to do so.

While an apology is rendered to the occasional professional reader for what may seem to be gaps in data or idiosyncratic assumptions, the volume is intended not as an exercise in social theory but rather as an overview for the general reader. Its statements come from ethnographic, historical, linguistic, and archaeological data interpreted from the viewpoint of that branch of anthropology that interests itself in the description and analysis of kin structures. This field is unfortunately largely alien these days to the bulk of historians, ethnographers, and even to most general anthropologists. However, a growing number of archaeologists, to their credit, have been paying increasing attention for some time to the interpretive potential the analysis of kin structure has for their raw data and its distribution through space and time (see, for instance, Emerson 1997:232–233, Jenkins and Krause 1986:106–109, 125–130, and Peebles 1970, in their discussions of Mississippian polities).

Many in the anthropological professions will also consider my coverage reductionist as a result of looking at the forest from far above rather than examining all its individual trees from close up and on the ground. Use of this broader view, however, does not imply that the details have not been considered in defining the bird's-eye view. The broader perspective could not have been arrived at without scrupulous attention to detail, and a concerted effort has been made to present *characterizations,* not caricatures, of each of the six native American societies described in this volume.

The attempt, therefore, is to see the forest in spite of the often obscuring individual trees, no matter how fascinating those trees may be. While such a view *is* somewhat reductionist, in that it does not detail all of the social differences that separate societies which otherwise share the same underlying social philosophy and structure, it does not do violence to an accurate data-based examination of the societies in question. It simply presents those aspects of native American societies that link and separate them from one another and, particularly, that have parallels in European, African, and Asiatic societies. The purpose of such a view is to enable comparison, without the obstruction of cosmetic detail. In this approach to the description of native American polities I also hope to show two continents as varied and as brilliant as anything the Old World ever produced.

The Focus

The particular descriptive focus used in this volume needs a brief introduction, explaining the scope, methods, and goals of the field of anthropology as I see it.

In the United States, anthropology has looked at the human phenomenon in a variety of ways over the years. From my vantage point—I entered the professional fray in the 1940s—anthropology began as a formal academic discipline with an emphasis on describing human cultural behavior holistically: the folkways and mores of a given social group as ideally stated and as implemented, its language and literature, its artifacts and structures both present and past, all as an interrelated package of symbolic systems, their linguistic and artifactual by-products, and the human actions that make such systems work. The methods of ethnography, linguistics, and archaeology were seen as inseparable techniques for gathering and interpreting interlocking data on the human behavioral present and past. This philosophy and its methodologies were initiated and fostered in the United States primarily by Franz Boas and a large coterie of his students in the period from the mid-1880s through the 1930s—men and women such as Margaret Mead, Ralph Linton, Ruth Benedict, Edward T. Hall, George P. Murdock, Mary Haas, and many others. With regard to its perception of the manner in which changes took place in human cultures, Boasian anthropology was multilinear and relativist, a point of view stemming from Boas's early training in the empirical sciences in Germany.

For reasons related, I would think, to the increasing specialization in American life in general after World War II, the holistic view gave way by the 1950s to what may be called *compartmentalized anthropology*, increasingly limiting research to the gathering and analysis of data on only a single, specialized aspect of culture—language, artifacts, religion, economics, politics, the arts, warfare, sports, and so on. In theory and method, ethnology, archaeology, and linguistics thus increasingly became separate disciplines, and their practitioners increasingly, though certainly not knowingly, distanced themselves from one another. Each discipline also became primarily oriented toward the description of its data in a synchronic time frame, paying less and less attention to the history and changes of that data through time. Such a highly descriptive, specialized approach was fostered by most universities, and the generation of university professors appearing in the 1960s and 1970s was largely made up of those trained in this compartmentalized view of man and his behavior, few conversant with all the branches of anthropology and fewer yet with any interest in a holistic examination of human cultures.

Then, in the 1960s and 1970s, diachronic approaches were reintroduced. Like their synchronic companions, however, these approaches were compartmentalized by subdiscipline. All concentrated on the interpretation of data through rigid, universalist evolutionary dialectics, rarely leaving room for either variation or irregularities. Such schemes, detailed in the extreme, were given as axiomatic and were added whole cloth to the subdisciplines to which they were said to apply. The underlying assumption, data-based as these practitioners saw it, was that man has evolved not only physically through the millennia but also culturally. "Evolved" was not taken to mean simply "changed," which might be multidirectional, but rather unidirectional, universal change in the same ways and types applicable to all human societies. This approach was soon referred to as the "cultural evolutionary" approach or as "processual anthropology." Such an evolutionary philosophy was not, of course, something new, for Oswald Spengler, Karl Marx, and many others had much earlier voiced such convictions, and the historian Arnold Toynbee had set the stage for a return to this point of view in the early and mid-1900s (see Toynbee 1972). The preeminent British archaeologist of the era, V. Gordon Childe, also used such an approach in his widely read descriptions of the development of human societies (e.g., Childe 1951).

In ethnography these earlier unidirectional evolutionary schemes were given a less literary and more data-substantive base by Leslie White in his *The Evolution of Culture* (1959) and, in a form more palatable to many anthropologists, by Elman Service in his *Primitive Social Organization* (1962) and *Origins of the State and Civilization* (1975). In archaeology Lewis Binford went yet one step farther, using a strictly Marxist scheme to view human cultures, branding all other views as simply incorrect (Binford 1972). In linguistics an even more drastic evolutionary scheme was devised by the philosopher-turned-linguist Noam Chomsky. Just as Binford called his Marxist evolutionary archaeology the New Archaeology, Chomsky seems to have thought of his universalist transformational-generative hypothesis as the New Linguistics. Actually his approach to language data and analysis was a modern version of that put forth by the Hindu logician Panini some twenty-five centuries earlier, with an added evolutionary component (Chomsky 1965). To many of us in the field then, the theories of White, Service, Binford, and Chomsky represented a return to the dataless philosophies of the Middle Ages and an abandonment of the empirical method we had worked so hard to develop and implement in human behavioral analysis. Younger generations of students and scholars, not having participated in the development of the discipline, and impressed by the vociferous missionizing methods used by the advocates of empirical abandonment, espoused the new causes with open arms. The result has been, in the 1970s and well through most of the 1990s, that much of anthropology, in all of its subdisciplines, leapt on the cultural evolutionary bandwagon, using highly mathematicized statistical methods, with carefully selected data only, to support this or that championed evolutionary axiom. Genuine empiricism seemed almost to have vanished from anthropological investigation, replaced by detailed a priori models and technical-sounding explanation.

By the late 1980s there was consequently little left in the way of meaningful, productive dialogue between the subbranches of anthropology, and even the technical vocabularies each developed became largely unintelligible to the others—one still, for instance, hears archaeologists talking about the "unintelligible jargon" of the linguist. Accompanying this change has been the compartmentalization of both meetings and publications of professional organizations, most notably the one-time unitary American Anthropological Association.

As the archaeologist Thomas Emerson has recently put it, these processual schemes have more than just a little dehumanized the past, and in the process "mechanistic societies have been created that operate with functionally motivated, clockwork precision and that respond, necessarily, only to external environmental stimuli" (Emerson 1997:2).

In recent years, however, to the relief of many of us, there has been the beginning of a return to a more holistic view of human behavior and its byproducts. Though this bent is being referred to as a "postprocessual" approach, it is the same thing that Franz Boas and others were talking about and using a century ago. In this almost full-circle return, material culture is once again seen not as something meaningful in and of itself, not as something participating in a rigid scheme of unilinear progression from one "stage" to another, but simply as "text," as "an encoding of the symbol systems that order the lives of those people who created the material culture," a by-product of "the interplay between and among people, their symbolic systems, and each other; the daily and moment-by-moment creation of systems of meaning" (Watson and Fotiadis 1990:614).

What this all means for this volume is that I am using an approach that is distinctly "postprocessual," one that attempts to take a holistic view of the societies under examination and to look at material culture as the result of symbolic systems in interplay with one another through the humans who created them and applied them to their lives. There are a number of ways—in fact a large number of ways—in which such a holistic view can be implemented. Simply because of my own background and training, I have chosen those symbolic structures that men and women have used to define their relationships to one another—their kinship systems—as the hub from which my analysis emanates. Through an examination of these systems as the defining focus for this volume, I suggest not only broad characterizations of the primary behaviors of the people of the individual societies looked at but also non-unilineal, non-evolutionary projections toward those societies' most likely political and economic futures. Some readers will fault me both for use of such an "old-fashioned" view and for abandoning cultural evolutionary schemes. I offer no apologies, for I feel that the resultant picture of native American societies provided by my particular "postprocessual" approach gives the reader a more humanized, less mechanistic view of the world we wish to investigate.

Kin Systems

Kin systems have been defined as sets of "mental rules known, if not accepted, by all members of a society and [the] real social relations that correspond more or less to these norms" (Godelier, Trautmann, and Tjon Sie Fat 1998:387).

The rules themselves are expressed through language as the set of terms that a people uses to describe and address other members of society. The actual implementation of those rules, on the other hand, is seen through physical, ethnographic, and archaeological data, which tell us if and how the rules have been put into effect through space and time. Needless to say, the actuality is rarely if ever the same as the ideal—implementations are the "is," while rules are the "ought" (Godelier, Trautmann, and Tjon Sie Fat 1998:4). Nonetheless, the "is" does not normally stray very far from the "ought," for all members of a society are expected to act in such a way that the social norms will be maintained, if only by lip service, in order "to reproduce the society as they reproduce their own numbers, and hence, up to a certain point, continually give it new life as they themselves endeavor to go on living" (Godelier 1998:389).

It is this focus of *The Americas That Might Have Been* that may seem alien to some social and political scientists as well as to some general readers, for to the minds of many, kin systems are but a peripheral, highly specialized fragment of overall social structure. To those who have dealt with such systems in depth, however, kin structures can be demonstrated to have far-reaching ripple effects on all of a society's broader social concepts and actions, be they political, economic, religious, military, artistic, or otherwise (Asch 1998:146; Godelier 1998:390; Hall 1959, 1966; Hofstede 1984).

This is so because kin terms provide a linguistic map that is at the same time a mirror of society at large, a subset of the social whole. Just as each otherwise specialized cell in a life-form contains the same underlying repetitive DNA configuration unique to the individual, all cells continually replicating the same overall message, so each kin-map expresses not only those unique concepts we call kin structure but also, in miniature, the overall logic of the individual society. It lets every member of the society know where he fits with regard to others in the community and what kinds of behavior are expected of him as well as what kinds of behavior he can expect from them.

Three characteristics of human language-use explain this mirror effect. First, the greater the number of people in a society who use a term or set of terms, the more important the concept underlying the term or term-set is. Kin terms are used by all members of all societies. Second, entities thought of as the same or closely similar are invariably given a single language label. Thus any two or more individuals lumped under the same kin term are thought of as falling in the same category. Third, the more important a concept is to the speakers of a language, the more frequently they refer to it—one does not, that is, spend a lot of time talking about things that one considers of no interest or importance. Kin terms are one of the most frequently used word-sets in all human languages.

Added to these characteristics is the fact that no human society uses more than forty-some kin terms. This small and finite repertoire greatly facilitates kin system analysis, and a number of widely used kinship algebras have been developed to accomplish such analysis (e.g., Lounsbury 1956, 1964a, 1964b; Tjon Sie Fat 1990, 1995, 1998). The realized behavior stemming from the kin-term rules can also be easily defined and described by the standard methods of archaeology and ethnography and can consequently be handled statistically.

The kin terminologies of the world, while numbering in the thousands, may be coalesced into probably no more than twenty subclasses, and these themselves are interestingly only variations of about half a dozen underlying basic types. Why this should be so is the subject of ongoing debate among scholars, but that it is a fact is acknowledged by all who have worked with kin systems. The terminologies and the basic types into which they fall have been well defined by a long line of professionals, beginning with Lewis Henry

Morgan and his seminal *Systems of Consanguinity and Affinity of the Human Family,* published by the Smithsonian Institution in 1871, continuing with the work of scholars such as Alfred Kroeber (1909), Claude Lévi-Strauss (1949), Robert Lowie (1928), and, particularly, George Peter Murdock in his classic *Social Structure* (1949). The publications continue unabated today, the most recent and important contribution being *Transformations of Kinship,* by a number of leading European and American scholars (Godelier, Trautmann, and Tjon Sie Fat 1998).

Kinship terms, then, constitute the primary data used to characterize the societies discussed in this volume. They provide the philosophical underpinnings for the overt behavior described from archaeological, ethnographic, and historical data.

The Mechanics of Kin

Kin terms may make distinctions between individual kin-members according to a number of criteria: (1) the *generation* to which a given family member belongs, (2) the *sex* of an individual, either the speaker or another kin-member, (3) whether one is related to another member of the kin-group by blood (*consanguinity*) or marriage (*affinity*), (4) whether an individual kin-member is directly related by blood to another kin-member (*lineality*) or related in a more distant manner, such as an uncle or a cousin (*collaterality*), (5) whether an individual kin-member is related through another kin-member of the same sex or the opposite sex (*bifurcation*), (6) whether a given kin-member is older or younger than the speaker (*relative age*), (7) whether a kin-member is living or deceased (*decedence*), and (8) whether two or more individuals use the same kin term to refer to each other (*polarity*) (Godelier, Trautmann, and Tjon Sie Fat 1998; Kirchoff 1955; Kroeber 1909; Lowie 1928; Murdock 1949). Individual systems will consider different combinations of these criteria in their terminology, reflecting their underlying concepts according to the general principles of language use described above.

Primarily on the basis of collaterality and bifurcation, Murdock (1949: 223–224) defined six basic kin-types, named for the peoples for whom they were first described: *Hawaiian* (or *generational*), *Eskimo* (or *lineal*), *Iroquois, Crow,* and *Omaha* (all referred to as varieties of a *bifurcate merging* type), and *Sudanese* (*bifurcate collateral* or *descriptive*). On the basis of the same criteria, the latest classification, by Maurice Godelier, defines four types, which are the same as Murdock's except that Crow and Omaha have been linked with the Iroquois type, renamed Dravidian, with Iroquois as a subtype: *generational* (*Hawaiian*), *lineal* (*Eskimo*), *bifurcate merging* (*Dravidian-Iroquois-*

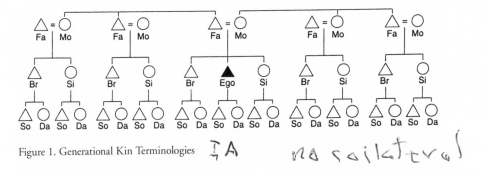

Figure 1. Generational Kin Terminologies *I A* *na saikttrol*

Crow/Omaha), and *bifurcate collateral* or *descriptive* (*Sudanese*) (Godelier 1998:395).

In looking at the kin terminology diagrams in the next several pages, it should be kept in mind that they are generic. That is, individual societies that are classified in one of the basic terminological categories on the basis of lineality, bifurcation, and the other kin-defining criteria, may or may not use the exact set of terms indicated for all of the kin-members so labeled in the sample diagrams. There are many variations on each of the basic themes, and minor differentiations do not invalidate their membership in the specific class to which they have been assigned on the basis of their underlying themes.

If one diagrams the kin-terms that are used in these basic types, an interesting overriding phenomenon becomes apparent. *Generational* (or *Hawaiian*) and *descriptive* (or *Sudanese*) systems do not distinguish between lineal kin (mothers, fathers, brothers and sisters, children) and collateral kin (uncles, aunts, cousins, nieces and nephews). *Generational* kin terminologies, shown in Figure 1, usually use no more than two sex-based reference terms per generation, so that all relatives are, in essence, lineal kin—all are fathers or mothers on the generation above EGO (the speaker), all are brothers or sisters on EGO's own generation, and all are sons or daughters on the generation below EGO. The criterion of collaterality is ignored.

Descriptive terminologies, on the other hand, as Figure 2 illustrates, use a separate, descriptive term for each individual related to EGO. All collateral relatives are referred to by labels which use only lineal terms—*father's-brother* instead of uncle, *mother's-brother's-son,* for example, instead of *cousin.* Thus descriptive systems, in spite of the name and in spite of the fact that some individuals *are* collateral, use only lineal terms to refer to all members of the kin-group. Notice that neither *generational* nor *descriptive* systems make a *terminological* distinction between lineal and collateral kin.

The degree of distinction between closely related lineal kin and more dis-

No registers! (handwritten annotation)

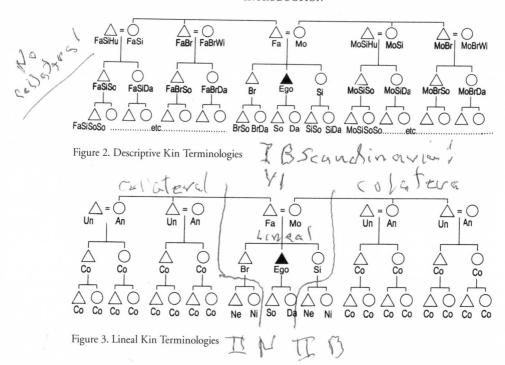

Figure 2. Descriptive Kin Terminologies

IB Scandinavian, (handwritten) *collateral* (handwritten)

collateral (handwritten)   *YI* (handwritten)

Lineal (handwritten)

Figure 3. Lineal Kin Terminologies   *IB N II B* (handwritten)

tantly related collateral kin may be referred to as *lateral spread*. With regard to lateral spread, both *generational* and *descriptive* systems are *unitary*—that is, there is no terminological differentiation made between lineal and collateral kin. Individual kin-members are described simply as members of a single, specific generation regardless of lineality or collaterality. When necessary to distinguish between the two unitary subtypes, *generational* or *Hawaiian* systems will be referred to as type *IA* systems, and *descriptive* or *Sudanese* systems as type *IB* systems.

In contrast are the kin systems referred to as *lineal* (or *Eskimo*) and *bifurcate merging* (or *Dravidian, Iroquois, Crow,* and *Omaha*). In the case of *lineal* systems, of which ours in the English-speaking world is one, collateral kin are usually referred to by one set of terms (uncles/aunts, cousins, nieces/nephews, etc.), while lineal kin are referred to by another set of terms (parents—mothers/fathers, siblings—brothers/sisters, children—sons/daughters), as shown in Figure 3. There is, in brief, a clear terminological separation of the two varieties of kinsman.

In the case of those *bifurcate merging* systems called *Dravidian* and *Iroquois,* shown in Figure 4, the same stricture applies, though in this instance a

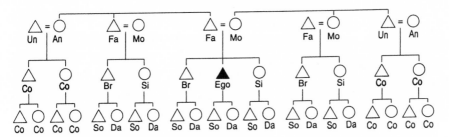

Figure 4. Merging Kin Terminologies

same-sex sibling of either parent (father's brother or mother's sister) is called by a parent term, mother or father, and the children of such individuals are referred to by EGO with the sibling terms brother and sister. In like manner, the children of such same-generation "cousins" are called son and daughter. By contrast collateral kin related to EGO through a different-sex sibling of either parent (father's sister or mother's brother) are referred to by EGO by collateral terms—uncle/aunt, cousin, niece/nephew.

Both the *lineal* and the *Dravidian* and *Iroquois* varieties of *bifurcate merging* kin terminologies, that is, show a two-way or *dualistic* lateral spread, since two subsets of reference kin terms are used on each generation, in contrast to the unitary spread of *generational* and *descriptive* terminologies, which use a single term-set for each generation. Further, lineal *Eskimo* systems show a narrow dualistic lateral spread in terms of the number of kin-category members described by lineal terms, while the *Dravidian* and *Iroquois* systems show a broader but still dualistic spread, pulling some but not all collateral kin into the lineal terminological fold. The former will be called type *IIN* (*narrow* lateral spread) systems and the latter type *IIB* (*broad* lateral spread) systems.

Those *bifurcate merging* systems traditionally referred to as *Crow* and *Omaha* show yet a third and different type and degree of lateral spread, as indicated in Figures 5 and 6. Essentially similar to the *Dravidian* and *Iroquois* terminologies, they skew generational reference upward on one side or the other of the kin-group—father's side for *Omaha*, mother's side for *Crow*, using a special third set of kin terms for that group of kin-members. Thus these kin terminologies have a three-way or *trinary* lateral spread, in contrast to the unitary spread of *generational* and *descriptive* systems and the dualistic spread of *lineal* and *Dravidian/Iroquois bifurcate merging* systems. The trinary systems of kin terminology will be referred to simply as type *III*.

Lateral spread has not been used before as a criterion for the definition of kin terms. If, however, it is indeed true that the inner DNA-like core of all

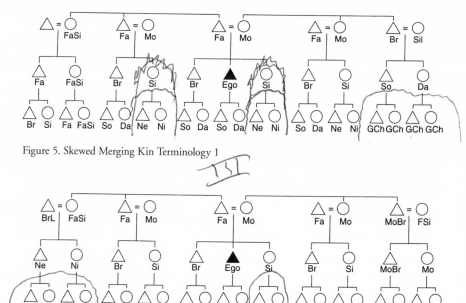

Figure 5. Skewed Merging Kin Terminology 1

Figure 6. Skewed Merging Kin Terminology 2

sets of language terms in the language of a given society is the same, as social data worldwide suggest, then the type and degree of lateral spread evidenced in a society's kin terminology should also be replicated in all other aspects of behavior such as politics, economic pursuits, religion, sports, the military, the arts, and so on. An examination of spread, in other words, should prove very useful in the overall description of a society, and it is specifically this approach that forms the nexus of the social characterizations and political projections discussed in this volume.

Social Change

Based on definition of their social systems in 1492, the last section of the book, *The Future of the Past,* suggests the possible political and economic directions the social systems of an unencumbered native American New World might have taken between 1492 and the present.

Does this mean that the philosophical inner core of those societies remained static and unchanged through this long 500-year period? Of course not. The processes of social change involve and shape all societies at all times, and they can lead to significant interlocking alterations in every aspect of socially prescribed behavior, including the language term-sets that are used to refer to those behaviors. Kin systems and their referent terminologies are not immune to these processes. The Russian anthropologist M. V. Kryukov has recently proposed a thorough, data-based schema for the investigation of kin system drift over time (Kryukov 1998), and earlier suggestions concerning the nature and directionality of such drift were proposed by the ethnologist George Peter Murdock of Yale and the University of Pittsburgh (Murdock 1949:323–352). Both the Murdock and Kryukov models are based on what Kryukov calls *synchro-diachronic* analysis, in which a series of separate time-based or synchronic data-sets (in this case kin terminologies) are gathered from a sequence of different time periods and examined diachronically through time to determine the types, numbers, and pace of alterations that have taken place from the earliest data-set to the latest (Kryukov 1998).

It is from the research of Murdock, Kryukov and others that we can define both the general pace at which kin terminology changes occur and the manners in which such terminologies and their overt realizations modulate from one terminological type to another. Murdock has demonstrated that social systems, including kin systems themselves, change not as a result of the imposition of a new social system from an outside culture or from peaceable diffusion of a new system from another society but rather by a process of internal readjustment stemming from long-term contact, peaceable or otherwise, with other societies and from the altered conditions of life such contact creates (Murdock 1949:198–224).

Murdock has also established that neither kin systems nor the overall social system in which they operate change whole cloth. The individual facets of such systems alter separately, differently, and at varying rates, depending on the nature of the outside pressures they are subjected to. Rules of descent, determining the manner in which goods, rights, and privileges are passed from one generation to another—through the father's or mother's line or both—are, for instance, relatively immune to change and alter only with exceeding slowness if at all. Marriage rules and rules of residence, on the other hand, defining where a newly married couple will reside, are particularly vulnerable to alteration and may change rapidly as a result of contact with outside societies which have different residence rules. Since changes in residence rules redefine the relationships between individuals in the society, they can eventually lead to alteration of the overall system itself and its individual aspects—the economic system, technology, property ownership and distribution, government, and religion, for example.

Kryukov's synchro-diachronic investigation of Chinese kin terminologies

(Kryukov 1972) and P. A. Lavrovski's similar much earlier analysis of changes in the Russian kin system (Lavrovski 1867) have defined the usual pace at which the alteration of social systems accomplishes itself. All indications are that kin systems and their terminologies change very slowly. The Chinese system, for which we have excellent written sources going back well over 2,000 years, for example, remained stable from approximately 200 B.C. until A.D. 400, a period of 600-plus years (Kryukov 1998:297–298), and the Russian system remained stable from an indeterminate period B.C. to at least A.D. 1100. That is, such changes seem to take between a minimum of 600–700 years and a maximum of 1,100–1,500 years to complete, and then only if urging historical forces prevail on the overall social system in question, as they did in the Chinese and Russian cases.

Can we, in addition, predict in what direction a given kin system and its related terminology will change over time—from type *IIB* to type *I,* for example? Can we suggest evolutionary, developmental schemes that dictate toward which type of kin terminology and behavior a social system will move? Many have been suggested—Kryukov 1998, Service 1975, White 1959, as well as the more well known classic evolutionary schemes of Karl Marx, Oswald Spengler, Arnold Toynbee, V. Gordon Childe, and others. None, however, has so far been conclusively demonstrated. We can only say that a change from one type of social structure to another can and will occur given the proper provocation. We do not, though, know with any degree of clarity even what constitutes a provocation for the change of any aspect of a social system other than to point out that the contacts a society has with other societies through space and time seem to provide the major impetus.

Social systems, in brief, are not static entities, and, yes, we know that historical and geographic factors play the major role in determining the nature, direction, and rapidity of social change. Even taking these factors into consideration, however, it would only be peripherally possible to predict the direction and pace of social change that specific native American societies might have undergone between 1492 and the present. In some instances archaeological evidence can be most enlightening in this regard, as it has been in defining the development and decline of the Mississippian city-states, but there are no demonstrably universal trends, Marx, Spengler, V. Gordon Childe, Toynbee, and others notwithstanding.

Thus, the core social philosophies of the native American societies discussed here, with minor exceptions discussed in Chapter 13, will be presumed to have remained relatively intact during the short 500-year period of our concern. Generally speaking, while there would certainly have been surface, cosmetic changes in the cultures of New World societies over the course of half a millennium, it would nonetheless seem unlikely that any major change in overall social direction would have occurred. At least what we are calling *unitary* societies would, in world outlook, likely have remained unitary, *dualistic* societies would likely have remained dualistic, and *trinary* societies would likely have remained trinary. Can we be certain of this? Again, of course not, because the kind of study this volume is concerned with, though data-based, is admittedly speculative. The likelihood that we are correct, however, is greater than the likelihood that we are mistaken, and the view of a presumed native American political future from this perspective provides, at least, a rational scenario, a scenario not considered before on the basis of objective data.

The Individual

At least some readers will have wondered by this point, particularly after the discussion on social change, what role, if any, the individual plays in society. Am I relegating the individual and his ability to innovate to a nonposition within social systems? Am I implying that all individuals in a society will blindly adhere to the social norms, acting like a mindless herd of cattle? The answer is a decided "of course not." While no individual in any society can, as it were, get out of his own skin to show behavior totally at odds with the expected social norms without being branded, and rightly so, as psychotic and dealt with accordingly, many individuals will, indeed, find solutions to cultural problems that are atypical and unique to them alone, solutions that at least on the surface remain within the accepted norms yet do not occur to the majority of the members of the society.

Most of us do this in limited realms of behavior: We find ways around expected behavioral norms that do not totally rock the boat. But the areas of behavior in which we do this are usually not momentous and do not affect society at large. Nor do we exhibit such idiosyncratic actions frequently. In most societies from time to time, however, there are also some individuals who become expert, through experience and experimentation, in manipulating the entire social system to their individual needs by seeming to follow the expected path and yet breaching even the most far-reaching mores, usually in the political, economic, or ritual-religious arenas.

How does an individual succeed in such behavior without being branded as a social outcast? Historical example makes it clear that all extreme individualists—we have come to call them either dictators or messiahs—succeed by presenting their own desires as expressions of society's most firmly held ideals, by appealing, that is, to what has come to be called "patriotism."

This term, by definition, means determined adherence to society's most dearly held ideals. When an individual becomes so expert in understanding what these ideals are, it is a short step to presenting his own social program as *the* road to implementation of those ideals. By such an appeal, particularly if made in times of general social stress such as warfare or internal strife, such individuals are enabled to rise to positions of leadership rather quickly.

One might expect such behavior to be more predominant and more successful in some types of societies than in others, and indeed this is the case, but individuals with this kind of ability to control and innovate occur in every society. They are most frequent in trinary social systems—Genghis Khan, Attila the Hun, Saddam Hussein, and Osama Bin Ladin—and least frequent in unitary systems—Mao Zedong and Slobodan Milošević—with dualists holding the middle ground—Napoleon, Hitler, Pol Pot, and Idi Amin. The rationale for these distinctions will be discussed in some detail in Chapters 4 through 6.

These examples are, needless to say, the exception, for most individuals do content themselves to "follow the rules" of their own accord and learn when and where they may break the rules without getting into trouble. These men and women rarely rise to positions of individual power in any social system but content themselves with their individual lives and goals. It is, however, the extreme social conservatives who rise to positions of control, and, consequently, it is often those individuals who, paradoxically enough, become catalysts for social change.

There were individuals of this kind in pre-Columbian native America, as will be seen in the descriptions of the six native societies dealt with in this volume.

Summary

In this volume we will assume, then, on data-based grounds, that world cultures belong to one of three broadly defined social-cultural types—*unitary, dualistic,* or *trinary*—described through reference to the lateral spread expressed in their kin terminologies, these same characteristics reflected in all other aspects of a culture's social ideals and actions.

This reductionist scheme is, interestingly, one also used in the political scientist's and economist's overall characterization of the nations of the modern world—the Free World, the Communist World, or the Third World. Free World nations are, if one examines their social structure, what we have defined as *dualistic* societies of both types *IIN* and *IIB,* all with capitalistic economic systems and something approaching representative government. Communist World nations, in the general definition of that word, view communal, group ownership of economic goods and property and something approaching government by committee as their social norm. Limited today to China and a small number of other nations, these are those states whose social structure we have defined as *unitary* societies of both types *IA* and *IB*. Third World nations are, with some exceptions, those with a *trinary* social structure, largely concentrated in the Near East and Central Asia, as well as North Africa and parts of Central Africa. It is interesting that such a tripartite defining scheme would have been devised on economic and political grounds alone, without reference to kin and other social structures and that kin system analysis would lead to the same point. This coincidence would seem to lend additional credence to the suggestion that what one aspect of social structure indicates as normative—in this case the economic and political system—is also indicated as normative by all other social structures. None of this, of course, necessarily lends a mantle of truth to the *Unitary-Dualistic-Trinary* model, but it does imply that it has pragmatic analytical utility, and that is the reason for its use in this volume.

(Handwritten annotations:)

Free World
II N IIB
Capitalist
Representative
Govt

Command
I
Communal
Group Ownership
Gov't by Committee

Third World
IIP
Tribel?
Islamic

Part I
IN THE BEGINNING

1

Men Out of Asia

Europeans and Early Americans

In the late 1980s and early 1990s, when Euro-Americans and their European confrères were preparing to celebrate the 500th anniversary of Columbus's voyages to the New World, a visitor from another world would be led to assume, on the basis of that jubilation and the interminable, often unresolvable, scholarly arguments, that these "Americas," wherever they may have been, were new to the eyes of man 500 years ago, a virgin land open to the happy settler.

Nothing, of course, could be farther from the truth. The Americas already had a population in the many millions when Columbus set foot on Guanahaní, the island he renamed San Salvador, on October 12, 1492. The Southern Hemisphere's largest civilized nation in territorial extent, the Inca Empire of Tawantinsuyu, was located in the Americas. The larger urban centers were ten times the size and population of the largest European cities: The metropolitan heartland of the Aztec Empire had in excess of 11 million souls, and the Inca Empire had a population of at least 12 million.

Native American scholars and scientists were investigating and debating topics as abstract and complex as any ever discussed in European universities of the age (León-Portilla 1979). The New World was hardly a land of vacant fields and forests populated by a few ignorant savages eagerly awaiting the largesse of Christian Europe.

The point is, of course, that while we must not give short shrift to the momentous occasion of October 12, 1492, which did indeed alter world history, it should be remembered that the Americas were *not* discovered in 1492. Discovery and settlement had come at least 12,000 and possibly as many as

20,000 years earlier, and, for better or worse, credit goes not to Europeans or Africans but, rather, to Asians (Billard 1993). The year 1492 marks only an accidental European finding of the New World—a very late one, and the second or perhaps third such European finding at that.

Why then the inordinate amount of attention to Mr. Columbus and his venture? Because, whether one views 1492 as an event to celebrate or an event to be despaired of, its impact was destined to be far more devastating than anything that had happened to the New World before or that has happened to it since. There is much still to unravel in the events of that fateful year and what came after.

Our calendar, however, has no Discovery Day in the broader sense, only a Columbus Day—as though the Men Out of Asia had never arrived, had never created their own lifestyles viable enough to last some 120 centuries and more. The common Euro-American view inculcated in us all from childhood ignores the fact of Asian discovery. These men and women have been viewed in our particular mythology of history as at best the Noble Savage, with emphasis on the latter word. Little, if anything, is seen as lost in their physical and cultural demise. It's as if the past really began just yesterday and began, at that, from a clean slate.

To continue this gloomy mood a moment longer, it should be well noted and remembered in this context that New Explorers, anywhere and at any time, tend to frown on what they consider the "inferior" and "alien" lifestyles of the "natives" they encounter. History makes it clear that such colonialist adventurers always attempt to re-create in some detail their own home turf, no matter how bizarre or unsuitable to the new cultural and physical locale. The charming gabled Dutch buildings of Jakarta and Surabaya, lolling in Indonesia's humid clime, attractive leaded windows carefully sealing the interiors from the frigid winters of Holland which never arrive, provide one incredible example. The northeastern pillbox homes of California, Arizona, Nevada, and Florida, marching row after narrow row, climatized with artificial frozen air and set amidst uniformly manicured lawns planted with midwestern grasses, offer another.

These are just the benign examples. The more insidious, directly life-threatening ones—the Roman conquest, the Crusades, the Mongol Invasion, the Nazi Holocausts (the never-referred-to Gypsies as well as Europe's Jewish peoples), Palestine, Viet Nam, Cambodia, Angola, Central America, Kuwait, Afghanistan, Iraq, and Wounded Knee—these genocidal bloodbaths need not even be invoked. One could, of course, go on forever, offending every settler in all the earth's "new" lands, past and present, bloody or benign. But this is not the point.

The point is that the newcomer tends to feel that his "new world" did not exist, or at least not properly so, until his own momentous arrival. In the Americas this meant the unconscious, or at times conscious, obliteration of all that came before. Just as natives of the Southwestern and Southeastern United States "Sunbelts" have seen their centuries-long lifestyles largely vanish, along with the landscape, in less than 50 years of "invasion" from the American Northeast and Midwest, so the Europeans of 1492 devoured the Welcome Wagon that met them. Less than 50 years later the Juggernaut had completed its rounds in the Caribbean Basin, and after another two centuries, little remained anywhere even to remind the Europeans that the Americas had not always been theirs.

A few feeble attempts were made, in retrospect, to halt such genocidal excesses—the *Laws of Burgos* of 1512, the *New Laws of the Indies* of 1542, or the meetings of the Spanish monarch with his advisors in Valladolid in 1550, for example—and the Spanish monarchs frequently requested that laws requiring humane behavior toward the Indians be enforced. But all of this came too late. Systems of de facto slavery, though given euphemistic de jure labels, were in place at least as early as 1501 (Gibson 1988:96–98). The damage had long been done and institutionalized as the *encomienda* and later *repartimiento* in Spanish lands, dividing up the population like so many cattle with forced allegiance to a European master, or as the native reserve in English lands, insulating the European from Indian contact and containing the Indian within restrictive, arbitrary boundaries. A few pockets here and there were inadvertently left, increasingly to become curious time-warped enclaves of the *noble past.* In later days these have been "protected" by the well-meaning but insipid and ineffectual assistance of those whom the Pueblo peoples refer to with disdain as *The Yearners,* those governmental and private groups and individuals who create in their own mind's eye an Indian past and personality that never existed and project it onto their charges. This peculiar brand of neocolonialism is still as much in vogue in Washington, Ottawa, Brasilia, Lima, or Guayaquil as it was in the first Spanish settlements on Hispaniola in the years just after 1492. The world's worst and surely most obscene example is what is happening today in Amazonia. With rare exceptions these relict societies had already been culturally and physically traumatized beyond recovery in an America no longer American.

Though it may sound so, none of this is said to dwell inordinately on the evils of Spanish, Portuguese, English, Dutch, French, Danish, Swedish, Russian, or Euro- and Afro-American settlement. The attempt is not to raise the banner of militant Pan-Indianism, though there is much to justify its raising. The point is made to clarify the fact that permanent cultural contact is rarely "good" from anyone's point of view and always destructive. By its very nature it puts in gear the mechanisms of change, and the old rarely survives in the face of the new.

Judgmental concepts of good and bad, right and wrong, while easy to invoke, have no honest place in viewing the panorama of human history and social differences. While we may quake and be appalled at human nature, we can only note patterns, and the most salient of these for New World history since 1492 has been the sometimes accidental but more often purposeful wholesale destruction of native America, reaching the end of its rampant and inexorable path just today. No other continent except Australia has seen the total destruction of almost all its native lifeways and peoples at any other time in known human history. The Europeanization of the Americas stands as a unique and astounding fact of human action.

None of this is said in neglect of the decimation of native American populations and the physical breakup of social entities caused by the inadvertent introduction of Old World diseases. These diseases have been shown to have been a powerful and major factor in the social disruption and loss of life throughout the native Americas in the decades and centuries immediately after 1492 (Dobyns 1983, Ramenofsky 1987, Smith 1987, Thornton 1987, Verano and Ubelaker 1992). In some cases the societies that Europeans saw had already been struck by European diseases which long preceded their initial New World carriers, so that our first views of many native societies are of cultures already in trauma. Thus there is evidence from the Southeastern United States and in the Inca Empire that disease-related population decline preceded an actual European presence (Dobyns 1983, Smith 1987:58–60). In Peru, for example, a measles epidemic that seems to have begun in or before 1500 caused massive loss of life 27 years before the arrival of Francisco Pizarro and his Spanish forces (Dobyns 1983). In other instances the new diseases came with their bearers, and decimation came only in the decades after conquest. So in the Valley of Mexico alone the estimated 1519 population of 11 million was reduced to 325,000 by 1579 at least in part as the result of smallpox and other introduced diseases (Ramenofsky 1987). Political and other cultural factors can, inadvertently or consciously, stem the spread of disease, and some diseases are endemic to specific societies, but bacteria and viruses know no national or cultural boundaries. In the New World they spread far more rapidly than the Europeans who carried them.

Nonetheless, epidemic-related population reduction, while it disrupts and destroys, and while it may in cases be culturally controlled, does not in itself disabuse one of an individual's innermost beliefs and behavior. Population reduction certainly does contribute to the disruption and alteration of social units, sometimes drastically so. If community elders die, some traditions and knowledge, some perhaps critical to overall cultural maintenance, may indeed be lost, but there has been no instance documented by archaeological or other data, anywhere on earth, in which such a reduction in and of itself caused the total breakdown of an underlying sociocultural philosophy (see Smith 1987 for a particularly fine discussion of this point). The onset of a state of cultural normlessness, *anomie,* demands an overt human agent and conscious effort. So, for example, the last surviving Yahi Indian of California, Ishi, befriended by the anthropologist Alfred Kroeber in the early 1900s, was still a Yahi in language, culture, and behavior in spite of the fact that there were no other members of his society with whom to interact. It takes more than disease to disabuse one of the soul.

Economic and political disruption and forcible Christianization were the tools of European expansion in the New World as they were in other regions to which Western Europe turned—a heritage at least partially of the Crusades. Lest one think this an overly harsh assessment, be reminded that, for example, Spanish clerics of the 1500s routinely read what were called *requerimientos* to their new charges—always in Spanish, a language the Indians did not understand, and usually read to them at an inaudible distance (Gibson 1988:97). These "requirements" uniformly stated that the Pope had given the Indian lands to the Spanish monarchs and went on to say that they, the friars, *demanded* (not requested or hoped) that the Indians accept Christianity and acknowledge the sovereignty of the King and Queen of Spain (Hanke 1938). Some of the more explicit *requerimientos* continued by adding that if the Indians did not do this the Spanish would take their lands by force and subject the people to the yoke of the Church and Their Highnesses, that they would make them, their wives and children, slaves, seizing their property and doing "all the harm and evil we can" (Hanke 1938). Should the Indians refuse conversion to Christianity, the *requerimientos* stated that the Spanish would wage "justifiable" war against them, and the resultant damages would be "your fault and not ours" (Gibson 1988:97, Hanke 1938). The modus operandi, in other words, was clear, brutal, and direct. That method of handling other peoples was certainly rooted in the fifteenth-century Spanish concept of *limpieza de sangre,* purity of blood, which led to the expulsion of the Jews and Moriscos or Christianized Moors from the Iberian peninsula in the years immediately following 1491. Promulgated largely through the Inquisition, the intent was openly to enforce a single faith for the nation as well. It was these concepts and methods that went with the Spanish to the New World and formed the basis for interaction with its native populations (Ewen 2001).

While the English and other colonizing countries did not verbalize their intentions quite as bluntly as the Spanish, the philosophy was the same. This was hardly benign conquest, and it was the grist of the mill that eventually destroyed much of native America. The phenomenon was not just an example of medieval European mentality in action but an essentially timeless expression of the Pogo philosophy "And, by God, if they don't want to be free, we'll force them to be free." This was reflected clearly as late as the so-called Indian wars of 1800–1891 in the American West and Florida and the brutal, literal "ethnic cleansing" of California natives well into the last quarter of the nineteenth century (Castillo 1978:107–115, Mahon 1988:144–162, Utley 1988: 163–184). The same philosophy, buried deep beneath the labels of anthropological and linguistic "research" organizations, characterizes present-day missionization programs and governmental "economic aid" programs throughout Indian America, North and South. The rapid demise since the 1960s of the native peoples of Brazil's vast Amazon Valley as a result of the economic, political, religious, and cultural conversion programs spawned by government agencies in Brasilia and missionary organizations from the United States, is a major case in point. European colonialism in the Americas is far from dead, and the tactics of implementation used in the 1500s have only been muted, slightly.

Let us be fair, however, for the phenomenon I have just described is not the sole property of the European world. It can be seen in just as virulent a strain in the Chinese invasion and occupation of Tibet in the 1950s and the subsequent violently enforced economic, political, and religious conversion of the Tibetan people, or in the Indonesian invasion and occupation of East Timor in the 1970s, or the Khmer Rouge genocidal bloodbath in Cambodia during the same decade. Europeans do not hold a limited license on forced cultural conversion. It is an unfortunate by-product of that human foible called *ethnocentrism,* the firm belief that one's own culture and society are moral and good and that all other societies and cultures are somehow inferior and in need of indoctrination toward a right way of life. The U.S. invasion of Afghanistan in 2002 and the joint U.S.–British invasion of Iraq in 2003 and the subsequent "democratization" policies of the U.S. and British administrations in those occupied lands provide up-to-date examples.

The First 12,000 Years or So

The Asian discovery of the Americas, it must be said, was no more a premeditated "Eureka" kind of event than the European rediscovery some 120 centuries later. It was an accident, as are so many great events. The Asian presence in the Americas was the result of the gradual migration of small groups of people, moving on to greener pastures, little aware that a new world almost the size of the old lay ahead of them. The migration began from Siberia, sometime in the dim and uncertain period between 12,000 and 20,000 years ago, and was complete by the early centuries before and immediately after the birth of Christ. During this long period American societies developed alone, uniquely Asian-American, and a bewildering number of native societies came into being. They showed greater language and cultural variation than existed then or now in all of Europe, Africa, and Asia combined. The monolithic concept of *The Indian*, a single entity all the same from the Arctic to Tierra del Fuego, is as bizarre a caricature as the concept of the *Inscrutable Oriental*. It was a simplistic figment of the European and later Euro-American imagination. It has never been so.

We know the route these first migrants took—across the Bering Land Bridge between Siberia and Alaska during the glacial ages—but the full details remain a mystery yet to be elucidated by archaeology. What we can say for certain is that these migrants came from North Asia, bringing with them the tools, social norms, and world outlooks of their Asian cultures. These, not European lifeways, were to form the woof and warp of the New World personality and the complex societies Columbus and the Europeans confronted in the years after 1492.

Between the early years A.D. and 1492, the Americas had few additional visitors from the Asiatic world, so far as we can tell. All the expansionist urges of the medieval Orient led not eastward but westward, toward Europe. They culminated in the near conquest of Vienna by the Mongols early in 1241 (Morgan 1986:1–2). Had not, in fact, the Great Khan Ogadai died suddenly in faraway Karakorum on December 11, 1241, causing a retreat of the Mongol occupying armies to join the *kuriltai* election council in Mongolia, Europe might well have become part of that mighty Asiatic empire and world history vastly changed (Chambers 1979:109–113).

What eastward Asiatic expansion there was led no farther than the island of Cipango, modern Japan, where the Mongols suffered one of their few crushing defeats, thanks largely to a devastating typhoon (Morgan 1986: 120–121). Medieval Asia did not participate in the rediscovery of the New World. Its interests lay elsewhere.

Nor does Africa seem to have participated in the settlement of the New World until the time of forced population movement through the Atlantic slave trade in the years after the first European settlement. Various ingenious archaeological and ethnographic theories have been put forth over the years to prove a pre-Columbian African presence in the New World, but so far none has held up under close scrutiny. From about 12,000 years ago until 1492, the New World was part of the Asian realm, both physically and culturally. Internal development over this long time period produced new and unique cultural patterns alien even to the original Asian homeland, but there is no inkling of anything European or African in that fabric until after 1492.

Europe, Spain, and Columbus

Late medieval and Renaissance Europe present quite a different picture than the medieval Orient. In the late 1400s Europe was ready to move outward— politically, economically, and, most important, philosophically and psychologically. The Age of Exploration was the natural culmination of a 500-year struggle toward national identity and economic success. Largely encapsulated in the tenets of European Christianity, which had become a rigid and strongly proselytizing agent for acquisitive change through the centuries-long period of the Crusades, the European *Zeitgeist* was looking for new worlds to conquer, worlds of concrete goods and bodies as well as of the mind and soul.

Contact had been made in the 1200s between the Roman Church and the Court of the Great Khan in distant Karakorum, and the Polos had demonstrated that overland contact with China and the Far East was possible and profitable (Morgan 1986:26–27). The journey, however, was long and fraught with difficulties and danger. The sea route around Africa had been found in 1488 and was to lead on to India in 1497. Columbus, in fact, was present when Bartolomeu Dias returned to the Portuguese court in December of 1488 and recounted what he had found on rounding the Cape of Good Hope. The tribulations of this route, too, seemed almost to outweigh its advantages, and the consequent urge to go west to get east became suddenly stronger in the mind of at least one man. Educated tradition implied that it should work, that the route was probably short, and that there was only the sea to contend with. A foresightful Columbus had already sought funding for this route in 1484 from the Portuguese Maritime Advisory Committee, only to be turned down.

All of this, of course, eventually conspired, in Columbus's person, to fulfill Seneca's prophetic words in his *Medea:* "An age will come after many years when the Ocean will loose the chains of things, and a huge land lie revealed; when Tethys will disclose new worlds and Thule no more be the ultimate"—a quotation to which Columbus's son Ferdinand later added a poignant hand-written note in his father's own copy of Seneca's work: "This prophecy was fulfilled by my father the Admiral in the year 1492."

But Thule was indeed to remain the ultimate westward land to Europeans for many years after the first centuries A.D., and Iceland and Greenland were the farthest afoot Europeans went in that direction until the year 986 (Magnusson 1980:181–220). In that year Norsemen from Iceland quite un-knowingly penetrated the eastern shores of northernmost North America (Magnusson 1980:212–247). Had all things been equal, the Icelanders and Greenlanders would sooner or later undoubtedly have pressed onward, south-ward from Vinland into North America's main landmass.

But the devastating Black Death of 1349 so decimated Northern Europe—killing, it is estimated, one out of every three—that European ties to Iceland and Greenland were temporarily severed, and the island Norsemen were forced to fend for themselves (Gad 1984:556–576; Kleivan 1984:549–555). There was neither energy nor manpower for westward exploration. By the end of the 1400s, the 3,000-strong population of Viking Greenland had vanished entirely, a mystery still largely unsolved, and the Norse of Iceland had been severely reduced in numbers (Kleivan 1984:554–555).

And so, with one possible exception, the Americas remained isolated from the European Old World until the epochal rediscovery by Columbus in 1492. The possible exception is the likely presence on the Labrador coast of Breton and Basque whaling settlements prior to the year 1500 (Curtsinger and Schlecht 1985, Grenier 1885, Laxalt 1985, Tuck 1985). Documentary re-search by Selma Barkham in the Basque archives at Bilbao, Burgos, and Oñate in Spain has revealed a definite and considerable presence at Red Bay, Labrador, in the early to mid-1500s, but how much earlier these intrepid ad-venturers were present in the Americas is as yet not known. That there was interaction with the native American Inuit people in the 1500s, however, is indisputable, for Inuit artifacts have been recovered at the Red Bay site (Tuck 1985:53).

But let us go back to our original premise. Let us suppose that Columbus hadn't rediscovered the New World and that no European had headed out into the Ocean Sea and its unknown perils. Let us also assume that the over-land routes charted to the Orient by the Polos had provided all the economic and psychological rewards that Europe needed. If there had been no contact with the Americas until yesterday, what would we find? What would the Americas be like today?

To say "what if" this centuries-long chain of events had not happened, this temperament that produced the mind and personality of a Columbus had not existed, is, of course, almost to negate the events of European history from the conversion of Constantine to Christianity in 324 to the final expulsion of the Moors from the Nasrid Kingdom of Granada, seven months to the day before Columbus's August 1492 departure from Palos, the same day that the caravel bearing the last of the Sephardic Jews of Spain departed the same port for the safety of Muslim Morocco. "What if" ignores the whole fabric of the Western European past and—perhaps unkind to say, but factually accurate— its acquisitive, proselytizing, and inquisitorial apogee, which came quietly and unbeknownst to all at the treaty of surrender signed by Abu-'Abd-Allah, the last Sultan of Granada, and Their Catholic Majesties Ferdinand and Isabela in the Hall of the Ambassadors of the Alhambra palace on January 2, 1492.

Nonetheless, knowing that our "suppose" did not happen, this is exactly what we are going to assume—that somehow, for unfathomable reasons, just as the Asians did not remain in constant touch with the Americas, just as the Norsemen and Basque whalers did not penetrate farther south than the Labrador and Newfoundland coasts, so the Western European secular and ecclesiastical elite did not reach that frenzied pitch of Outward Urge for the Faith and for exploitation that did, in fact, hold it in thrall.

Let us imagine a Europe still embroiled in internecine strife, still battling the more civilized and tolerant Moor, still certain that Asian riches could come from overland trade—a Europe perhaps still full of missionizing zeal for the souls of man and economic zeal for his body and belongings, but one in which such urges were directed inwardly within the Old World itself. If this had been so, then let us look at an America pristine in 1492 and in the years that followed. Let us extrapolate from that world to an America never conquered between 1492 and the present.

2

America 1492

When Columbus landed on the Bahamian island of Guanahaní on October 12, 1492, there were among the estimated 3,000-plus native tribal groups in the Americas twelve polities of various sizes and kinds similar to what we think of as *countries, nations,* or conglomerates of *city-states* actively pursuing their courses in the New World. Though the term *nation-state* is a Western European concept, and one that did not come to fruition even there until the 1500s, it is not far from correct to say that these twelve American polities were characterized by the same essence that characterizes European states today. They were conscious aggregates of individuals speaking the same or closely related languages and with essentially the same cultural norms and practices. They were striving to express this unity through political and economic independence, and they were either urban entities or something close approaching that settlement type.

Of the twelve, six had largely succeeded in the venture and would compare readily to the largest and most sophisticated of European, Asiatic, or African states of the 1400s. Of this *Big Six,* as I shall call them, two, the Pueblo Towns and the Mississippian Cities, were in North America; two, the Aztec Empire and the Maya Kingdoms, were in Middle America; one, the Taíno Kingdoms, was in the Caribbean; and one, Tawantinsuyu, the Inca Empire, was in South America.

All of the Big Six were urban—five of them brilliantly so—with large groupings of people concentrated in highly stratified urban settlements. As in the Old World, some were literate—the Maya and the Aztec—and some were not, though all had large literatures verbally transmitted from one generation to the next. All possessed carefully defined political and economic structures. All had an erudite class and an organized system of schools. All were as concerned with things religious as was Western Europe, though usually in ways less universalist, less xenophobic, and more tolerant of differences than the European Christianity of the times. All of the attributes we associate with nationhood were abundantly present in all of the Big Six as well as in nascent form in the remaining six. One, Tawantinsuyu, *Land of the Four Quarters,* was the largest political entity the Southern Hemisphere has ever seen.

As in the Old World, these states were not static things but were constantly changing, vibrant social organisms, spreading and shrinking through space and time, struggling with their own internal problems and vying with each other for regional political and economic power.

The five mainland powers—the Pueblo Towns, the Mississippian Cities, the Aztec Empire, the Maya Kingdoms, and Tawantinsuyu—were the outgrowth of earlier, sometimes more spectacular, urban cultures. The Chaco Canyon pueblos of New Mexico gave rise to the historically known modern pueblos. The earlier Poverty Point settlements led ultimately to the cities of the Mississippi River Valley in the period from 1000 to the middle 1400s. Teotihuacán and Toltec Tula in central Mexico were forerunners of the México State founded by the Aztecs in the 1200s. The Maya cities of Guatemala, Honduras, and Belize and the Maya-Toltec cities of Yucatán gave rise to the Maya States of the 1400s, and Tiahuanaco in Bolivia, an Aymará city, was the clear forerunner of Inca Tawantinsuyu. All of those earlier societies were in many ways greater than their fifteenth-century descendants. Their offspring, however, consciously retained and profited from much of the grandeur and sophistication of the earlier cultures, framed in what were more pragmatic national settings. These forerunners were like Greece and Imperial Rome to Europeans.

The list of the 12 polities follows, with the Big Six italicized.

North America

1. *The Pueblo Towns* of Arizona and New Mexico
2. *The Mississippian Cities and Towns* of the Mississippi River Valley
3. The Northwest Coast Towns of British Columbia

Middle America and the Caribbean

4. *The Empire of the México* (Aztecs) in Mexico
5. The Tarascan State in Mexico
6. The Mixtec Kingdom of Mexico
7. *The Maya Kingdoms* of Mexico, Belize, and Guatemala
8. *The Taíno Kingdoms* of Hispaniola and Puerto Rico

Figure 7. Major Native American Societies, 1492

South America

9. *Tawantinsuyu* (the Inca Empire) of Peru, Ecuador, Bolivia, Argentina, and Chile
10. The Chibchan Tairona Towns of Colombia
11. The Chibchan Muisca Towns of Colombia
12. The Guaraní Towns of Paraguay

Columbus himself saw only the Taíno Kingdoms on the islands of the Greater Antilles, semiurban and well organized but not of the calibre, from our point of view today, of the remaining Big Six. It was left for later explorers and conquistadores to make contact with the larger polities.

The League of the Iroquois in what is now New York State might, with some reservations, be added to this list. Possibly formed long before the arrival of the Europeans for mutual protection and trade among all the Iroquois-speaking peoples—the traditional date for its foundation is A.D. 1390—the league was a unified power to contend with until the end of the American Revolutionary War. The lack of fully urban centers is the only characteristic of the league that makes it not a candidate for unified nationhood (Fenton 1978:296–321, Trigger 1978:344–356).

Between, around, and among these polities and chiefdoms were other native American peoples, organized but not yet in 1492 on the verge of urban nationhood. Several were, much later, to embark on that usually abortive path but only in the period 1600–1900 in reaction to European and Euro-American encroachment. These were (1) the Cherokee of North Carolina, Georgia, and Tennessee; (2) the Creek Confederacy of Georgia, Alabama, and Mississippi; (3) Kalaallit Nunaat (the Inuit Eskimo people of Greenland); (4) the Dinétah (Navajo) of Arizona and New Mexico; and (5) Nunavut (the Inuit Eskimo of north-central and eastern Canada).

Of the original twelve plus the Iroquois Confederacy and the later five native American societies that achieved a considerable degree of political and economic independence, the only ones to survive into the twenty-first century have been the Pueblos of the American Southwest; the Eskimo of both Canada, as Nunavut, and Greenland, as Kalaallit Nunaat; the Navajo in Arizona; and the Guaraní in Paraguay. All except the Guaraní and the Greenlanders are, however, dependent on the largesse of other governments and exist within a peculiar, ambivalent framework allowing neither full self-government and cultural expression nor full economic and moral support from the Euro-American master governments. Thanks to Denmark's enlightened policies, the Greenlanders' future seems assured, and Guaraní has the distinction of being the sole native American language to have official status in any American state, its native Paraguay.

The Maya of Yucatán, Belize, and Guatemala, as well as the Inca of Peru, through variant effective tactics, have kept the essence of their social norms intact, and they may yet redeem parts of their former national independence. It will likely take a bloodbath to achieve it, a prognostication particularly applicable for the Inca of Peru through the determined efforts of the nativistic movement known as *El Sendero Luminoso,* "The Shining Path." This movement is popularly and erroneously interpreted as another bloodthirsty, money-hungry South American drug ring or simply a group of Marxist thugs, compared by the self-styled but unknowing media cognoscenti to the Medellín and Cartagena drug cartels. Regardless of its methods—predictably callous with regard to human life, as in all societies that act well in unison—its goals are about as similar to those of the drug cartels as green cheese is to the moon. The goals of El Sendero Luminoso are nationalistic, not self-seeking.

The native insurgents of Guatemala, with a totally different underlying social system and philosophy, are less motivated to act in unison. The political success of Maya insurgency, though still in abundant evidence (Jones 1989), is consequently less certain. The Maya independence movement has, however, already been recognized in Guatemala with the 1992 Nobel Peace Prize award to Rigoberta Menchú, an outspoken and highly intelligent Mayan activist.

The Americas of 1492, in short, presented a widely varied and complex cultural and social panorama to the incoming Europeans, a panorama whose nature, contrasting with that of the newcomers, would lead to the inevitable dissolution of the New World's greatest native polities. It is this picture that will be described in the following chapters.

Part II
THE INNER MAN

3

Native Philosophies of Life

The four chapters in Part II are stage setters. Their purpose is to provide a general description of the social systems that are known to have characterized native American societies in the past as well as now. Most of the examples in these chapters, however, concern recent historical events in modern European, African, and Asiatic societies with which the reader is already familiar—chosen because they show the general social characteristics we wish to explain. The chapters in the following section of the book, "The Matrix of Lives," will describe the same social philosophies at work in the native American Big Six.

The reader will also find the statements in this and the following three chapters to be rather repetitive. With due apologies, I have purposely said the same thing a number of times in different ways with the expectation that such repetition will etch the primary concepts with which we must deal indelibly on the reader's mind.

The Forest vs. the Trees

To begin, it is worth pointing out, as we did in the introduction, that there is enough archaeological and ethnohistorical data available to describe the workings of most of the larger independent American polities at the end of the fifteenth century in considerable detail. To do so society by society in this chapter, however, would cause the fabric of the forest to vanish because of the individual trees. We will consequently leave such a discussion to the six chapters of the "Matrix of Lives" section and concentrate our attention here solely on an abbreviated description of the larger overall views, distilled from the whole by description of the overriding social philosophies of thought and action most readily seen in those societies' kin systems. It was these concept sets that characterized native American life then, as they still do today.

One should also not lose sight of the fact that the Big Six were but the tip of the iceberg, the most successful of the native American societies. There were hundreds of other smaller native groups productively following their own lifeways as well. The lack of data and description of these equally valid social expressions should not be taken as an indication that they were unimportant. It is again, rather, a case of wanting to show the dominant characteristics of the most visible American societies that had developed organizational structures similar to the European nation-state at the time of European intervention.

The social philosophies of the Big Six, delimiting behavior in every walk of life, were in some cases not dissimilar to European philosophies, but most were distinctively different, some radically so. It is here that one can see the rationale for native American actions, what the peoples' goals were and how they reached toward them. It is these underlying philosophies that determined the manner in which the American societies interacted both with each other and with the European invaders.

Such social philosophies, however, it should hastily be pointed out, do not *determine* anyone's behavior. They do not dictate how an individual must behave. Rather they give a set of viable socially accepted options from which to choose a course of action. One may not, however, go outside such options without incurring disapproval or punishment from the other members of the society. The goal in this section is to describe the broadly defined sets of positive options available to members of the native American Big Six in 1492.

Social Systems and the Scheme of Things

The considerable amount of data we have from social anthropology, archaeology, ethnohistory, and native literatures indicates that in all the cultural and linguistic diversity of the pre-Columbian New World, only the three social option sets we described earlier (*unitary, dualistic,* and *trinary*) were used. These are not just New World themes, however, for they also occurred then and do now in European, African, Asian, and Pacific societies. They are distributed, though, in a quite different manner in native America than in other parts of the world.

We have suggested that solid data make it evident that these three varying themes and their incidence around the world form everywhere the fabric of human alliances and consequent international, intercultural relationships. It was clearly the differences between these themes that determined the nature of European-American interaction in the fifteenth and sixteenth centuries, and it was such contrasts that created the New World problems that appeared rapidly after 1492.

While the definition of social themes described here knowingly neglects some of the idiosyncratic dissimilarities that separate otherwise similar societies, the themes are, nonetheless, statements of social ideals, and these are what we wish to emphasize. The fact that worldwide no human social group actually operates in a such a simplistic manner does not negate the importance of such themes, and their presentation without cosmetic detail allows us to see better the commonalities that link, separate, and differentiate societies from one another.

It is also such commonalities in interaction that define cultural problems and their resolutions. Any interaction, whether peaceable or forceful, if protracted, will alter the social system of both contact partners over time. We have discussed the extremes earlier—the obliteration of one people's culture by invading settlers from another culture. At times, such as the Norman Conquest of England in 1066, a new culture results from the blend of invader and invaded, built largely on the norms of the invader but incorporating large segments of native social beliefs and practices as well.

More often than these extremes, however, one sees a subtle interplay of contact through trade and general social interchange. Under such circumstances an infinite variety of mixings of native and nonnative cultural norms may occur.

The point is that the picture we will paint here of America's Big Six in 1492 is a purposefully simplified one. The simplification, however, has been done with an exceedingly fine comb to ensure that the accuracy of the data is neither skewed nor stretched. The result is a canvas in outline rather than one fully filled in, but the outline is true to life, not fiction, and the colors and forms one sees express reality as we know it from the surviving archaeological, ethnographic, and historical data.

From the perspective of viable option sets for the solution of social problems and for handling the everyday affairs of the world, *unitary* societies, anywhere, see each situation in which a decision must be made as amenable to only a single solution. Such a solution is pragmatically applicable only to the specific time at which the decision is needed and not dependent upon any constant, universally valid principle. It will simultaneously contain both positive and negative components. *Dualistic* societies, on the other hand, see two viable, polarized solutions, one absolutely good, the other absolutely bad—without a viable middle road. Such solutions do not vary from time to time; they are seen as universally valid, regardless of the time at which the decision is needed. *Trinary* societies, unlike either *unitary* or *dualistic* societies, see each problem as solvable by one of three alternatives, one good, one bad, and one a preferred compromising middle ground. The alternative solutions are not time dependent but are based on a set of constant, universally applicable norms.

How can we be so certain that only these three problem-solving philosophies characterized native New World societies? We can because of the wealth of surviving ethnohistoric, linguistic, and archaeological information. A great deal of what we know—a surprise to most—comes not from the inferential secondary data of history and the spade of the archaeologist but, rather, directly from the surviving oral and written literatures of many of these early peoples, which is voluminous in the extreme. The people, in a very literal sense, speak for themselves.

For example, the surviving repertoire of Aztec literature, put down in Latin script in the Náhuatl language during the years immediately following the Spanish conquest of Mexico, is greater in volume than the total surviving repertoire of Classical Greek, which so eloquently expresses the Western European philosophy of life. It equals in bulk all the surviving writings of the Romans throughout their long history. It is also as varied in subject matter, including histories, legal and business treatises, mythologies, philosophical works as profound as those written by any Socrates, Plato, or Aristotle, educational, instructional, and moral tracts, social descriptions, medical treatises, religious writings, and poetry as beautiful as that of any other world literature. We have lesser but similar works for the Maya, the Iroquois, the Navajo, the peoples of the Pueblos, the Kwakiutl, and many other native American peoples. From such centuries-old works, in conjunction with the details of everyday life provided by archaeology and the ethnohistorical record, a surprisingly vivid and detailed picture of native American social philosophies emerges, and the *unitary, dualistic, trinary* descriptions are abundantly verified.

Here we are also able to find the terms that each people used for members of its kin-groups—the immediate and more extended family, social leaders, and other groups within the society. From Zuni literature, for example, we know that kin are divided into three groups: one's direct line from one's parents, one's relatives on the mother's side, and one's relatives on the father's side. Examination of the names for members of other social groups indicates the same use of a three-way division, and, in fact, any aspect of Zuni life that one looks at is talked about with terms that describe its components in a three-compartmented manner. If we perform the same examination with the kin-naming labels of Maya societies, however, we will find that they are segmented into only two groups—one's direct-line relatives and everyone else. In Maya societies one will find that whatever aspect of culture is examined, it will be talked about in terms that describe its components in a dualistic, two-compartmented world.

Thus the definition of *unitary* (as with the Aztec), *dualistic* (as with the Maya), and *trinary* (as with the Zuni) social themes comes from standard anthropological analysis, particularly kin-naming, and is built on the exhaustive data bank provided by the literatures of the societies themselves. Such an analysis of social systems may seem complex, and at times it is, but the rewards are great, for from such scrutiny emerges a definition of the underlying philosophy of the people who use the social system.

Summary

The very basic description of *unitary, dualistic* and *trinary* social systems and their underlying philosophies presented here may have left the reader wondering what all this really has to do with native America in 1492. The answer will become increasingly evident in the following chapters. We will see the widely variant *unitary, dualistic,* and *trinary* social philosophies and systems in operation in an American setting, most of their inherent pitfalls abundantly apparent.

In this framework we can see why native America reacted to European intervention in the ways it did and why the results were so devastating. The results were not an "accident" of history, but, like most of history, the foregone conclusions of social contact and confrontation.

In the following chapters, two polities—Tawantinsuyu (the Inca Empire of the Quechua people of Peru) and the México Empire (the Aztec Empire of the Náhuatl people of Mexico)—represent the unitary theme; two—the Maya Kingdoms of the Maya peoples of Central America and the peoples of the Mississippian Cities and Towns—represent the dualistic theme; and two —the Pueblo Towns of the American Southwest and the Taíno Kingdoms of the Greater Antilles in the Caribbean—represent the trinary theme.

Evidence from all parts of the world also tells us that these underlying option sets stubbornly defy change and endure for centuries through all but the most devastating and permanently disruptive adversities. They are what give voice to the culturally *inalienable rights* of a society. In the Americas the descendants of the Big Six American polities still adhere to the social patterns of their ancestors, and it seems safe to suggest that regardless of the cosmetic, surface differences that would obviously have developed during the passage of five centuries, the Americas would have been looking at us today through the same social filters with which they viewed us in 1492.

4

Unitary Norms
The Asian Perspective

Of the Big Six, the México or Náhuatl people of the Aztec Empire of Mexico and the Quechua people of the Inca Empire of *Tawantinsuyu* in Peru were both, in spite of great differences in outward cosmetic culture, unitary societies. The same underlying type of social system also occurs frequently on the less-organized tribal level in many other parts of the Americas. The unitary worldview is, in fact, characteristic of all those societies around the world that utilize kin-naming terminologies referred to as *generational* (Type *IA*) or *descriptive* (Type *IB*), as described in the introduction.

In the rest of the world, most native Pacific and Far Eastern societies, with the exception of Japan, Korea, Tibet, Bhutan, Cambodia, and Mongolia, utilize such systems and their accompanying unitary reflections in the other aspects of their cultures—the governmental system and politics, the economic system, the religious system, the military system, and the arts and literature.

The world's largest and most powerful unitary state today is China, with a *descriptive* or unitary *IB* social system (Kryukov 1972, 1998). Unitary states of either subtype, *IA* or *IB*, as can be seen from the map in Figure 8, are rare in Europe and Africa, *IA* occurring in Europe only in historically quite modified form in Serbia and Montenegro and type *IB* occurring only in Scandinavia.

The tenets of unitary logic constitute what most Western Europeans other than Scandinavians view as illogical, accompanied by what is often perceived as either self-serving, sometimes even devious, or opportunistic action. This is because unitary peoples are the world's best pragmatists—the end, carefully conceived, always justifies the means, equally carefully executed. Unitary peoples invariably solve problems with whatever solution will produce positive results *at that particular time,* not on the basis of presumed universal rights-vs.-wrongs. European and Euro-American societies, which belong to dualistic

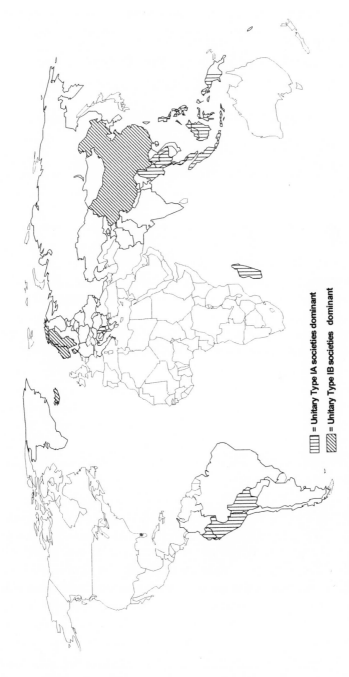

Figure 8. The World's Unitary States, 2004

⊞ = Unitary Type IA societies dominant

▨ = Unitary Type IB societies dominant

social systems, do not understand or know how to cope with such fluctuating norms, norms not pinned down to concepts of absolute, unchangeable and inflexible value sets. That inability has led not surprisingly to the caricatured concepts of the hyper-*Pragmatic Scandinavian,* the volatile *Quixotic Yugoslav,* and, particularly, the *Inscrutable Oriental.* We do not know how to deal with such societies, and we generally do not fully trust their governments, for we have learned that a promise or decision made today may be completely reversed later, even tomorrow, and what seems a firm contract today may be broken without compunction six months from now. Often perceived as betrayal by nonunitary peoples, such fluctuation is simply seen as logical, intelligent, and normal social-preservation behavior by unitary societies.

A major reason for the lack of trust the majority of Western societies places in unitary systems is that these societies come as close to literal all-encompassing economic, political, and cultural communism as one can imagine, not just in terms of the distribution and ownership of goods but also in terms of broad social rights, duties, and privileges. We are *not* referring to the self-styled Marxist Communism promulgated by Marx himself or its Lenin-altered practice in the former Soviet Union and Eastern Europe over the past 70-plus years. That philosophy, which became in effect Marxist Fascism in the hands of European societies, has almost nothing in common with literal communism other than the euphemism of the name. Neither Russia nor the other Eastern European societies have ever practiced communism in the social sense of the word, and it is enlightening to note that these societies have all in recent years returned to the Western European, dualistic, nonunitary fold where they all by nature belong—a foregone social conclusion expected and prognosticated by many over the past five decades.

The true communist societies of Asia and the Pacific, and even those few in Europe, are unitary in the sense that every member of society is ideally considered of equal importance and worth. Men and women are different-but-equal partners in society and life at large. Some unitary societies place greater emphasis on males than females—China, for example—and some place greater emphasis on females, but by and large the duties and privileges of both sexes are much the same. Scandinavian societies provide prime examples of the implementation of such social equality. There is in unitary societies usually only a single social class—*The People*—though in the larger unitary societies specific groups are "elevated" by election, sometimes by birth, to greater levels of social responsibility, with emphasis on the latter word. Such individuals, however, are raised to this position explicitly to *serve* the people—never to become a privileged, hereditary ruling class. The truly democratic monarchies of Denmark, Sweden, and Norway are examples of this "born-to-serve" philosophy in action. There is, consequently, no such thing as a "social ladder" to success. Success can come equally to all who honestly participate in following accepted social norms and striving toward accepted social goals.

As pointed out earlier, even such seemingly mundane things as the kinship terms of unitary cultures show a oneness. Among other things, this means that a person can show the same affection toward a cousin's children as to one's own and that one can go to uncles and aunts as freely as to biological mother and father for parental advice and help—aware, of course, that a father's brother or mother's brother is a different kind of "father" than a biological father, but that difference is not considered a major factor in determining his behavior or one's own.

Setting some individuals below the social norm, even in slavery, does occur in these cultures but comes almost exclusively as punishment for crimes of "individualism." The social group—from family to nation—is infinitely more important than the individual. Difficult as it may be to fathom, competition and individual expression, if participated in at the expense of the group, are considered *the* most antisocial behavior possible and are stringently, at times ruthlessly, suppressed. We saw this principle operating to its fullest in China in Tien An Men Square in June of 1989 and, earlier, in the famous trial of the Gang of Four in 1976, when Chiang Ching, Chairman Mao's widow, and three others were tried and convicted explicitly for "crimes of individualism." In Western European and Euro-American societies they might have been rewarded for their insights.

Temporal and spatial boundaries are of little concern to unitary societies. Neither is viewed as a segmented system in which ownership or control of parcels belongs to individuals. Rather both are looked at as natural continuities belonging to society at large. Time, for example, has no *past* or *present* or *future,* and though such concepts may, of course, be indicated by various kinds of circumlocutions, they are rarely needed, since context generally makes it obvious to the hearer what is meant. Spaces are the property of the group at large, and the group's ownership boundaries stop only wherever the group stops, or wishes to stop, not where someone else's ownership begins. Even economic goods often belong to families or other social units rather than to their individual members. The individual use of goods is dictated largely by need, not simply by acquisition or individual desire. Both the Chinese economic system and the Scandinavian "welfare state" serve as examples.

Emphasis in the manufacture of goods is on uniformity of use effected in enduring, traditional style. Utility alone, economy of price or function for their own sake, and stylistic innovation are attributes rarely considered except for export trade to countries in which such characteristics are known to be important.

Warfare and the urge toward territorial expansion are frequent, since no land is seen as belonging to any particular individual or set of individuals. Because of the lack of emphasis on the individual, loss of individual life in warfare is unimportant so long as the group survives and achieves its goals. The lives of the conquered, for the same reason, are unimportant. They may be obliterated or absorbed into the social whole, often through a system of forced indenture and reeducation. The two-century-long period of Viking expansion from Scandinavia westward into the Atlantic, southward into Britain and mainland Europe, and eastward into Russia is a case in point, as is the 900-year Polynesian settlement of the entire central and eastern Pacific and the Chinese occupation and absorption of Tibet in the 1950s (Bellwood 1979, Fitzhugh and Ward 2000).

Any tipping of the scales toward individual expression is considered dangerously antisocial. All are expected to think, act, and look as much the same as possible. The job of political leaders is to ensure the survival of the system, not to rule as individuals and not to protect the rights of the individual. The Cult of Personality, as the Chinese call it, is severely punished, as Madam Mao found to her dismay.

The former Yugoslavia (now Serbia and Montenegro), ruled by committee, was Europe's only partial example of a modified *IA* unitary state until its predictable dissolution. Though historical events in the Balkans over the centuries have altered the original system considerably, Serbia and Montenegro still exhibit this underlying social philosophy.

It is also of interest to note that both China and Yugoslavia early on broke their close ties with Russian Communism, which with its rigid party class structure of Ins vs. Outs was "communist" by label alone and quite alien to the genuine social communism of unitary societies.

Unitary cultures see unity in all they behold. Concepts of absolute good vs. bad, right vs. wrong, even yes vs. no, do not exist, as they do with us, as simple, clear universal polar opposites. "Rightness" and "wrongness" are always conditional, dependent upon the circumstances of the moment. A "yes" answer today may be a "no" answer tomorrow. *Yin* and *yang* do not, as we erroneously suppose, refer to polar opposites within a whole. They refer, rather, to the fact that all shades of possible interpretation and action, including opposites, are simultaneously inherent in any event, mixing and mutating to meet the moment. In psychological parlance, unitary societies are *Gestaltist,* and, as pointed out earlier, strongly pragmatic societies when it comes to alliances—an enemy today may be a friend tomorrow and today's ally may become tomorrow's nemesis, in both politics and economics.

The Chinese languages provide numerous examples of this lack of binary oppositions. No distinction, for example, is made between action words (verbs) and naming words (nouns). When a word is used in what to us is a verbal fashion, it does not have to be positioned clearly in time. The context and the addition of other words indicates such nuances when necessary, but it rarely happens, for the idea of positioning an action rigidly and specifically in a time slot is alien to Chinese, as it is in the languages of most unitary groups.

In unitary cultures there is never need for compromise, for any situation will in itself fluctuate in Gestalt manner between paramount good, paramount evil, and everything in between, depending on the circumstances at the time. It is the duty of the members of such societies to get the most from any situation. The very idea of compromise is both puzzling and meaningless in such a context. It is always the whole that counts, never its individual components. The keynote to unitary thought is certainly pragmatic self-submersion in a relative world. As we shall see later, this is not only a Chinese philosophy of life, a Scandinavian philosophy of life, but also the philosophy underlying the social systems of both the Inca and Aztec peoples and is what has enabled their cultural—if not national—survival to the present.

5

The Dualistic View
The European Norm

Of all the chapters in the book, this is the one that will cause some readers the greatest discomfort. To some, in fact, it will probably seem downright offensive. To readers of both kinds I offer an apology beforehand, for no affront is intended. Such negative reaction is likely to be engendered because the social characteristics discussed reflect the way of life that most of us who were born into the European, Euro-American, and Afro-American world consider right and proper. Consequently any description of that lifeway, other than one completely favorable, may be construed by some as a biased attack.

The offense some may feel is based on a human universal: the feeling that the tenets of one's own culture are inviolable, the only morally correct natural order of things. This sentiment, mentioned earlier, is referred to as *ethnocentrism.* It is the strong belief that one's customs are part of universal human nature and, therefore, inherently good. This belief is accompanied by the feeling that other behaviors will tip the applecart and that disagreement with one's own norms signals animosity.

The statements made here, however, stem not from personal bias, or even from personal opinion, but rather from the data-based reports and accounts of a large number of highly respected sociologists, anthropologists, psychologists, and other kinds of social observers over a period of several centuries (see, for instance, Gastil 1975 and Hofstede 1984 for summaries of such data-based assessments).

The second social theme found in the native Americas is a system shared by the majority of European nations as well as many African nations today and throughout their histories. This system emphasizes *binary* or *dualistic* pairs of concepts and actions. Dualistic is clearly the better term, for it is not just a matter of seeing things in pairs—binary—but more a matter of seeing things in terms of opposing pairs. These are the social systems labeled *IIN* and *IIB* in the introduction. Just as the members of unitary societies are the world's true Pragmatists and Relativists, so the citizens of dualistic societies are the world's true Absolutists, seeing only two polar opposites for every situation— one positive and absolutely good, the other negative and absolutely bad. There are no in-betweens, and when they seem to occur they are invariably lumped with the negative. Individuals in these societies who cannot "make up their minds," who are "fence-straddlers" or middle-of-the-roaders, are seen as ineffectual and not in tune with positive social action toward desired community goals. They may, in fact, be seen as out-and-out enemies of the system or, worse yet, enemies of the state.

Examples of this type of reaction on the part of dualistic societies to outsiders can be seen in the U.S. Patriot Act of 2001, with its expression of extreme ethnocentric concern and fear of both outsiders and those within the society who do not adhere to the norms. More insidious examples, however, are abundantly evident—the treatment accorded "non-Aryan" peoples in what was euphemistically called "National Socialist" Germany during the 1930s and 1940s, the treatment meted out by the Khmer Rouge to anyone with a foreign, specifically European, "taint" in Cambodia in the 1970s, or Idi Amin's ethnic cleansing in Uganda in the 1970s. Such xenophobic fear of outsiders is, regrettably, typical and to be expected in all dualistic societies and cultures worldwide.

In the Americas of 1492 both the Maya Kingdoms of Yucatán, Belize, and Central America and the towns and city-states of the Mississippi River Valley in North America, two of our Big Six, held to this worldview, as do the Eskimo peoples of North America and Greenland and many of the Chibchan peoples of Colombia and southern Central America. Such dualistic social systems are, however, rather rare in the Americas. They are most frequent in Western Europe and include Spain, Portugal, England, the Netherlands, France, and Russia—the main colonizers of the New World.

The system is so typically European in nature, in fact, that it may said to form the primary cornerstone of European cultures and to be the most distinguishing, readily noticeable characteristic of European peoples, the only exceptions being the unitary Slavic peoples of Serbia and Montenegro and the trinary peoples of Albania, Kosovo, and Malta. Almost all the countries one could care to name west of the Ural Mountains exhibit politically, economically, and culturally (in the usual sense of that word) either narrow dualistic type *IIN* norms or the broader type *IIB* norms. The world's dualistic states today are shown in Figure 9.

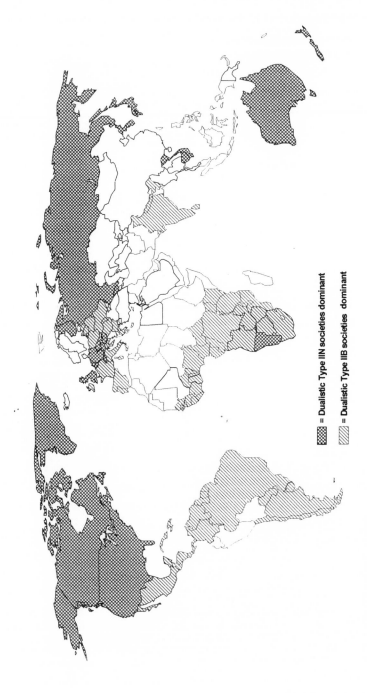

= Dualistic Type IIN societies dominant

= Dualistic Type IIB societies dominant

Figure 9. The World's Dualistic States, 2004

Narrowly defined (*IIN*) dualistic behavior is typical of the Germanic peoples of Germany, Austria, the Netherlands, Belgium, Luxembourg, Liechtenstein, and parts of Switzerland, as well as of the Finno-Ugric peoples of Hungary, Finland, and Estonia and the Georgian and Armenian peoples of the Caucasus. The Slavic Czechs, Slovaks, and Russians also belong to the *IIN* group.

Social type *IIB* nations, with a much broader interpretation of what constitutes "right" and "wrong," include Celtic Wales, Scotland, the Isle of Man, and Ireland, Slavic Poland, the Ukraine, Belarus, Moldova, Bulgaria, Croatia, Macedonia, and Slovenia, as well as Greece and all of the Romance-language-speaking countries—France, parts of Switzerland, Italy, San Marino, Spain, Andorra, Portugal, and Romania. In the Middle East, only modern Israel, with a European-derived *IIN* social system—an instance of historically driven kin system change from an original trinary model over the last 1,500 years—is characterized by this social theme. In the Far East, Japan, Korea, Tibet, Bhutan, and Cambodia all have narrowly defined *IIN* systems, while the various peoples of India are predominantly *IIB* in culture. Most of the countries of sub-Saharan Africa are also *IIB* societies. In the New World, all the modern Euro-American nations follow the dualistic social philosophy, the United States and Canada with a blend of *IIN* and *IIB* peoples, the former always predominating in government and economics, while all of the Latin American nations except Ecuador, Peru, and Bolivia have *IIB* social systems, as do all other areas of the world settled by Europeans—Australia and New Zealand, for example. Ecuador, Peru, and Bolivia are the only New World nations in which unitary native American peoples still dominate demographically (though not politically).

As can be seen, the two dualistic patterns, importantly, are thus the behavioral patterns that most of us on both sides of the Atlantic are used to, for they represent the core of the social systems in which we were raised, regardless of the surface differences which separate, for instance, an Englishman from a Spaniard, a Finn from an Italian, a Kenyan from a Greek, a Punjabi from a Hungarian. The differences are cosmetic; the underlying philosophy by which they govern their lives is the same. These are the behavioral norms that we tend to think of as "natural," the way God Made Man. Derived from the Indo-European and Finno-Ugric peoples of the Black Sea and Ural Mountains regions and the ancestral Bantu-speaking peoples of sub-Saharan Africa some 5,000 to 7,000 years ago, these social norms have been around for many millennia, and their tenets were those that drove the actions of all of the European colonizers of the Americas. Thus, just as the unitary pattern may be called essentially an Asian social pattern, so the dualistic pattern may be called a European and African social pattern. This is, of course, a clear example of reducing things to their minimal common denominator, but it is also socially and culturally accurate.

Unlike unitary cultures, in which men and women are seen as social equals, men and women in dualistic cultures are seen as both temperamentally different and socially unequal. In *IIN* societies men dominate. In *IIB* cultures, on the other hand, it is most often the woman who plays the leading role, more often than not, like Lucretia Borgia or the more benign Italian, Irish, Spanish, or African grandmother, behind the scenes, for these are the world's on-the-surface "macho" societies. In both types of dualistic society the sexes are seen as unequal in duties and rights, regardless of which sex dominates.

Dualistic social systems, not surprisingly, have two social classes—the Haves and the Have-Nots, the Ins and the Outs, both with widely differing privileges. In narrow *IIN* societies, such as the United States or Great Britain, it is possible to climb a "social ladder," so that Have-Nots can, with considerable effort, become Haves, and Haves can easily become Have-Nots if they are not careful. In such societies class membership is usually established by one's economic or political acumen, which may, of course, change. In the broader *IIB* dualistic societies, such as Spain or the societies of India, however, class membership is set rigidly by birth—one is born into, and forever remains, in one class or the other. In general, it may be said that all dualistic societies exhibit wide economic, sometimes political, religious, educational, and general cultural social class differences. These differences are frequently not openly acknowledged, but their tacit recognition is reflected in the treatment accorded the individual dependent upon his social class.

While both subvarieties of dualistic society pay considerable overt lip service to the concept of equality and democratically applied "Human Rights," regardless of one's social class, in actual practice not only does this rarely occur, but the "Outs" are routinely subjected to various kinds of social and, in some cases, physical ostracism and abuse. We do not like to acknowledge this, but it is a documentable characteristic of all dualistic societies around the world through the centuries.

Perhaps the most notable characteristic of dualistic cultures is the attention they accord to individualism. All are highly individualistic societies—one might almost say *egoistic*—and the desires of the individual are far more important, when push comes to shove, than the overall rights of the group. One is not only encouraged to compete, in all realms of endeavor, but, in order to succeed in dualistic societies, one *must* compete. Such a highly individualistic, competitive norm is the polar opposite of the role the individual plays in unitary societies—the flip side of the coin, as it were. While having a "mind of one's own" and expressing it openly is anathema in unitary societies, it is the end-all and be-all of dualistic cultures.

As described in the introduction, dualistic cultures use kin-naming labels that separate the family into two groups, one the immediate lineage of parents, brothers/sisters, and children, the other the less closely related blood relatives we call uncles/aunts, cousins, and nieces/nephews. As in other binary pairs in such cultures, one set of terms represents an In-group—lineal relatives—while the other set represents an Out-group—collateral relatives. Though it is not necessary to take this difference too much to heart, it does mean that first preference will normally go to one's own parents, siblings, and children, and that the uncle/aunts, cousins, and nieces/nephews will be viewed only as "relatives." This distinction is of considerable importance when it comes to the ownership, inheritance, and transfer of privately owned property.

The definition of who is and is not lineal kin is much broader in *IIB* societies than it is among *IIN* peoples. Nonetheless, the dictum that lineal kin are more important than collateral kin still holds. The members of dualistic societies, consequently, hold greater reservations about interacting with strangers, who are of course Outs, than they do with their own more narrowly defined In-groups.

Governmental ruling power lies with some Have or In group, never with a Have-Not or Out group, and the In group will pick its most outspoken and individualistic members as its leaders, whether those leaders have the title of monarch, president, or prime minister. All groups, in fact, have an individual leader—a corporate CEO, a committee chairman, a university president, the bishop of a church, the captain of a football team. Rule by committee, the norm in unitary societies, occurs only euphemistically in dualistic cultures.

Economic goods and real estate belong to individuals, with a great, frequently inordinate, emphasis on legal systems, which provide highly detailed judicial and contractual definition of individual property rights in a bewildering multiplicity of legally defined situations. Litigation per se is thus, not surprisingly, of great frequency and importance in dualistic societies.

Manufactured goods emphasize utility and economy of price and function. Style fluctuates constantly. These are technical, engineering-oriented societies in which the mechanical attributes of products are more important than the scientific principles underlying their design and workings. Dualistic societies are not science-oriented per se. What is particularly important is the alteration of product types and styles through time. As General Electric says, "Progress is our most important product." Change for change's sake is of great concern in all dualistic societies. Lip service is paid to tradition, but progress lies in change. Individuals from the past are seen as less intelligent than those living at the present, and those in the future will be yet more intelligent. The Past, that is, is seen as less perfect than the Present, and the Future is invariably seen as going to be better than the Present. Thus products occur in an often bewildering number of varieties, and they change their style and presentation almost continually—the latest automobile style, the latest clothing styles, constantly upgraded computer software systems, for example.

The importance of change for change's sake is embedded in the great importance of time and timeliness in all dualistic societies. To be completely acceptable in such societies, actions must be accomplished within a defined schedule, on a well-honed time line. We go to work at a specific time; we leave at a specific time; we have lunch breaks at a specific time. Even recreational activities are planned along a time line. Spontaneous work and spontaneous recreation are not the norm. Both must be planned for well ahead of time.

Such an emphasis on time is carried over to timeliness—fulfilling one's work and recreational activities according to the agreed-upon time line. In *IIN* dualistic societies, for example, one may be only three to ten minutes "late" in meeting one's time-defined obligations. If one begins the obligation later than the agreed-upon time, one must proffer an apology and a convincing explanation. Such a strong time orientation is typical not only of the individual in dualistic societies but of all organizations as well. We are all familiar with the economic, political, educational, medical, and other social plans formulated by city, state or provincial, and national governments. If the implementing governmental organization or agency does not meet its schedule, then we expect a clear explanation of the rationale for not doing do. We may, in fact, even "fire" or otherwise rid ourselves of the individuals we see as responsible for such time line breaches. The same stricture applies to business organizations—in fact, to all of the organizations of dualistic cultures.

Warfare and territorial expansion are frequent, as in unitary cultures. Unlike unitary systems, however, in which the individual is of no consequence, individual heroism and leadership are emphasized and rewarded in dualistic systems. Military and military veterans' organizations are, consequently, accorded very high prestige. Conquered peoples are, on the other hand, not surprisingly in this either/or philosophy, cast in the role of *Outs* and are, therefore, "bad," "wrong," and "inferior" by definition. While conquered peoples used to be killed or enslaved, these days it is considered more politic to bind them by long-term treaties of "peace" that subject them to both political and economic subjugation and long-term cultural deprivation with attempts to bring the social fabric of the conquered society into forcible compliance with the social norms of the conqueror. The treaties following both World War I and World War II provide prime examples, as do the invasion, occupation, and attempted Americanization of Iraq in 2003. The individual leaders of conquered states are generally put through mock trials, after which the foregone conclusion is carried out—they are executed, imprisoned for life, or exiled (that is, de facto enslavement). The torture and killing of civilian populations of conquered societies is also, regrettably, frequent, though rarely these days either admitted or documented.

It is worthy of a side note to point out that in newscasts late in 2003 well-known news commentators studiously discussed what the military occupying forces in Iraq should do if Iraqi *free* elections should return an Islamic council or a military dictator to power. All of the commentators were in agreement that the United States should nullify such a free election and require subsequent elections until a "democratic" government is returned. They were also in agreement that any individual not clearly and specifically subscribing to American democratic ideals should not be allowed to run for office, and there was even some suggestion that perhaps they should not be allowed to vote. No mention was made of the widely contrasting cultural differences that separate the United States and Iraq, nor was there mention of allowing Iraqi voters to make the ultimate decision regarding the type of government under which they would prefer to live. It was made clear, in fact, that any new Iraqi Constitution must *require* all Iraqi citizens to subscribe to the same rights, privileges, and duties required of U.S. citizens by the American Constitution —shades of the Spanish colonial *requerimientos*! Such exclusionary policies are typical of dualistic societies, in which the militarily subjugated Outs and Have-Nots are routinely deprived of rights and privileges unless and until they conform to the requisite social norms of the conqueror.

It should also be noted that, with their emphasis on individualism and its expression, dualistic societies not infrequently produce leaders with a dictatorial bent, particularly in times of trouble—impending warfare, postwar trauma, or internal political strife. In these times men such as Adolf Hitler in Germany, Pol Pot in Cambodia, Idi Amin in Uganda, Francisco Franco in Spain, Oliver Cromwell in England, Napoleon in France, Benito Mussolini in Italy, Vladimir Lenin and Joseph Stalin in Russia, Juan Perón in Argentina, Fulgencio Batista or Fidel Castro in Cuba, and a long, long list of others have successfully bent the public will toward their personal views and wishes. This is readily accomplished in a dualistic society both because extreme individualism is a highly prized social expression and because these particular men, for a variety of reasons inherent in their personal backgrounds, discovered early on that insistence on keeping to the social ideals was the most highly rewarded behavior in their societies. If one could by actual or euphemistic label and behavior convince the public that one was the champion of moral correctness, that one could right the social ills of the times, then political leadership could quickly follow. It should be added as a corollary that such behavior is also fleeting in dualistic societies, for other individuals inevitably follow who will be able to puncture the bubble of "patriotism" stimulated by the current leader in power. Every period of internal or external crisis routinely brings forth new individuals convinced that they have the proper moral solutions to the crisis at hand.

Slavery is also a frequent practice in dualistic societies, those enslaved coming either from other cultures or from the *Have-Not* segment of the society in question. It is often difficult to detect the presence of out-and-out slavery in dualistic societies, however, since the word itself is usually disguised as "penal servitude," implemented in "correctional" institutions, or avoided entirely in favor of various euphemisms such as "work-service," "community service," "work contract," and so on. Nonetheless, the servitude to which *Have-Nots* are subjected, deserved or not, can be seen daily in roadside work gangs and similar scenes, which have little if anything to do with "correction" or rehabilitation and all to do with coercive punishment for breaking society's norms.

All things in dualistic societies are dual. The languages of dualistic cultures—Japanese, Korean, and all of the Indo-European languages such as English, French, Greek, Hindi, or Russian, for instance—have a two-way distinction between naming words (*nouns*) and action words (*verbs*), and within the verbs there is always a distinction between past events and nonpast events. It should also come as no surprise that the either/or binary number system that operates our computers was designed, developed, and brought to the massive fruition it has today by dualistic cultures, led by Japan and the United States.

Our own social system and those of most other American, European, and sub-Saharan African nations are excellent examples of the dualistic theme at work. To us things are either right or wrong, good or bad, positive or negative, clean or dirty, light or dark, left or right, black or white. Criminals are either innocent-or-guilty—there could be no such thing in a dualistic system as "half-guilty" or, harder yet to imagine, "half-innocent," a perfectly legitimate conclusion in many nondualistic societies. Ours is an *is*-or-*isn't* system. The world and all that is in it is seen in black and white—grays and all in-betweens are thought of as black, and, therefore, as both negative and unacceptable. Though it is perhaps unkind to point it out, this is strongly reflected in the attitude of the peoples of dualistic cultures to men and women of any color except their own.

As mentioned, compromise is consequently neither a choice nor a virtue in such societies. It is a weakness. There is no worse insult than to be called "wishy-washy" or "spineless," not to have a "mind of one's own."

The keynote to dualistic systems is, then, *egoistic competitive absolutism.* In this context it should be of more than passing interest to an American, Canadian, or British audience that both the Japanese and Korean social systems, in spite of their historical links to and borrowings from unitary China, are more dualistic even than Western European social systems, and it should come as no surprise that these two nations are succeeding in outcompeting all the rest of us other dualists these days. Another foregone social conclusion!

The descriptive outline of dualistic societies presented in this chapter also characterizes the dualistic societies of native America, abundantly evident in the actions of the Maya Kingdoms and the Mississippian City-States, discussed in Chapters 9 and 10.

6

The Trinary Compromise
The Near Eastern Norm

The third, and very frequent, native American social theme is the *trinary* theme. Of the native American Big Six, two followed a trinary theme—the majority of the Pueblo Towns of New Mexico and the Taíno Kingdoms of Hispaniola and Puerto Rico. The trinary social theme also occurs widely in smaller native American societies on both continents, particularly North America.

This theme represents a globally widespread way of life of considerable importance, and to the mind of some its social philosophy may ultimately hold the key to human problem-solving. It occurs primarily in the Middle East (see Figure 10) and includes most of those societies which the Western World refers to these days on economic grounds as Third World countries. In Africa and the Middle East, these are Morocco, Western Sahara, Tunisia, Algeria, Egypt, Sudan, Ethiopia, Eritrea, Djibouti, Mali, Mauritania, Niger, Somalia, Chad, Burkina Faso, Senegal, Guinea Bissau, The Gambia, Guinea, Lebanon, Syria, Jordan, Palestinian Israel, Saudi Arabia, Kuwait, Iraq, Qatar, the United Arab Emirates, Bahrain, Yemen, Oman, and Turkey. In Central Asia they are the Turkic- and Mongol-speaking peoples of Kazakhstan, Turkmenistan, Uzbekistan, Kyrgyzstan, Azerbaijan, and Mongolia; the Indo-European-speaking peoples of Afghanistan and Tajikistan; and the Indic-speaking peoples of Pakistan. In Europe only two nations—Albania and Malta—represent the trinary norm. In the Serbian province of Kosovo and the nation of Bosnia-Herzegovina, trinary peoples dominate demographically, but their political control of their destinies is precarious. In the context of recent years, it is of interest to note that the entire Arabic-speaking world belongs to this interesting social type, as, by extension, do most but not all Muslim nations.

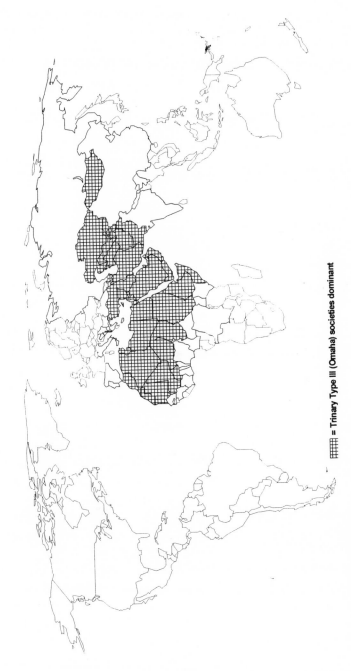

Figure 10. The World's Trinary States, 2004

The most obvious and all-pervasive characteristic of the trinary social theme is *compromise*. In trinary societies there is, in addition to the two polar extremes, a middle, compromising solution for every decision-making situation and every problem, if we will look for it. This middle ground is preferred in every instance, for in such solutions, although no one may perhaps "win," neither does anyone "lose"—there is something for all. Neither the yin-yang *relativism* of Oriental unitary societies nor the individualistic *absolutism* of the Western dualistic societies can tolerate this philosophy. Both have historically been inimical toward its expression and use over at least the past two millennia.

Again, even the kin-naming terminologies of trinary societies show a three-way split: lineal relatives (parents, brothers/sisters, and children); father's relatives (paternal uncles/aunts, their children, and their children's children); and mother's relatives (maternal uncles/aunts, their children, and their children's children). Each of these three categories has a special set of terms limited to that category, and each type of relative is accorded a slightly different treatment. The languages of trinary societies also show this three-way definition of the world. There are *verbs* (action words), *nouns* (naming words), and *particles* (encompassing any language form that does not fit into the other two classes). There are three verb aspects: imperfect (usually present time), perfect (usually past time), and future. There are three noun numbers: singular, dual (only two), and plural (more than two); There are three noun cases: subject, object, and possessive. Most words in many trinary society languages consist of only three primary consonants, referred to in Arabic as triliteral roots.

This three-ness pervades all. Christianity, for example, which had its roots in the trinary Near East, has a Trinity for its Godhead. Ancient Egyptian society, also a trinary society, divided its pantheon into nine groups of three deities each. Islam, while monotheistic, also holds to belief in two other divine types, the jinn and the angels, and both Christianity and Judaism, like ancient Egyptian, have nine groups of angels with three types in each group.

It should thus come as no surprise that in these societies there are three social classes: a ruling elite, which is often, though not necessarily, hereditary; a professional class consisting of business, military, and often educational and religious leaders; and the rest of the members of society. Each class has carefully and intricately defined social rights and responsibilities, ensuring adequate social participation and protection for all inasmuch as possible. One's class membership is most frequently determined by birth, and there is rarely a "social ladder" to be climbed.

The middle or professional class is especially prominent in trinary societies —the Arab merchant, for example, or the Turkish or Mongol warrior. This class is usually the mainstay of trinary polities, and in the Americas it was exemplified by the far-flung native trade networks that linked societies as far apart as the Amazon and Orinoco basins in South America with the South-eastern United States or Mexico and Central America with the North American Midwest.

Trinary societies tend to combine the characteristics of both unitary and dualistic cultures in the sense that they emphasize both the overriding importance of the individual *and* his obligation to maintain the welfare of the group. Group duties and privileges and individual duties and privileges are delicately balanced, neither taking precedence over the other. Thus trinary cultures are neither totally individual-oriented nor totally group-oriented but are, rather, compromising.

As pointed out on several occasions, compromise is viewed as a weakness in Western, dualistic societies, an inability to reach a decision. In the unitary societies of the Far East there is no need for compromise, inasmuch as every situation has its own wide and fluctuating range of solutions. In trinary societies, however, compromise, in even the smallest decisions, is viewed as the only normal, rational manner of satisfying the greatest number of people. The phrase *You can please some of the people all of the time, and all of the people some of the time, but you can never please all of the people all of the time* is taken quite literally.

Such compromising problem-solving is usually not effected directly between two adversaries but rather, as one might assume, through a third, disinterested mediating party, an ombudsman or middleman—the role, for instance, that Jimmy Carter played in the Sadat-Begin Camp David Accords of 1979 or that Iran's Ayatollah Khamenei offered to play in mediating the Kuwait crisis or—the classic case—the role King Solomon took in resolving which woman was a child's mother.

As in all the attributes of this three-way system, there is a careful balance between individual rights on the one hand and group welfare on the other. Individual wealth, for example, is important, as it is in our dualistic culture, but in a trinary culture the possession of wealth obligates the individual to redistribute a specific portion of it—*zakat* in Arab countries—to the less fortunate members of the group.

In some trinary cultures, such as those of the Arab world, the male is strongly dominant, while in others the female dominates with equal strength. Both varieties are found in the New World, though the female-dominant variety is the more frequent. In neither instance is the intent to subjugate, denigrate, or control the nondominant sex. Though we in the West like to think of the Islamic seclusion of women in this light, and while abuses certainly occur, as in all social systems each sex has clear-cut responsibilities to the other and to society at large as well as clear-cut expectations from members of the opposite sex.

The manufactured goods of trinary societies emphasize function, style, and, most important, the underlying principles that give the good its utility. Trinary cultures are technical cultures, and it is from them, through the medieval Arab world and Muslim Spain, that Greek, Roman, and Hindu science was passed to Western Europe. Dualists have injected utilitarianism into the manufacturing process, but the principles come from a trinary base.

Land and other real property is usually owned by the group—the family, the business organization, or the nation. A man's home is consequently not only his castle but remains his family's tangible identity, often generation after generation. There are, for example, homes in the city of Fez, Morocco, that have been owned and occupied by the same families since they retreated there from Muslim Spain over 500 years ago, some with the keys to their earlier Spanish homes in the Kingdom of Granada still hanging on a peg in the entryway. This same attachment to group-owned real estate forms the basis of the strong feelings of homeland and nationhood felt by the members of most trinary societies. Fervent patriotism is a keynote in such polities.

This, in fact, is precisely why Kuwait was important to Kuwaitis during the recent Gulf War, and why it was also so important to Iraqis, for the latter viewed that country as a piece of their own national patrimony from which they had been too long alienated by the exigencies of nineteenth- and twentieth-century European colonial politics.

The expected solution to the Kuwait impasse should have been compromise through a third-party mediator, which was, in fact, suggested by Saudi Arabia shortly before the outbreak of the Persian Gulf hostilities and again by Iran after the hostilities had begun. The Saudi solution, granting something to both parties but the totality to none, was the ceding of Buiyan, Failaka, and other small Gulf islands to Iraq in exchange for that country's formal statement renouncing claim to the remainder of Kuwaiti territory. Such a ready solution was rejected out-of-hand, as should also have been expected, by the leaders of the dualistic societies attempting to "solve" the problem. To dualists compromise smacks of "giving in," which, of course, is to them not a tolerable solution. Dualists, more than most, feel that their solution is both the "correct" one and the only one. Even seasoned diplomats from these cultures rarely bring themselves to compromise, for such is not part of the dualistic mind-set.

Was Kuwait an economic and oil problem? Partly, of course, but much more a problem of social differences—a trinary Iraq vs. a dualistic Western alliance. Simplistic? Yes, perhaps. Naïve? No, just social reality. Hence the Gulf War.

The Kuwait impasse is, of course, simply one of many such maladjustments of social reality in the Middle East at this time in history. When the Gulf War was over, the reality remained, no longer as the Kuwait Problem but as the Iraq Problem and the Palestinian Problem. Again compromise has been suggested, but the other players—Israel and its Western allies—are all dualistic polities, and compromise is hence out of the question. Without compromise, however, the next step was obvious, and the expected dualistic-trinary confrontations became historical fact with the American-British invasion of Iraq in 2003 and the heightened conflict between Israel and Palestinians in the same year.

Unlike dualistic societies, in which warfare usually occurs as a result of ideological differences between adversaries, in trinary societies it tends to be fought over territory, for ideological impasses between trinary polities are routinely handled through diplomatic compromise. Any territory seen as the national patrimony or as a logical extension of that patrimony, however, can be a prime candidate for conquest. All of the expansion of the Mongols, the Huns, the medieval Arabic world, and the Turks—all trinary peoples—resulted from the urge to add territory to what they deemed their natural geographical domains.

Trinary warfare, particularly against nontrinary societies, can be brutal and unusually violent, but the conquered are normally allowed to continue their own lifeways. Only if the conquered concertedly oppose conquest are they treated without mercy—and the complete destruction of cities and their entire populations has in the past been the normal method for dealing with territorial enemies who did not submit. With submission, however, peaceable coexistence was customary—the Muslim treatment of the Christian and Jewish populations of Spain after its conquest in A.D. 711, such coexistence lasting until 1491 and the reconquest of the Kingdom of Granada by Christian forces. The Turkish conquest of Byzantium and the city of Constantinople in 1453 provides another example, the Christian population allowed to live in peace so long as opposition to the conquering Turks did not occur. The Greek Orthodox Patriarch, for example, was allowed to continue his residence in Constantinople, administering to his church from that city, and he does so up to the present day.

Interestingly, in spite of this penchant for genuine tolerance and compromise so long as trinary ideals and norms are not challenged or tampered with, once they are abridged the reaction is usually quick and violent—the Mongol wholesale destruction of the towns of medieval Persia which did not welcome the Mongol newcomers, for example, or the reaction of the Arab world to the twentieth-century intrusion of Israel and its dualistic norms after an absence from the region of some 2,000 years. Israeli dualism, with its to-be-expected absolutism, could not deal by compromise with an Arab Palestine. It was not, as we have been taught, an "anti-Semitic" confrontation of Islam and Judaism, for the two religions have been close allies and co-protectors for over 1,400 years. The problem arose because Arabic Palestinians expected genuine share-and-share-alike compromise, which Europeanized Israel could not supply. The norms of Arabic culture were challenged, and the Arabic world reacted with the expected remedy all trinary societies have used for millennia—violence.

When European dualistic colonialism became so demanding in the late 1900s and early 2000s that it abridged trinary Arabic and Islamic norms, the expected violence erupted, expressed through the hyperconservative El Qaeda network. Terrorists from the dualists' point of view, its members are from their own view simply protecting the integrity of their trinary societies in the requisite manner—difficult perhaps to understand, and impossible for dualists to accept, but nonetheless true. The violence that has gripped the Western European and Euro-American world increasingly since the end of World War II does not reflect the worldwide rise of lawless, murderous terrorists but, rather, the conflict between dualistic and trinary societies. The tactics used by the trinary attackers may be brutally violent in the extreme, but this could have been foreseen by anyone familiar with the histories of trinary societies. We saw the same in the so-called Indian wars in the United States in the midyears of the nineteenth century. When the norms of the native American societies of the far Midwest and Southeast—all trinary societies—were abridged and their very survival threatened, the reaction took the form of truly barbarous atrocities against the Anglo-American invaders. Again not terrorism, regardless of its horror and brutality, but simply the natural reaction of any trinary society when its sacred territory and social norms are threatened.

At the time of Spanish intervention in the New World, both the Pueblo Towns of New Mexico and Arizona and the Taíno Kingdoms of Hispaniola and Puerto Rico, discussed in Chapters 11 and 12, along with the many smaller American trinary societies thriving in the American Midwest, West, and Southeast, exemplify the trinary mode in the New World.

Part III
THE MATRIX OF LIVES

Now that the stage has been set, and the framework for our cultural descriptions has been defined, it is time to look at native American societies as they were in 1492 and the early 1500s. We have purposely chosen, bear in mind, to describe only a select number of those cultures, those that were at the end of the fifteenth century similar in structure to the emerging nation-states of Europe. These specific societies have been picked both for that reason and because the structural similarities to their European counterparts enable comparisons meaningful to today's reader.

We have purposely chosen two societies from each of the three basic social types described in the first part of the book: two *unitary* societies—the Inca Empire of Tawantinsuyu in South America and the México or Aztec Empire of Mexico; two *dualistic* societies—the Maya Kingdoms of Central America and the city-states of the Mississippi River Valley; and two *trinary* societies—the Pueblo Towns of the American Southwest and the Taíno Kingdoms of the Greater Antilles. These selections were also made because they include two societies from each of the three main geographical areas of the Americas—America north of the Rio Grande, Central America, and South America and the Caribbean.

In our discussion of the characteristics of the six societies described in this section of the book, comparisons are drawn, both with similar distinctive traits in European cultures and with traits largely or partly shared among the native American cultures themselves, to enable the reader to achieve better understanding of the social philosophies of the cultures we are describing.

7

The Empire of Tawantinsuyu

I will be no man's tributary. I am greater than any prince upon the earth. Your emperor may be a great prince: I do not doubt it, seeing that he has sent his subjects so far across the sea; and I am willing to hold him as my brother. As for the Pope of whom you speak, he must be mad to talk of giving away countries which do not belong to him. As for my faith, I will not change it. Your own god, as you tell me, was put to death by the very men he created. But my god still looks down upon his children. (Anonymous 1930 [1563], Hyams and Ordish 1963:222)

Thus replied the Emperor Atahualpa to the *requerimiento* read to him by the Dominican priest Vicente de Valverde just before noon on Saturday, November 16, 1532, in the public square of the Inca garrison town of Caxamarca.

Late in the afternoon of the previous day the Spaniard Francisco Pizarro and some 200 soldiers had arrived at Caxamarca, whose population of 10,000 had left the city some days before for the military camp just outside the town where the Emperor was staying. On their arrival, finding the city deserted, the Spanish encamped in several of the large barracks in the city, and Pizarro sent his assistant, Hernando de Soto, to the Emperor's camp to tell him that they wished to meet him the following day.

To this Atahualpa agreed. Thus shortly before noon on the sixteenth, Atahualpa and almost half of the 10,000 inhabitants of Caxamarca returned to the city and gathered in the town's public square for the first encounter between the Spaniard and the Inca Emperor. The Spanish, however, did not greet the incoming entourage but remained secluded in their barracks, watching as the Emperor arrived in the city and prepared to meet with them.

When the waiting Emperor and the people had filled the square, Valverde, the Dominican priest, entered alone, Bible in hand, and through his interpreter Felipillo proceeded to read the standard *requerimiento* from the Spanish Crown, telling the Emperor that Inca lands belonged to Spain, to whom they had been given by the Christian Pope, and that he, Atahualpa, and his subjects were required to profess submission to the Spanish Crown and to embrace Christianity.

The Emperor's response, quoted above, did not please Valverde, who, noting the great number of Indians both in the square and outside the town, returned to Pizarro in his barracks, where he is quoted as saying, "Do you not see that while we stand here talking to this haughty dog, the fields are filling with Indians? Fall on at once! I absolve you!" (Anonymous 1930 [1563], Hyams and Ordish 1963:223). What followed was one of the most treacherous attacks recorded in New World history. Pizarro gave the signal to his men to attack the crowded plaza, from which there was only a single exit, and with cannon, gun, and sword the Spanish quickly dispatched the panicked crowd of some 5,000 unarmed men, women, and children, capturing the Emperor and holding him hostage. Nine months later, on August 29, 1533, after having paid the Spanish a "ransom" of some 1,326,539 pesos of gold and 51,610 marks, or 12 tons, of silver, melted down from items removed from the Coricancha, the holiest temple of Cuzco, the Inca capital, Atahualpa was again betrayed and garroted to death (Hyams and Ordish 1963:244). So much for Christian and European largesse.

This example of man's remarkable barbarity to man is an example of the unfortunately routine treatment accorded conquered New World peoples by the invaders from Western Europe. Many nowadays would either sweep such episodes under the rug or explain it all away as simply part of "the way people were in the 1500s," but such rationalizations miss the point—that dualistic peoples *always* view those they conquer as less human unless, on demand, they embrace the dualistic beliefs and practices of their conquerors with fervor.

With this traumatic introduction to Europe, the Andean empire of the Inca, called *Tawantinsuyu,* "Land of the Four Quarters," vanished into oblivion. We are fortunate, however, in having copious contemporary documentation on Inca society and lifeways, and these records let us see a prime example of a unitary society in action, with all of the attributes described earlier for the Asiatic unitary cultures—individual needs subordinate to group needs; groups linked by strong, well-defined reciprocal obligations, rights, and privileges; an overriding emphasis on voluntary work for the benefit of the group; widespread use of means-justifies-the-ends policies and actions; land, goods, and services communally owned; and an all-pervasive belief in *tinku*, the constant mutating and merging of all things in a single all-pervasive natural continuum, analogous to the yin-yang principle of Chinese thought.

During its short life of no more than three centuries and a few years as an organized polity—from approximately the 1200s through the death of Atahualpa in 1533—Tawantinsuyu was one of the most brilliant unitary systems the world has ever seen. Spreading from southern Colombia in the north to central Chile in the south, a distance of some 3,500 miles, and with a population of 11 to 12 million souls, it was also the largest native state in the Americas in both size and population and the largest Southern Hemisphere empire the world has ever known.

The four *suyu* or administrative quarters into which Tawantinsuyu was divided were *Chinchaysuyu* in the north, *Antisuyu* in the east, *Cuntisuyu* in the west, and *Collasuyu* in the south. *Chinchaysuyu* included most of what is now Ecuador and most of coastal Peru to the north of the capital city of Cuzco. *Antisuyu* was comprised of a small region to the immediate east of Cuzco. *Cuntisuyu* consisted of the Peruvian coast to the west of the capital, and *Collasuyu* included the western section of what is now Bolivia, most of Chile, and large stretches of northwestern Argentina.

The boundaries of the four quarters radiated outward from the center of the main plaza of the capital city of Cuzco, high in the Andes in what is now south-central Peru. With some 40,000 inhabitants, Cuzco was a cosmopolitan urban center in every modern sense of the word. When the Spanish under Francisco Pizarro first approached it in 1532 with a small force of mercenary soldiers, their reaction was utter disbelief. In the distance they beheld a large city perched high in the cloudy mountains, towering buildings glistening with gold and silver in the sun. The physical size and splendor of the Inca metropolis was beyond anything European imagination could summon up. The Spanish chronicler Cieza de León, who accompanied that first sortie of troops, says that had he fully described the city in all its stupendous detail, he would not have been believed (Cieza de León 1973). Europeans were simply not used to the opulence and splendor of a city like Cuzco. To them it was a strange, alien vision from an impossible dream, for no European city of the time could compare in its magnificent use of stonework and the prolific use of gold, silver, and precious stones for architectural embellishment.

The inhabitants of Cuzco were the Inca themselves, Quechua speakers indigenous to the region, and though today we use the name *Inca* to refer to all of the inhabitants of Tawantinsuyu, the term then actually applied only to the empire's ruling Cuzco Quechuas. The city, divided into an upper or *hanan*

Figure 11. The Empire of Tawantinsuyu in 1532

sector and a lower or *hurin* sector, was inhabited by ten extended Inca family lineages, five in each sector. It was from these that the Emperor and the highest administrative officials of the realm were chosen, and it was in Cuzco that all primary administrative decisions affecting the empire were made, here that the central accounting of agricultural, work, and textile taxation was done, here that the primary religious structure of the empire, the Coricancha, was located, and here that the special educational schools of the empire were situated.

If we extrapolate from uncertain native tradition, Cuzco was founded sometime during the first quarter of the fifteenth century—1438 is the usual date given. Its Inca rulers quickly began to conquer and consolidate the other Quechua and non-Quechua peoples of the Andean region into what became the empire of *Tawantinsuyu,* the Land of the Four Quarters, a process still ongoing when the Spanish arrived in 1532. Native history, however, in keeping with unitary norms, was not time-oriented and was clearly rewritten from time to time to account for the current ruler's needs. Thus the founding date of Cuzco is only approximate, but the area is known to have been inhabited for at least several centuries prior to the date of the official founding of the city.

In terms of population, Tawantinsuyu incorporated not only a nexus of some 40,000 to 50,000 speakers of the Cuzco dialect of Quechua, the Incas themselves, but 11 to 12 million more citizens of widely diverse ethnic and language affiliation. Though integrated into the Inca realm and as rapidly as possible indoctrinated in Inca ways, all of the non-Inca citizens of Tawantinsuyu were subjects, inhabiting some eighty provinces within the four quarters of the empire.

To bind these diverse ethnic units into a cohesive whole the Inca used a number of pragmatic means-justifies-the-ends practices, instituted either benignly or, if the circumstances demanded it, with force. The leaders of conquered peoples were, for example, required to learn and use *Runa Simi,* the Cuzco dialect of Quechua for all formal communication. It became the official, unifying language of the realm, a required lingua franca. To ensure the success of this policy, the children of leading families from non-Inca communities were brought to Cuzco to learn Runa Simi and be reared as Incas. Once educated, they were returned to their families and local communities, where they assumed positions of leadership. Other highly pragmatic means to bring newly conquered people into the fold included the forcible resettlement of entire populations to areas where they could be more readily controlled, often to regions in which they were surrounded by Quechua-speaking peoples. The ultimate goal of these administrative policies was to weld the diverse population into a loyal, Quechua-speaking empire, to train each succeeding generation of the conquered to become more and more Inca in thought and behavior.

By far the most direct and pragmatic method used by the Inca of Cuzco to control their own as well as all the subject peoples of the empire was through the empire's highly bureaucratic form of government, which operated strictly according to the underlying principles of Inca culture. Primary government officials included the Emperor himself, the governors of the four *suyu* or quarters, who were called *apo,* and a large battery of junior officials called *kuraka,* who governed the smaller divisions of the four quarters. There were also vast numbers of religious, accounting, and other officials, all of whose duties and responsibilities were spelled out in great detail by the Inca principle of recip- rocal obligation, which we shall discuss subsequently.

The Emperor, The Inca, was chosen by his predecessor from one of the ten large royal lineages of Cuzco, called *panacas,* whose members were descen- dants of the earlier emperors. Members of the *panacas* were considered Inca- by-Blood, and their primary duty was to govern for the common good in accordance with the rules of Inca culture. From their ranks came not only the Emperor but also the governors of the four *suyu,* the *apo.*

Royal succession was normally in the male line but not necessarily from father to son. There was no automatic rule of succession in any office, and demonstrated ability was the major criterion for filling all offices, that of the Emperor not excluded. Individual governing members of the *panaca* class, including the Emperor, were subject to replacement if they did not rule for the benefit of the people at large.

The Spanish erroneously equated members of the *panacas* with European nobility, but the equation was true only in that European nobility and Inca *panaca* members governed. Birth into European nobility gave one individual rights and privileges well above those of the ordinary man, with little in the way of well-defined reciprocal duties toward one's subjects, and inheritance of these rights and privileges was normally from father to eldest son, regardless of the abilities of the inheriting offspring. Birth into an Inca *panaca,* on the other hand, gave one only duties. Any rights and privileges came only later, after an ability to rule for the common good had been amply demonstrated.

Members of the royal lineages or *panacas* were educated in Cuzco in the *Yacha Wasi,* the House of Teaching or Royal School, and only those who showed aptitude were ever likely to become more than just another govern- ment functionary. Such training emphasized not the privileges that did indeed accrue to a successful ruler but, rather, the social responsibilities of the Inca- by-Blood. The four-year curriculum was in charge of *amautas* or philosopher- scholars. The first year, for both Quechua and non-Quechua students, was devoted to learning *Runa Simi,* the Quechua language, in all its niceties. The second year was spent in acquiring a thorough knowledge of the philosophy and workings of the state and the state religion and its ritual. The third year was devoted to learning use of the *quipu,* the system by which both mathe- matical accounts and historical events were meticulously recorded on an in- tricate system of knotted strings; and the fourth year was devoted to practical application of the *quipu* to all varieties of accounting, mathematical, and historical problems under the careful guidance of the teachers (Hyams and Ordish 1963:113). The State, governed by such trained *panaca* members, was thus a heavily bureaucratic organism which operated with a benign Machiavellianism that in its pragmatism out-Machiavellied Machiavelli.

By far the most important and pervasive of the principles underlying not only Inca government but the Inca way of life in general was the concept referred to as *tinku*. It defined the universe as an interlocking, constantly mutating natural continuum in which two entities join to form a single unit—as male and female join to form a reproductive unit, for example. The offspring of such a union will themselves then join with others to form new reproductive units, and so on for eternity, in a universal, never-ending process that applied to both living and nonliving things. It is a kind of cause-effect statement in which the participants in each union are obligated both to each other and to the new units that spring from them and those units are, in turn, reciprocally responsible both to the unit of their origin as well as to the new units which they themselves form and beget or give rise to. This concept of reciprocal obligation of work and service was and remains today central to the Inca way of life, as it is in all unitary societies.

The basic social unit in which reciprocal obligations operated was then and now the *ayllu*, a community consisting of related families descended from a single ancestor, real or imaginary. The royal *panacas* of Cuzco were *ayllus*, and all Quechua-speaking communities were organized in the same manner, though non-Cuzco *ayllu* members were referred to as Inca-by-Privilege rather than Inca-by-Blood, as members of the *panaca ayllus* were called.

All members of an *ayllu* jointly owned the land on which they lived as well as its natural resources, and they shared work obligations and the fruits of that labor in a series of reciprocal exchanges of goods and services. The economic, political, religious, and broader social functions of the community were managed not person by person or family by family but through the administrative organization of the *ayllu*, with officials similar to the mayors, clerks, accountants, and chiefs of police of our cities and towns. There were religious officials as well, to organize the religious festivals of the *ayllu*. It was through such leadership that all decisions regarding the community's workings and well-being were made.

It was also from the ranks of the non-royal *ayllus* that most administrative positions in the empire below the level of *apo* were filled. Incas-by-Privilege could also attend the Royal schools in Cuzco and thereby earn greater privilege and rank if they showed the necessary aptitude and energy to perform the prescribed reciprocal duties to their communities adequately. From the graduates of these schools came legions of efficient administrators, merchants, engineers, soldiers, and priests.

As said earlier, the local officials of each of the four *suyu* were under the guidance of an *apo,* an Inca-by-Blood who was drawn from the highest levels of those *panaca* members matriculating successfully from the training schools in Cuzco. The *apos* were responsible directly to The Inca, the Emperor, and resided in Cuzco in four major city wards corresponding to the four quarters of the empire. Below the *apo* were the governors of the provinces of each of the *suyu* and below them the administrators of the provincial subdivisions, which as pointed out earlier were called *kurakas.* These lower levels of State officialdom might be filled either by Incas-by-Blood or those Incas-by-Privilege who had shown their ability to govern and had completed the curriculum of the Royal Schools in Cuzco with distinction.

It can not be overemphasized that all of the officials in this vast imperial bureaucracy were in their positions because of their demonstrated ability to serve the needs of their constituents. Nor can it be overemphasized that they could and would be rapidly replaced if they failed in these responsibilities. Membership in the ruling circles of Tawantinsuyu might, indeed, confer certain privileges on the office-holders but only so long as they continued to serve the groups for which they were responsible. The individual was always expendable, the group was not.

All citizens of the State, whether members of an Inca-by-Blood *panaca,* a royal *ayllu,* or an *ayllu* of the Inca-by-Privilege, had the responsibility to supply labor, agricultural goods, and manufactured goods to the central government in lieu of monetary taxes. Such goods and services were, in effect, the currency of the realm. The central government, in turn, had the responsibility to collect such goods and to see to it that they were equitably allocated and redistributed where they were needed. Poverty was essentially unknown, except to those who, through crimes of individualism, had refused to pay their due to the State. Poverty, that is, was a punishment, not a natural economic condition.

The citizens of Tawantinsuyu, whether members of native *ayllus* or non-Quechua conquered peoples, were accounted for in what might be called citizen-units of 10, 100, 500, 1,000, 5,000, and 10,000 individuals, each under the direction of a *kuraka.* Every citizen was accounted for and contributed his share not only to the welfare of his own *ayllu* or non-Quechua local group but also to the State in the form of voluntary nonmonetary taxation.

This was done willingly as a result of the philosophy of reciprocal obligation, which was instilled in all from the time of birth.

The first form of voluntary taxation for the communal good was the *mit'a,* a specified annual number of days of labor on the part of all able-bodied males in the military or on public works. The latter might include the construction of public buildings, roadways, bridges, the important storage warehouses for agricultural produce called *qollqa,* maintained by the State, assistance in the transport of goods along the highway system, or, for specialists, work in the manufacturing of goods. The government provided the individual's living needs and food during the *mit'a* period.

The second form of voluntary taxation consisted of required labor on state-owned agricultural or pastoral lands for a certain number of days per year. The *kuraka* of each citizen-unit was required to keep account of labor performed and goods produced and report such data periodically to the provincial governors, who in turn reported to the *apo* of the *suyu* in which the work was done. It was this accounting that in turn justified the redistribution of both agricultural and manufactured produce to the individual *ayllus* and other local groups. Normally one-third of State produce went to the State temples, one-third to the State bureaucracy itself, and one-third to the *ayllus* of the citizens who had performed the services.

Individuals were allowed and expected to work their own communal lands as well. No land belonging to an *ayllu* was usurped by the State. State lands were kept scrupulously separate, obviating possible cause for revolt on the part of the people at large. Property of all kinds belonged exclusively to the *ayllus,* and under the Emperor Pachacuti laws were passed prohibiting the inheritance of goods from one individual to another among the Inca-by-Blood. All goods accumulated by an individual went to his *ayllu* at that individual's death.

It is little short of amazing that in a distance equal roughly to that between New York and the Panama Canal Zone and with a population close to 12 million such a collection and redistribution system could work as well as it did. The Inca were well aware that the crop and resource potential of their realm differed not by region but rather by altitude. They accordingly divided the Four Quarters, the *suyu,* into similar longitudinal economic regions, linking similar regions in each of the Four Quarters by a paved dual 10,000-mile highway system which remained unsurpassed anywhere else on earth until the advent of motorized travel in the mid- and late nineteenth century. One spur of the highway system ran through the highlands from the southern border of Colombia to southern Chile, and the other branch ran down the coastal lowlands from Tumbes on the Ecuadorian border to just north of the Maule River in south Chile. Each section of this remarkable engineering feat was linked by a latitudinal east-west connecting highway. All along the system at intervals of one day's travel were sturdily built warehouses and inns, many of which survive today. Along these routes the resources and goods of the empire were moved for collection and redistribution with both amazing speed and incredible precision.

Though the Quechua-speaking Inca began their amazing spread throughout the Andes region in the 1200s, the majority of the realm was pieced together during the century immediately preceding European intervention. The greatest ruler and empire-builder, and certainly one of the most notable Americans of all time, was the Emperor Pachacuti (1438–1471), who succeeded both in consolidating and in extending Inca conquests. His was the credit for taking the native Inca system of reciprocal responsibilities and obligations and extending its potential to create the governmental and economic system that the Spanish found in 1532.

Cuzco, the amazing capital city of Tawantinsuyu, from which as we have said literally radiated all roads to the rest of the empire, served as the organizational center for this massive gathering and redistribution effort. It was a city of great beauty as well as efficiency, filled with administrative buildings, the royal residences of The Inca, block after block of massive storehouses, and other public buildings. The most imposing of these was the Coricancha, the Golden Enclosure, housing the State temples and schools and administrative offices, At least the lower walls of many of these structures, including the Coricancha, survive today. In Cuzco lived both the ruling Inca, representatives of all the ten royal *panaca ayllus,* the rulers of conquered lands, the *apo* of each of the Four Quarters of the empire, and the priestly and learned classes.

The system worked well, and Tawantinsuyu was a functional, smoothly running, literal communist welfare state such as the world had never seen before nor has seen since.

The Incas were masters of practical engineering, as their surviving masonry structures, amazing rope bridges, and highway system testify. Particularly notable was the art of building with interlocking stones without mortar. When a major earthquake struck Cuzco in 1950, most of the Spanish colonial and later-period buildings were readily toppled, but the much older Inca masonry structures went completely unscathed.

The Incas were also master workers in fabrics, a heritage from earlier ages held in common with all the peoples of the Andes. While the *mit'a* was a form of taxation of able-bodied males, textile taxation was the major form of reciprocal service performed by the women of Tawantinsuyu, whose fabrics have always been noted for fine workmanship, durability, and exceedingly fine decoration.

Perhaps surprising to most, Inca physicians were quite fluent in many branches of practical medicine. Such expertise is common in unitary societies the world over, as Chinese medicine and the pharmaceutical practices of many smaller unitary cultures indicate. Dentistry among the Inca was particularly advanced, including the use of silver crowns, but the most well known Inca medical practice was the use of cranial trepanation to effect cures in instances when the patient would otherwise have died—the repair of serious head wounds or the removal of tumors, for example. Modern Peruvian surgeons have actually used Inca medical instruments to perform cranial surgery with excellent results. From what we know, we cannot say that Inca physicians and surgeons were interested in science for its own sake, but they became sophisticated practitioners of what experience taught them effected a successful cure—pragmatists of the first order, as one would expect.

Inca religion, which like Japanese Shinto believed that all was holy, *huaca* in Quechua, especially revered the Sun God Inti and the Creator God Viracocha. The Emperor Pachacuti is said to have codified Inca religious beliefs and created a State religion devoted to the worship of Viracocha. While the latter was viewed as a universal deity, in actual practice the Inca were very tolerant of the beliefs of their conquered subjects so long as Viracocha was publicly acknowledged as the paramount deity. The *huaca* or Holy Objects of conquered peoples were brought to Cuzco and housed in the Coricancha along with the shrines of the Inca gods—whether for honor or as hostage is open to question, but the practice insured the loyalty of subject peoples and helped weld them into something resembling national unity. Inca religious practices, one should hasten to add, also allowed human sacrifice. Barbaric to us, one must remember that in all unitary societies the life of the individual is unimportant by the side of the survival and welfare of the group. Thus if the sacrifice of a single life was seen as overcoming a group crisis, then that life was taken. The individual whose life was forfeit, so far as we can tell, went quite willingly to his death—another part of the philosophy of *tinku* and reciprocal obligation. The person was drugged with coca and usually left to freeze to death in a semicomatose state on an open mountain peak.

The vast realm of Tawantinsuyu was, like all other large unitary states, formed by military might through the exploits of a series of Inca rulers, of whom Pachacuti (1438–1471) and Tupa Inca Yupanqui (1471–1493) were the most aggressive and important. Inca warfare, like that of all unitary societies, was frequent and, because the life of any and all individuals was expendable, brutal in the extreme, but the conquered were taken in and over time assimilated into the empire. Those who did not resist and who survived the initial military onslaught were usually not only allowed but obligated to live on their traditional lands in the manner to which they had been accustomed. They were simply formed into citizen units, their former rulers serving as the equivalent of *kurakas* or *ayllu* leaders. As pointed out earlier, their children were often taken to Cuzco when young and educated in the Royal Schools of the Coricancha. When converted by young adulthood, they were returned to their people, among whom they served as leaders.

Special government officials from Cuzco, known as *tokoyrikoq*, were charged with keeping tabs on the members of the enormous government bureaucracy. Their duties cut across bureaucratic lines, and they were especially charged with investigating all State and local affairs. They acted, in effect, as the empire's FBI and General Accounting Office.

In somewhat similar manner, entire settlements of Quechua-speakers were made in conquered lands to act as regional spies and to hasten the process of converting the local inhabitants into good Quechuas. These *mitma*, as they were called, provided a positive example of exemplary Inca behavior, and only particularly loyal citizen units served as *mitma*. They were exempt from control by the local *kuraka* and reported directly to officials in Cuzco.

Military garrisons were established throughout the empire, but diplomacy was especially used to win the rulers of newly conquered lands to the Inca way. Often recalcitrant rulers and their entire families were brought to live in Cuzco, where they were allowed the trappings of royalty—a kind of velvet-gloved house arrest.

In spite of what seems to us the extreme rigidity of this highly regimented, bureaucratic, Big Brother society, it must be noted that the majority of the non-Quechua peoples conquered by the Inca were apparently happy with their lot. There were exceptions, of course, particularly in Ecuador in the north and in Chile in the far south, and the Spanish took full advantage of these newly conquered, dissatisfied segments of the population. Most of the non-Quechua peoples at the heart of the empire—Peru, Bolivia, and Ecuador —were themselves members of unitary societies before the Inca conquest, and the nature and rigors of Inca rule were consequently the expected social norm.

Generally speaking, the Incas learned to avoid long-term contact with dualistic peoples—the Amazonians across the Andes to the east, the Chibchan cultures of Colombia to the north, and the Araucanian cultures of Chile in the south. When the Inca found that their methods of governance simply would not work in these social surroundings, they seem to have quietly left them to their own devices.

Inca history, in our sense of the word, is very sketchy, for the official history of the Inca State, as propounded amply to the Spanish in 1532, is typical of all state histories, unitary, dualistic, or trinary—it ignores what it wishes to ignore, glorifies what it wishes to glorify, and reinterprets events to suit the needs of the current dynasty. Since time and what we perceive as its flow is of little or no concern to the people of unitary societies, no historical time line is found in the Inca chronicles, and we have very little idea of the span included in the official Inca histories.

In terms of overall success as a yardstick for measuring the adequacy of a social system, it is hard to find anything overt to criticize adversely in the Inca world of Tawantinsuyu. It had its harsh points, as do all social systems, but its efficiency as a method for creating and maintaining an equitable public welfare state was amazing. Nothing, even the modern Chinese unitary state, can compare to it today. Inca unitary life still survives in the Andean highlands of Peru, where the *ayllu* transcends the individual, where village and family welfare come first. They still call themselves Runa, The People, and look forward to a time when their values will once again govern their land. They refer to Quechua as *Runa Simi,* Human Speech, to distinguish it from Spanish, which is called *Alqo Simi,* Animal Speech! Though Tawantinsuyu is gone, the unitary Inca survive, numbering yet in excess of 7 million souls.

8

The Empire of the México

A distant vision of unbelievable beauty unsurpassed by anything they had ever seen: that was the Spanish invaders' first impression of Tenochtitlán, the imperial capital of the Aztec Empire in the Valley of Mexico. The city, as seen by the advancing expeditionary force of Hernán Cortés on November 8, 1519, from the banks of the great lake of Tezcoco, seemed to float on the water. Bernal Díaz del Castillo, who accompanied that momentous expedition, describes his reaction:

> During the morning we arrived at a broad causeway and continued our march toward Itztapalapa, and when we saw so many cities and villages built in the water and other great towns on dry land and that straight and level causeway going toward Mexico, we were amazed and said that it was like the enchantments described in the legend of Amadís, on account of the great towers, temples, and buildings rising from the water, and all built of masonry. And some of our soldiers asked whether the things we saw were not a dream. (Díaz del Castillo 1963)

The Spanish were dumbfounded by the city's vast extent—modern estimates of its population are put at 200,000 to 300,000, five times the size of the largest European city of the times. Like Buda and Pest or Minneapolis and St. Paul, the capital was a dual city on a single island—Tlatelolco to the north and Tenochtitlán to the south. Tlatelolco served as the main marketing and commercial center of the capital, and Tenochtitlán served as the administrative center of both the city and the empire. The palaces of the emperors were located in Tenochtitlán, and all major ceremonies, political and religious, were held there.

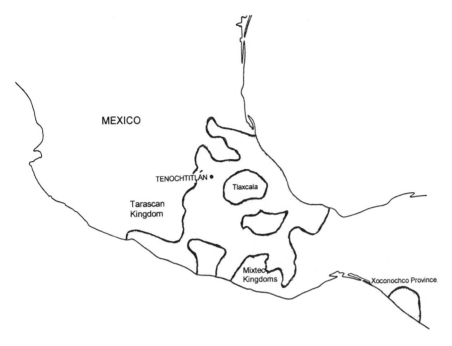

Figure 12. The Aztec Empire in 1519

The Spanish marveled at the city's careful plan, its aqueducts of roaring freshwater from the springs at Chapultepec and Coyoacán on the western edge of the lake, the vast dike across the lake built by the Emperor Nezahual-coyotl of Texcoco to separate saltwater from fresh, the city's system of waste disposal, its immaculately clean streets and gleaming buildings. The pyramidal towers of the temples shone against the intense blue sky, and the many massive causeways leading several miles across the lake to the city were crowded with people coming and going. Description of the city once inside is even more lavish. We are told of endless networks of canals linking every section of the city, well-built houses of stone and mortar, some several stories high with interior patios planted with flowers, roads lined with trees and flowering bushes, the city's metropolitan zoo—the aviary alone had ten large enclosures, around the tops of which were walkways with hanging gardens—botanical gardens, and libraries of books.

The empire itself, with a population of some 11 million, was comparable to Tawantinsuyu, though its geographical spread was not as great. Permanent effective power was limited to the Valley of Mexico and the immediately adjacent regions, but political control of other Aztec as well as subject cities spread as far as the Gulf of Mexico to the east, the Pacific coast in the west, and as far south as the Pacific coast of San Salvador.

Settling the vast Valley of Mexico in the mid-1200s as seminomadic intruders from Nayarit in northwestern Mexico, the fortunes of the Méxica, as they called themselves, improved remarkably in the early 1400s, when a series of successful wars brought the city of Tenochtitlán supremacy under the fourth Aztec ruler, the Emperor Itzcoatl. During his reign (1427–1440) and those of his successors, Motecuhzoma Ilhuicamina (1440–1468) and Axayacatl (1468–1481), the other Náhuatl-speaking cities of central Mexico came under the control of the Méxica, and so it remained until the arrival of the Spanish a century later in 1519.

The successful consolidation of power under the dynasty of Tenochtitlán was largely the result of the diplomatic acumen and military expertise of one of the most extraordinary leaders native America has ever produced. His name was Tlacaelel. The nephew of the Emperor Itzcoatl, Tlacaelel became the primary advisor to the imperial throne through the reigns of his uncle Itzcoatl, his half-brother Motecuhzoma Ilhuicamina, and his nephew's son Axayacatl. Just as the Inca Pachacuti formed and delineated the Inca State, so Tlacaelel did for the Aztec State, serving in the capacity of Secretary of State or, shades of the Ottoman Empire, Grand Vizier. Statesman and strategist, Machiavellian in the extreme, Tlacaelel preferred to serve for the glory of the State rather than assume more personal dictatorial powers, which he could well have done had he so desired. The Méxica Empire and its underlying philosophy was largely his invention.

We are fortunate in the first-hand information we have of Aztec life in all its aspects. Unlike other native American societies encountered by Europeans, which we see largely through the writings of their Spanish, French, or English conquerors, with all the mistaken interpretations of native ways and thought to be expected when a foreigner looks at a new and alien society, we have literally thousands of pages of documents from members of Aztec society just after the advent of the Spanish.

We are indebted to a number of highly motivated and intelligent Catholic priests for this information. Three men in particular, all Franciscan friars—Fray Toribio de Motolinia (1495–1565), Fray Bernardo de Sahagún (1499–1590), and Fray Diego Durán (1537–1588)—have left us remarkable documents in the words of the members of Aztec society to whom they talked. Sahagún's accounts (Sahagún 1950–1970) are especially valuable, for, like a good modern-day gatherer of ethnographic data and oral history, he took down what his informants said, as nearly as possible, word for word. All three men learned to speak the Náhuatl language fluently when they first arrived in Mexico, all realized that traditional Aztec culture was vanishing and would be completely gone within a generation or two, and all wished to record what they could of the history of the Empire, the customs, thoughts, and beliefs of the people, and the manner in which Aztec life had been traditionally carried forth.

Sahagún worked at compiling his firsthand reports over a period of twenty-two years, from 1547 to 1569. Durán recorded firsthand accounts of Aztec history, though not in his informants' exact words as Sahagún had done, as well as detailed descriptions of Aztec religion and ceremonial rites (Durán 1964, 1971), and Motolinia's history remains one of the most important firsthand documents of the times (Motolinia 1951). Yet another friar, Alonso de Molina, produced a dictionary of the Náhuatl language in 1571 that is still unparalleled (Molina 1977).

Thanks directly to the overt efforts of the Inquisition at home in Spain, however, none of these works was published. They did not see the light of day for 300 years, not until the late nineteenth century. Their content, however, once known, revolutionized the study of Aztec life and the history of the Aztec Empire. We have more reliable ethnohistoric data on the Aztec and their pre-Columbian empire than we do on any other native American society at any time. It is thus possible to describe Aztec society as it was in 1519 and the several centuries just before and after that date with considerable certainty and detail.

We know that the empire was governed by the same kind of unitary bureaucracy that kept Inca Tawantinsuyu intact, its main concern the maintenance of the national welfare through a complex interplay of decisions and actions by the constituent groups within the social system.

The ruling classes of Mexico were as well trained as the Inca elite, and though imperial succession remained within the dynasty, at times from father to son, the choice of succession was made by election by members of the emperor's Cabinet, the leading priests, and his War Council, and only those within the royal lineage who had been carefully educated and who had demonstrated an ability to deal with people and problems were chosen to rule. By a series of diplomatic alliances through marriage with the royal families of the subordinate Aztec cities, the dynastic line of Tenochtitlán carefully and with purpose also assured itself backing throughout the empire.

Though government under the royal dynasty was concentrated in the person of the *Tlatoani* or Emperor, his power was not without its checks and balances. The emperor was advised by a Cabinet, the *Tlatocan,* which consisted of four members of the royal family eligible for the succession. The most important member of the Cabinet was the *Cihuacoatl*, the Woman Serpent or Vizier. This was the post that Tlacaelel filled. The *Cihuacoatl* was something of a Minister of the Interior, charged with the management of the internal affairs of the Empire, while the Emperor himself made decisions largely having to do with external relationships of the State with other cities and kingdoms. There was also a War Council for advisement specifically on war and territorial expansion. Additional advisement came from the *tetecutin*, who were members of other, nonroyal, noble families, and from members of the State judicial system. The emperor and the Tlatocan Council appointed judges for a large and far-ranging court system consisting of neighborhood courts, the State Court (the *Teccalco*), and a Supreme Court of thirteen senior judges (the *Tlacxitlan*).

Aztec society had become, that is, highly bureaucratic and stratified during the century preceding Spanish contact. Below the emperor and the *tetecutin* noble families were a series of lesser nobles, the *pipiltin*. And beneath these were the *macehualtin* or the ordinary people. Such hierarchies of social classes are typical of most large unitary societies—Tawantinsuyu, or modern-day China provide comparable examples.

The vast and intricate bureaucratic structure of Aztec society has led most modern researchers to conclude that the México people were not in the least egalitarian (Coe 1984:155, for example), that class differences meant wide differences in social privilege. While the latter is true, for class distinctions were rigid and well defined, the first assumption is not. Aztec morality mandated egalitarian treatment of all members of the community, whether nobles or commoners. Sahagún's and Durán's Aztec informants repeatedly emphasized that class membership gave one not just certain limited privileges but, more important, responsibilities and obligations. Behavior harmful to any segment of society was not condoned but, on the contrary, quickly and often brutally punished. Such prescribed behavior was a social requirement, and even the emperor and nobility were not above its requirements. They were simply first-among-equals.

The reciprocal responsibilities that linked and separated the members of Aztec society were expressed in a philosophical principle called *ometecuhtli/ omecíhuatl*, Lord and Lady of Duality, a concept almost identical to that of Quechua *tinku* and Chinese yin/yang. This principle was conceived of as the sole source and rationale for all that existed, as the only "reality" there was, all other explanations being illusion (León-Portilla 1979:387).

Ometecuhtli/omecíhuatl, promulgated under Tlacaelel's tutelage, provided the underpinnings not only of Aztec government but of the Aztec way of life in general. Precisely like Inca *tinku,* it defined the universe as an interlocking, constantly mutating, all-pervasive, natural continuum in which two entities join to form single units, a process that continues on for eternity in a universal, never-ending progression that applied to both living and nonliving things. It is a kind of cause-effect statement in which the participants in each union are obligated both to each other and to the new units that spring from them, and those units are, in turn, reciprocally responsible both to the unit of their origin as well as to the new units that they themselves form and beget or give rise to. This concept of reciprocal obligation of work and service was as central to the Aztec way of life as it was to the Inca way of life. This was the *moral imperative* of Aztec life, and it overrode all distinctions of social class.

The capital of Tenochtitlán was divided into four quarters—Cuepopan, Mototlan, Teopan, and Aztacalco—which were in turn divided into numerous residential neighborhoods or wards, called *calpulli,* Big House, each a largely self-sufficient neighborhood in the overall economic and political machine of the city.

The member residents of each *calpulli* were closely related individuals from large extended families, often including as many as several thousand people, all of whom were descended from a single real or fictitious ancestor. Each *calpulli* was a town within the city, and each had its own elected leader, the *calpullec,* who had broad governing powers and who was entrusted with seeing to it that the needs of all *calpulli* members were met and that every member contributed his or her share of labor and services toward the overall welfare of the group. Political and economic decisions affecting the *calpulli* itself were effected within its structure. Only those life activities touching on the larger society were governed by national policy, formed in the administrative center of the capital.

Calpulli affairs were correlated and kept track of by a special *calpulli* official known as the *tequitlatoque,* a kind of Secretary of Outside Affairs for the ward. His duties were similar to those of the Inca *kuraka,* though the *tequitlatoque* was a member of his own *calpulli,* not, as the Inca *kuraka,* an outsider imposed from above by the State bureaucracy.

Like the Inca *ayllu,* the *calpulli* owned its own land communally, individual plots being assigned to specific families for the raising of locally used produce. Private real property was unknown among the *macelhualli* or commoners, though the *pipiltin* or nobility and those above them in rank did own certain lands privately. Even these, however, were passed on from the owner to his own community at his death. Within the *calpulli,* goods of all kinds belonged to *calpulli* family units or to the *calpulli* itself. Also, like the Inca *ayllu*, the members of a *calpulli* were required to help support the State at large. This was done not through taxation but through occupational specialization and the performance of obligatory labor for the State. The *tequitlatoque* organized the *calpulli* labor forces, keeping account of the work done for both the *calpulli* and the State. Community tasks could include the construction of public buildings and waterways, causeways and aqueducts, or service in the military or civil service when needed. As in the Inca State, every member of Aztec society had a reciprocal obligation to his own community, the *calpulli*, and to society at large.

Individual *calpullis* tended to devote themselves to a specific trade or business, so, for example, in Tlatelolco there were seven *calpulli* devoted solely to the business of wholesale and retail trade. Another neighborhood was occupied exclusively by feather workers. Through such craft specialization, goods needed by the State were produced by a specific *calpulli* in exchange for other goods which it needed, which would come from another *calpulli* through the State bureaucracy or from tribute from conquered peoples or from foreign trade. The tremendous variety of agricultural and manufactured products gathered by the State in this manner were also used for support of the royal *calpullis*, the State temples, and schools.

The redistribution of goods to the individual *calpullis* was handled and accounted for by the *tequitlatoque*, and the entire redistribution procedure was effected through a marketing system of staggering proportions. The Spanish estimated that the central market of Tlatilolco alone saw 30,000 souls a day and 60,000 on every regular twice-weekly market day.

Agricultural practices were highly professional, extremely intensive, and more than successful. The Aztec and their predecessors had learned early that reclamation of land from the large fresh- and brackish-water lakes of the Valley of Mexico could provide them with all the agricultural land they needed, and that very near their urban settlements. Canals were built to allow the water of shallow swampy areas on the edges of the lakes to drain off, leaving the higher parts of the fertile lake bottoms above water. These embryo islands were used for the growing of crops. Over the years, as increasing amounts of lake-bottom soil were heaped on them with the help of woven substructures, they became permanent fertile islands, the famous *chinampas* or floating gardens. Irrigation was, of course, not needed, inasmuch as the roots of one's plantings were readily supplied with water from the lake. Yields were extremely high.

Chinampas on reclaimed land were immediately adjacent to one another in great numbers, producing large fields with crisscrossing natural canals between them. As the years passed, *chinampa* areas of many hundreds of acres were created around the shores of Lake Texcoco. The only surviving *chinampa* region today, however, is the well-known one at Xochimilco, on the south shores of the lake.

The variety of produce known to have been cultivated and harvested on the *chinampas* of Lake Texcoco is indeed remarkable. Vegetables and fruits of all kinds were the principal crops, along with flowers in profusion—the Aztec, then and now, outdo even the British in their love of blossoms of all kinds. Grains were also grown, though usually on natural land, the major ones being maize and amaranth.

Fish and game, particularly the former, from the lakes and hills and mountains of the Valley of Mexico were also major food sources for the more affluent upper classes, but the common man rarely had the pleasure of their presence on his table. Chocolate and other exotic imported commodities were also the privilege of the noble classes. Just as Russian caviar is today not within the grasp of all, chocolate was a precious product, so precious, in fact, that cacao beans served as a major form of currency in the marketplace as well as in foreign trade.

The craft specialization of the Aztec and the conquered peoples of the empire was extremely varied and of very high workmanship and quality. As is so often the case with the manufactured products of unitary societies, the appearance and physical appeal of the item was of as much importance as its utility, in some cases of greater importance. Manufactured goods were, in general, works of art. It is, in fact, often impossible for one unfamiliar with Aztec life to assign a use to a specific artifact, just as is the case, for example, with many beautiful and exotic Chinese jades. The artisan's aesthetic taste for form, color, and texture often outweighed any underlying utility.

The Aztec were also fine metal workers and lapidaries, and the sculpting of all varieties of stone and precious gems was a refined art. Fabrics of feathers and unusual furs and fibers were also frequently made. Ceramic wares were beautifully made as well. These craft traits were not limited to the Aztec. All the neighboring unitary cultures of Central Mexico show them as well—particularly the Mixtec and Zapotec—as do the dualistic Tarascan people.

Education for both sexes was universal and mandatory, provided on the *calpulli* level as well as on the State level. The *calpulli* schools, called *culcacalli,* House of Song, were intended for the ordinary citizen, providing an overall education for the young. Other *calpulli* schools, called *telpochcalli,* provided military training for the young men of the ward. In contrast, the State schools, the *calmecac,* and the temple schools, in the central administrative section of the city, like the Inca *Yacha Wasi,* were devoted to the training of State officials and their children. Here, too, there were both elementary level schools and secondary schools. The secondary schools, like the *telpochcalli* of the *calpulli,* were specialized, offering training in military affairs, law, engineering, and practical science. Education on both the *calpulli* and State level was completed at the age of twenty. From what we know—and Bernardo de Sahagún, major chronicler for the Aztec, gives us detailed descriptions of the educational system of the empire—these institutions were at least as advanced in both knowledge and instructional technique as any of Europe's medieval universities.

It was in the empire's school system that the necessary behavior traits of a desirable member of society were taught. The reciprocal social obligations demanded by the principle of *ometecuhtli/omecíhuatl*—the most important of which were self-restraint, respect for others in mind and deed, and humility— were thoroughly imbued in all students, commoner and noble alike, to judge from Sahagún's informants. Not even members of the royal lineage and the other royal *calpulli* were exempted from these Spartan requirements.

Literary efforts flourished, many in hieroglyphic written form, a kind of prompt book rather than the full-fledged writing of the neighboring Maya. The subject matter of Aztec literature is as varied as that of any European language. Philosophical tracts, for example, are frequent and profound, discussing the nature of humans and the world in which they lived. The surviving works of the statesman Tlacaelel and the philosopher Nezahualcoyotl rival those of any thinker of any time, and Aztec poetry compares favorably with that of any of the world's other great literatures. The volume of surviving Aztec literature is greater than that which we have for Classical Greece, approaching that of Roman literature.

The occupation of scribe in the *calmecac* was a particularly prestigious one, usually filled by men of considerable education and wisdom. Books were written on *amatl,* paper made from the inner bark of the fig tree, though records of abbreviated kinds were also sculpted on stone.

The copious surviving instruction to the young details the exemplary life, which is one of moderation and consideration for one's fellows, of adhering to *calpulli* and State norms. Extremes of all kinds are constantly warned against. The educational instructions to those reared to be rulers and officials of the State reflect a highly humane view of life, one in which the avoidance of excess in any form is of paramount social value. This, in short, is just the kind of educational system one expects in a unitary culture (Sahagún 1950–1970).

Unlike Inca religion, which was essentially simple and direct, Aztec religion was extremely complex. It had the same pessimism and concept of sin and inherent human evil that characterized medieval Christianity. The clergy were celibate, as in Catholicism, and the Spanish clergy recorded their surprise and pleasure at these aspects of native belief, noting the presence even of confession and concepts of atonement. Atonement, however, came not only through confession, ceremony, and acts of contrition but, to the horror of the Spanish, through the public sacrifice of human beings, numbering in the thousands each year on more than a dozen public Holy Days. It was this which colored and still colors the European view of Aztec Mexico, though it must be remembered that to sacrifice one's life for the welfare, real or imagined, of the public whole is the greatest of honors in unitary societies, not the unspeakable horror with which we view it. The individuals who met their fate in this manner were considered special human beings, accorded the most solicitous treatment once chosen, often living a year prior to their sacrifice in luxury, and seem to have gone to their death content that they were serving their people in the best of ways. Death for the State was seen as a necessary part of life, something to be valued, not an excess or an antisocial act of revenge or punishment. After death under the sacrificial knife, the souls of the victims went to a special heaven, where they became gorgeous hummingbirds which accompanied the sun on its daily journey across the skies.

Warfare became the mainstay of the Aztec State after the conquests of the Emperor Itzcoatl (1427–1440). Under Tlacaelel's guidance the War God Huitzilopochtli became the paramount deity, and the greatest service an Aztec youth could aspire to and render to the State was successful service in the wars of the empire. Captives of battle were routinely sacrificed at Huitzilopochtli's altar, and the survivors formed tributary states. While the conquered were usually allowed to retain their own leaders and customs, they were obliged to help support the economic needs of their Aztec overlords through the supply of both agricultural and manufactured products. Special tax collectors called *calpixque* were in charge of enforcing these requirements, and backsliders were dealt with harshly. The very backbone of the Aztec State became tribute from such subsidiary societies, and the collection machine was one of great complexity.

As important to the economic well-being of the México Empire as tribute were the goods brought home by merchants, who came to form a special social class, the *pochteca*. These traders traveled throughout Middle America, making shrewd economic purchases for the State. Like the Inca *tokoyrikoq,* they also became espionage agents of considerable skill as well as forgers of new and important diplomatic alliances. The *pochteca* became a powerful force in Aztec society, and they were both highly respected and greatly feared.

Like the Incas, the Aztecs had their greatest imperial success with the other unitary societies that occupied large areas of central Mexico. When confronted by the dualistic Tarascans of Michoacán, to the west of the Valley of Mexico, the dualistic Maya to the south, and the many trinary-culture desert tribes to the north, however, their tribute-machine simply did not work, and the México Empire limited its borders to lands largely occupied by other unitary peoples.

The empire came to a sudden and violent end in 1521, and the disruption was so thorough and so devastating that Aztec society was unable to recover. Unlike the Inca of Tawantinsuyu, who were never absorbed into the mainstream of Spanish society and culture in the Andean countries and who have consequently maintained their separate identity over the centuries, the Aztec of the México Empire were taken in by their Spanish conquerors, and today modern Mexico prides itself on being neither Hispanic nor Indian but an inextricable blend of both. Aztec culture still survives in greatly modified form, but the full genius of the culture has vanished forever.

9

The Maya Kingdoms

Though there were more than half a dozen urban dualistic societies in the pre-Columbian New World, only two controlled large geographical areas—the Maya peoples of Middle America and the Mississippi River Valley peoples of North America. In this and the following chapter, we will describe both of these societies, which, in spite of their seemingly exotic natures, followed the same underlying social norms that characterize most European, Euro-American, and African states today.

The Maya region then and now was comprised of all of the present nations of Guatemala and Belize, parts of Honduras and El Salvador, and the Mexican states of Chiapas, Tabasco, Campeche, Yucatán, and Quintana Roo. This large region can be subdivided into three major geographical-cultural areas: the Southern Area (highland Guatemala, fronting on the Pacific coast); the Central Area (centered in Chiapas, Tabasco, and Campeche states in Mexico, and, particularly, the Department of the Petén of lowland Guatemala, all of Belize, small parts of Honduras and El Salvador, and large parts of southern Yucatán); and the Northern Area (central and northern Yucatán and Quintana Roo). The peoples of the Southern Area are aptly referred to as the Highland Maya—primarily the Quiché, Cakchiquel, Kekchi, Pokomchi, Ixil, Chuh, and Tojolabal peoples. The Central and Northern Areas are inhabited by the Lowland Maya—the most important being the Chol, Chontal, Tzeltal, Tzotzil, and Chorti peoples in the Central Area and the Yucatec people in the Northern Area.

While cities and their surrounding kingdoms developed in all three areas, it is those of the Central and Northern areas that interest us most, partly because we know more about them than we do the Southern Area highland cities and partly because it was in those regions in which Maya culture showed itself most brilliantly. We are particularly interested in the Northern Area kingdoms, for these were the ones that faced the brunt of Spanish intervention in the early and middle 1500s. The cities of the Central Area kingdoms, over sixty in number, had been largely abandoned during the period of about A.D. 900 to 1200, but some sixteen kingdoms were still following an urban way of life in northern and central Yucatán, Quintana Roo, and Belize when the Spanish arrived in 1528.

The Classic Period of Lowland Maya culture, centered in the cities and kingdoms south of northern Yucatán, largely in the Petén region of Guatemala in the Central Area, lasted from approximately A.D. 250 to shortly after A.D. 900—the last dated monument bears a date the equivalent of 909. The Maya groups responsible for this florescence were the Cholan peoples—Chol, Chorti, and Cholti. There followed a period of some 300 years during which depredations and invasions by the Toltec people of central Mexico brought havoc to the Yucatec peoples of the Northern Area and brought a series of problems not yet fully understood to the kingdoms of the Central Area— problems probably related to excessive dynastic strife that brought on collapse of the economic base of most kingdoms. By the time the Spanish arrived a little over 300 years later, in 1528, the period of classic glory in the Central Area had long been over and the vicissitudes of the previous centuries largely gone. What remained was a group of Northern Area kingdoms centered around large urban settlements. Much of the technical and artistic tradition of earlier times was still intact, though perhaps not in the spectacular manner we are used to associating with the great Classic Maya Central Area kingdoms of Palenque, Tikal, Yaxchilán, Piedras Negras, Copán, Quiriguá, and many others. It is from the data we have for both the Classic Period cities of the Central Area and the later cities of the Northern Area that we can piece together a rather full description of Maya culture as it existed both during the Classic Period and at the time of Spanish intervention.

Today, however, the view we have of Lowland Maya society is very much at variance with the earlier, long-held traditional view. The new view is built on the traditional base, but the tremendous amount of new archaeological and epigraphic data unearthed and analyzed in the last three to four decades has forced us to a radically different interpretation of these fascinating people. We should hasten to add that knowledge of Maya society is not and has not been for at least a century at the level of a total mystery, in spite of the fondness of popularizers for instilling that concept in their readers. We know today almost as much about the Classic Maya of the Petén region of Guatemala and their latter-day relatives in the Yucatán peninsula as we do about the ancient

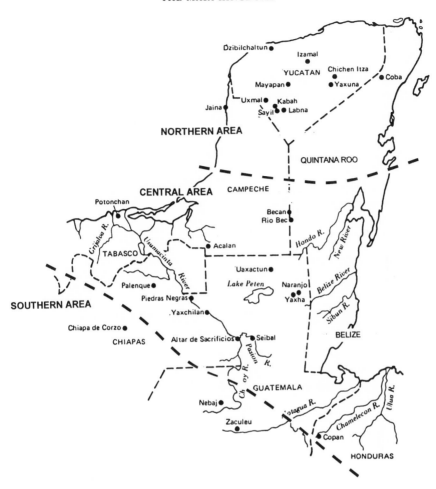

Figure 13. Maya Kingdoms of the Classic Period (ca. A.D. 250–900)

Egyptians. There is still much that needs elucidation, but the main lines and many details are quite clear.

For many years the Lowland Maya were portrayed as a highly docile, peaceful people, ruled by theocrat-priests from ceremonial centers and obsessed with marking the passage of time—every hieroglyphic monument is covered with a series of finely honed dates in a calendrical system next to which ours pales as mere child's-play. As it turns out, the reasons for such time markings, we now know, are not at all the reasons we had originally thought. It is not time itself with which the Maya were obsessed but a time line of events in the lives of the kings and queens who ruled the Maya kingdoms.

We had also thought first that each Maya city was a completely separate political unit, operating independently of the others, but later opinion turned to the notion that cities had grouped together to form larger confederacies, only seven or eight in number. Both assumptions, now that we have considerable documentary information from the Maya inscriptions themselves, were incorrect. Instead what we see is approximately sixty independent kingdoms in constantly fluctuating alignment or war with each other. Many monuments make it clear that though a kingdom might be independently ruled by its own dynastic family, its independence was dependent upon the largesse of the ruler of a yet larger and more powerful neighboring kingdom. These overlord kings seem to have had the last word in major decision making. The state of affairs is remarkably similar to the manorial system of medieval Europe in the 1200s through the 1500s, in which princes, dukes, earls, barons, and even some kings, though technically independent of one another and of more powerful kings, gave allegiance first to one over-king or emperor and then to another, depending upon a large number of political and economic circumstances.

It had also been thought that the beautifully designed urban complexes of both the Highland and Lowland Maya were ceremonial and market centers, to which the ordinary people came only on market and ceremonial Holy Days, occupied permanently only by a small priestly ruling class. This belief was based both on limited archaeological excavation and on the model of modern Maya market towns in highland Guatemala. Considerably more excavation and site surveys now indicate that, to the contrary, these centers were true cities. We know that the surviving complexes of spectacular temples, palaces, and administrative buildings were surrounded by hundreds and in some cases thousands of less durable homesteads, spreading out for many miles from each urban core. These were cities in every modern sense of the word.

In the last years of the nineteenth century and the early years of the twentieth, our data also seemed to indicate that the individual had little worth in Maya society, that it was only maintenance of the overall social norms that counted. We assumed that these norms were unitary, focused solely toward the needs of society at large, like those of the Aztec and Inca. Again, as a result of the expanded archaeological database and our increased knowledge of the content of the texts of Maya hieroglyphic monuments, we now know that this, too, was not so.

When we succeeded in unraveling the basic intricacies of Maya hieroglyphic writing, we found a world of highly competitive individualism. Now that we understand much of what the inscriptions say, we know that they are celebrating the rule of hereditary dynasties of rulers, glorifying the exploits of individual monarchs from ruling families. We even know the names of a great many of them and have in cases been able to compile partial biographies and royal genealogies of the leading families (Coe and Van Stone 2001, Martin and Grube 2000, Proskouriakoff 1960).

A number of royal tombs have also been found and opened, revealing a glory and panoply of New World King Tuts that vividly demonstrate the un- usual, important, and overriding role the individual played in Maya society. This importance is beautifully indicated as well by remarkable works of art, including strikingly lifelike portrait masks, paintings, and sarcophagus sculp- tures.

Maya society was not only highly individualistic, it was also a decidedly two-class society—the Haves (the nobility or *almehen*) and the Have-Nots (the rest of the people), reminiscent again of medieval European nobility and serf, with no in-between middle class, the eventual European bourgeoisie. These principles of individualism and dualism are vividly revealed in Maya concepts of family and property as delineated in the surviving Maya chron- icles and documents from all time periods, most notably perhaps the *Titles of Ebtun,* a voluminous compendium of legal documents defining property rights, division, and inheritance in Yucatán during colonial times (Roys 1939).

Each person, noble or commoner, traced his descent through both his fa- ther's and mother's lineage to a founder of each line, male in the father's family, female in the mother's. In addition to given names, each individual had a dual family name, identifying his father's lineage and his mother's. Both real and perishable property were individually owned. Ownership of both types of goods might come to the individual either through his personal efforts or through inheritance from his father's or mother's lineage. At the time of Span- ish intervention the bulk of real property descended through the male line, as did rank and political power. There is, however, increasing evidence from Classic Period monuments that many powerful rulers of earlier times, such as the ruler of Naranjo known as Lady Six Sky (A.D. 682–741), were women, and that the ownership of goods as well as rank and privilege was determined not so much by one's gender as by one's abilities.

When the Spanish arrived, there were some 250 male-line families in Yu- catán, with a small number of extremely powerful lineages, such as the Cocom and Xiu, at the helm. These families constituted the nobility, the *almehen,* and from them came the ruling dynasties of the sixteen individual kingdoms. The rulers themselves were referred to as *halach uinic,* Real Man, though in earlier times they had been called simply *ahau,* King. Each *ahau* or later *halach uinic* ruled from his own city, controlling a considerable area around it and, like the medieval European lord, owning large tracts outright. These tracts were worked by peasant labor in return for protection and other services, in a distinctly manorial way. At the time of the Spanish conquest, each of the sixteen kingdoms was governed in this manner.

The dynasties of most of the kingdoms of the 1400s and 1500s traced their ancestry either back to the time of the Mexican invasions from Tula and other Toltec cities of central Mexico in the late 900s or to the Itzá, who invaded and overran all of the peninsula in the early and middle 1200s. The descendants of many of these families survive today, quite conscious of their illustrious forebears.

The smaller settlements in each kingdom were governed by an official called a *batab*, appointed by the *halach uinic* and usually coming from a noble family closely related to the ruler himself. Government on this level consisted of the *batab* and a council of local lesser nobles. As in Aztec Mexico, each settlement was divided into four quarters, and members of the local governing council were chosen from each of the quarters. One of the *batab*'s major roles was that of War Lord, and he was expected both to keep the borders of his segment of the manorial province secure and to supply a ready force of fighting men to his *halach uinic* in the event of interkingdom war.

Beneath the *almehen* were the commoners, who, as we have seen, played almost no role in governance of the affairs of the kingdom—only a single commoner was chosen annually as a member of each town's council. Maya kingdom government shows almost no signs of democratic decision making. The closest parallel is again medieval Europe of the 1300s.

Unlike the unitary societies of the Inca and the Aztec, the ordinary man in Lowland Maya society did not belong to a large residential neighborhood held together by kin ties. There were no *ayllus* or *calpulli*. The largest residential unit seems to have been the male-line/female-line family, emphasizing the male line. It was to those blood kinsmen only that the individual could look for mutual help in time of need.

The Maya kingdoms, then, were governed ironhandedly by a ruler, perhaps subservient to an over-king, and a small advisory body of other upper-class citizens. These were cities that struggled against one another over the centuries for control of agricultural lands and general economic as well as luxury goods. Warfare was frequent and usually fought not over boundaries with neighboring states but over alleged or real hurts to the honor of the male-line family of the *halach uinic* or to win the alliance of smaller, less powerful kingdoms. Warriors became an important subclass in society, and formal interkingdom

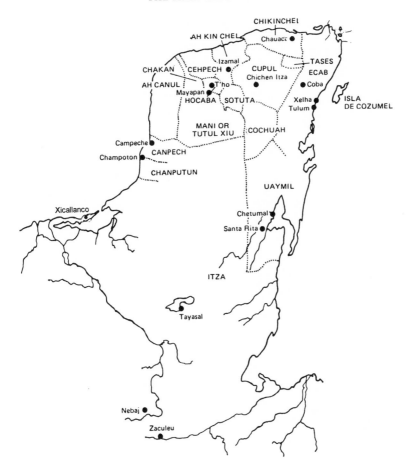

Figure 14. Maya Kingdoms at the Time of Spanish Intervention (1528)

warfare seems to have been conducted, European-style, on a field of battle with contingents of infantry in battle array.

When threat came not from within the community of Maya kingdoms but rather from outside, other forms of resistance were used to maintain social and cultural stability. In most dualistic cultures, full-scale invasion from a foreign source brings about covert, stubborn guerrilla activity—the reaction, for example, in the German-occupied countries of Europe during World War II. This, in fact, was the Maya reaction to Spanish intervention from the start, and it led to an ongoing resistance movement among the Maya which lasted for four centuries—from the early 1500s until the mid-1900s, a formal peace treaty signed only in 1936. In spite of that treaty, the Maya resurgence movement is by no means dead today (Jones 1989). Such underground resistance is a usual, automatic, culture-preserving reaction of dualistic societies, and in Yucatán and Quintana Roo it made it impossible for the Spanish to achieve any real conquest of the Maya, regardless of the overthrow of the Maya cities and kingdoms.

In interkingdom warfare during the Classic Period in both the Central and Northern Areas and during later times in the Northern Area, the conquered were enslaved, as the famous murals from the city of Bonampak show us in graphic detail. Many captives met their death as sacrifices to the Maya deities, but many also ended up in the Middle American slave market, usually sold into bondage to the Aztec. Just as Maya society was divided into the Haves and the Have-Nots, the Ins and the Outs, so peoples, kingdoms, and cities other than one's own were Outs by definition and therefore fair game for any kind of exploitation one might successfully impose on them. Hieroglyphic monuments give us fascinating insights to the interkingdom and interdynasty strife that consumed so much of Maya life, and the delightful lifelike statuettes of warriors from the island of Jaina off the Campeche coast provide timeless impressions of the importance of that class in Maya society.

Cities were large, well-planned communities with massive, well-engineered buildings of considerable architectural merit, with temples, schools, markets, military barracks, ceremonial ball courts, and cultural centers (Proskouriakoff 1946). Most were largely self-sufficient from the point of view of both agricultural and manufactured goods. We used to think that only slash-and-burn, milpa-style agriculture was practiced by the Maya, that the farmer would have to move on to new lands as the soil became exhausted, which, because of the nature of most tropical forest soils, occurs every two or three years. This, in fact, was often used as a rationale for what seemed the sudden abandonment of most of the Classic Period cities in the southern lowlands around A.D. 900. We now know, however, that their abandonment was neither sudden nor complete and may be laid largely at the feet of a combination of ruinous, long-running, shifting alliances, interkingdom wars, and subsequent political and economic collapse and ultimate invasion from both Tabasco and central Mexico.

Recent archaeological work has specifically indicated that Maya agricultural practices, while partly milpa or slash-and-burn, were much more sophisticated. Evidence of permanent raised fields has been found in the vicinity of many major sites, and these rather than milpa fields seem to have been the norm. Maize, beans, squash, and a multitude of vegetables and fruits were cultivated. Cotton was an important crop, used for producing cotton fabrics, which were not only used domestically but served as a major trade item outside the Maya area. The agricultural economy was a varied one not dependent upon the vagaries of nature. There is no evidence for either the import of foodstuffs or the need for internal redistribution of such commodities within the Maya realm.

The Maya depended on a cash economy rather than a barter system. Cacao beans, as in Mexico, were the coinage of the times. While the Yucatán Maya themselves do not seem to have been great traders, the Chontal Putún Maya of Campeche and Tabasco, to the southwest, were. The Aztec trading port of Xicallanco was located on the Laguna de los Términos in Chontal lands, and the Chontal Putún seemed to have served the role of Maya *pochteca,* for we know that they moved goods by sea around the coast from Honduras on the Caribbean side of Yucatán to Xicallanco on the Gulf coast of Campeche, gathering goods at numerous coastal and inland points as they traveled. These fascinating people have been called the Phoenicians of the Caribbean. They were master seamen, noted for their large, seaworthy canoes, which the Spanish had encountered long before they came to Yucatán in 1528. The major end buyers of Maya goods through this system were the Aztecs. Maya Chontal Putún trader and Aztec *pochteca* articulated at Xicallanco.

The major goods exported through the Chontal trading system were salt (Yucatán was the major salt producer in Middle America), cacao, honey, cotton fabrics (for which, as we have already pointed out, the Maya have always been noted), feathers (particularly of the gorgeously plumed Quetzal), flint, obsidian, shell, and jade (largely from Guatemala's Motagua Valley). Of equal importance was the slave trade, which the Chontal Putún also ran in flourishing manner as a result of the constant interkingdom warfare. All of these commodities were apparently brought to seaport locations from the interior of the Maya lowlands. At least in northern Yucatán there was also a network of narrow but effective paved, raised highways, called *sacbe,* linking the major cities and facilitating such transport considerably.

Maya science was well developed, though not along what we would consider empirical lines, for complex ritual and myth were its philosophical underpinnings. Astronomy was as much astrology as science. The pharmacopoeia was as much myth and legend as medicine. Nonetheless, one should not leap to the erroneous conclusion that the Maya were not science-oriented. They were, and their achievements are at least as impressive as those of ancient Egypt, Sumer, or Babylonia. The mathematical and calendrical system devised by the Maya and their Olmec forebears was far in advance of anything used in the ancient Near East and considerably more sophisticated than that in use in Europe during the fifteenth century.

The Maya alone among native Americans developed a writing system capable of recording the spoken word in all its intricate beauty, a system that, like the Chinese script, could be equally applied to all the mutually unintelligible as well as the partly intelligible Maya tongues and dialects. The documents and monuments of the Classic Period all use the language of the Central Area sites, a Cholan language, and it remained the language of writing throughout its entire 1,500-year history from approximately A.D. 250 until the Spanish destruction of the last Maya stronghold, Tayasal, in 1697.

Gorgeously painted manuscripts on folding gesso-coated palm-leaf panels recorded history, mathematical tables, astronomical and astrological information, and religious and literary works. Spanish zeal in the person of Bishop Diego de Landa of Yucatán succeeded, in true Inquisitorial fashion, in consigning this invaluable fountain of information to the flames in holocausts of burning books which must have made Fr. Torquemada, back home in Spain, green with envy. Only parts of four of these volumes have survived. Monuments in stone, the famous Maya stelae, recorded biographical information on the lives of important rulers and historical information on their kingdoms and their alliances, carefully embedded in a context of intricate chronologies and ceremonial information. We also have a Maya equivalent of the so-called Egyptian *Book of the Dead,* revealing a mythology of history and the afterlife as complex and interesting as that of any religious system anywhere at any time. This comes to us largely as painted scene and hieroglyph on a large series of ceramic vessels (Robicsek and Hales 1981).

Maya art is varied, of very high quality by anyone's standards, and generally noteworthy (Schele and Miller 1986). Murals, painted ceramic wares, and manuscripts show considerable artistic ability and great imagination. Jewelry is outstanding, especially in jade, and ceramic wares show an unusual variety of forms, techniques, and styles. In a few instances we seem to have been able to pinpoint multiple works by single artists, though we are in total ignorance of their names. Individual style, however, was clearly recognized and of importance.

Maya religion, like that of the Aztecs, involved a multiplicity of deities representing most of the aspects of the world of nature. Like the Aztec pantheon, that of the Mayas demanded blood atonement, physical sacrifice of both animals and men, and while we do not have quite the same detailed accounts of the Maya sacrificial ceremony that we have for the Aztec, we have enough to let us know that Maya religion, too, was one in which many hundreds lost their lives annually to the gods. How much of this is natively Maya and how much a result of the centuries of Mexican domination and influence after A.D. 900 is uncertain, but Spanish accounts indicate a system super-ficially similar to that of Aztec Mexico at the time of the conquest.

It is to the credit of Bishop Landa and other churchmen that we also have a fairly full account of Maya culture in Yucatán at the time of the Spanish intervention in 1528 under Francisco de Montejo. The greatest glories of the Classic Period were long over, but much of the sophistication of those times still characterized the cities which Montejo, his son, and his followers saw and destroyed.

Sometime around A.D. 900, the Toltecs, from Tula in central Mexico, in-vaded the Maya area, arriving by sea along the Campeche coast, and became the conquering rulers of Yucatán. There they founded the city of Uucil Abnal and forced Uxmal and the other northern Maya cities into submission. Most of the cities, in fact, seem to have been abandoned at about this time. Some-time in the early 1200s the Toltec themselves were displaced by a new invader, the Itzá, about whom our information is still rather sketchy but who were probably Putún Maya Chontal speakers from Tabasco and Campeche. Suffice it to say that they occupied and rebuilt Uucil Abnal as Chichén Itzá and built a new city, Mayapán, as well. Unlike the Náhuatl-speaking Toltec, who had become at least bearable over the three centuries of their occupation, the Itzá, Maya kinsmen or not, were never welcomed and were, in fact, cordially de-spised. Battles between the native Maya and the Itzá continued from the early 1200s until the mid-1400s. At that time Mayapán was destroyed, the Itzá driven from the land, and native Maya rule restored. The surviving Itzá re-treated to the island city of Tayasal in northern Guatemala, where they re-sisted Spanish rule until 1697.

The society that Francisco Montejo found in 1528 and that finally fell to his son, Francisco Montejo the younger, in 1542 and 1546, was a resurrected Maya culture with strong Mexican influences from the time of the Toltec and Itzá invasions. By and large the Maya people and the essential characteristics of Maya culture survived the double onslaught of Toltec and Itzá, as they were to survive the Spanish conquest itself. Today the Maya remain a strongly vi-able physical and cultural entity throughout northern Middle America. Even today Maya is the most frequently heard language on the streets of Mérida and throughout the towns and byways of the Yucatán peninsula.

When the Spanish came, the Maya were ready to deal with them, and though the Maya cities and their kingdoms fell one after another and became the source of plundered stone for Spanish towns, the Maya people and the

Maya way of life survived. Guerrilla warfare made it impossible for the conquerors to subjugate the defeated either physically or spiritually. The urban way of life was gone, relinquished to the Spanish, but the Maya simply retreated to the less accessible lands of eastern Yucatán, Quintana Roo, and Belize. As late as 1860 the Maya rose against their oppressors, coming close to taking all of Yucatán. Throughout the 1900s there were continued sporadic but concerted efforts to reinstate the Maya way, which may yet win out, both in lowland Yucatán and in highland Guatemala. Unlike the Aztec, whose inner culture is largely gone, or the Inca, who survived simply by retreating into the mountains, the Maya survive largely because they understand their conquerors and are able to fight fire with fire. Though Hispanic dualism is not the same as Maya dualism, the Maya are individualists, and they have learned how to compete against their rulers.

10

The Mississippian Cities and Towns

During the period A.D. 1000 to 1500 a number of native American communities, not surprisingly called Mississippian by archaeologists and ethnologists, developed along the length of the Mississippi River from the Gulf of Mexico northward to the confluence of the Mississippi, Missouri, and Ohio rivers and beyond, as far as Wisconsin in North America's heartland and as far as the Georgia and Carolina coasts in the Southeast. By the time Europeans reached the New World, its greatest days of glory, like those of the Classic Maya of Middle America, had passed, but enough of the Mississippian cultural tradition was still alive then to enable us, with archaeological and ethnohistoric data, to recall a time when large towns and cities, some of such size, social complexity, and regional power that they may, in the opinion of this writer, rightly be called city-states, grew, prospered, and proliferated along the course of the Mississippi, and urban development in native North America reached its high point.

The term *Mississippian* can be understood in a number of ways—as a simple geographical term incorporating all the vast length of the valley of the Mississippi River and its tributaries, as a description of the peoples themselves who occupied the towns and cities along those rivers, or as a social-cultural system and tradition. When we use the term in this chapter, we are largely talking about the last definition, the Mississippian cultural tradition, for both the other usages of the word are not completely accurate. Many large and important Mississippian settlements were far removed from the Mississippi Valley—Ocmulgee and Etowah in Georgia, Toqua and Dallas in Tennessee, Moundville in Alabama, the Jonathan Creek site in Kentucky, the Angel site in southern Indiana, the Lake Jackson site in North Florida, or the Spiro site in Oklahoma. The differences in the artifactual inventories of individual Mississippian sites also make it evident that we can not talk about a single "Mississippian people," for more than one ethnic, linguistic population is clearly involved—the Caddoan people in the western regions, the Tunica and Natchez in the lower Mississippi Valley, ancestral Muskogean peoples in Alabama, Georgia, and North Florida, perhaps Iroquoian peoples in Tennessee, and ethnically unknown but probably Caddoan or possibly Siouan peoples in the upper valley. We are rather certain only that the Algonquian peoples, who by the time of European intervention inhabited much of the northern reaches of the Mississippi Valley, were not participants in the Mississippian tradition (Emerson 1997:193–194).

Yet, in spite of such geographical and ethnic variety, the population of all of the Mississippian cities and towns shared an overriding set of social characteristics—political, economic, religious, and organizational—that, in and of themselves, define the essence of Mississippianism. This set of characteristics has been aptly referred to as "a prevalent variety of socioreligious organization cross-cutting other cultural and ecological boundaries" (Knight 1986:681).

As seen in the previous chapters, we have ample firsthand historic documentation for the cultural tradition of the Quechua-speaking Inca, and for the Aztec and Maya of Middle America much the same, as well as written documentation in the Náhuatl and Mayan languages for the latter two. All three, unlike the Mississippians, represent single or closely related ethnic-linguistic populations, and in all three instances the archaeological data support our analysis of the cultures from the ethnohistoric base provided by Spanish and native observers.

For Mississippian societies between A.D. 900 and 1500, however, we have almost no sources other than archaeological on which to rely for a cultural reconstruction. There are no written or even surviving oral records, and Mississippian cities and regional power bases were long abandoned and deserted by the time Europeans arrived. Some sociopolitical aspects of the tradition were indeed still present in the impressive chiefdom of the Natchez people of the lower Mississippi Valley, the Coosa chiefdom of northwest Georgia, and, to a lesser extent, in the cultures of other native American peoples of the Southeast. The core beliefs and rituals of Mississippian religion (if it is correct to call it that) remain alive to this day among some of the surviving Muskogean peoples, but by and large, Mississippian culture as a definable, cohesive tradition was gone by the time of European intervention.

We do have Spanish accounts from the time of de Soto's epochal expedition through the Southeast in the early 1540s, but they refer to what may be called

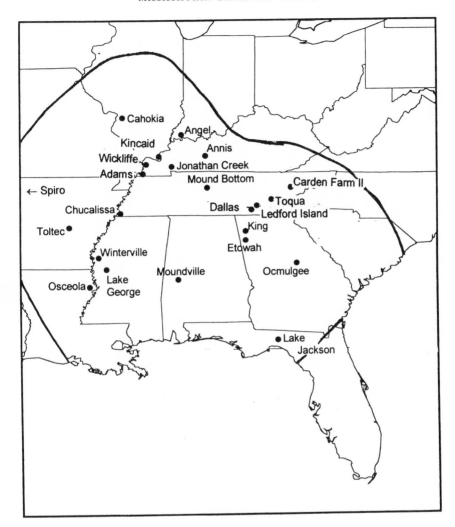

Figure 15. Mississippian Cities of the Classic Period (A.D. 1000–1400)

post-Mississippian times, and the contacts of the expedition members were with peoples by that time only residually Mississippian.

Thus archaeological data and inferences from the surviving aspects of native Southeastern socioreligious life are all we have to fall back on in reconstructing the lifeways of Mississippian communities. Yet, from the truly monumental work that American archaeologists have done over that past five decades, there emerges a clear delineation of not only the essence but also the details of Mississippian life and thought. The essence has perhaps been most succinctly expressed by Tom Emerson, who says, "If there was a single over-riding theme in the cosmology of the Southeastern Indian groups [i.e., the Mississippians], it was the organization of the natural and supernatural worlds into dualistic categories that often were expressed as sets of oppositions . . . the structuration of the Mississippian world in dualistic sets opens wider parameters for understanding the cultural milieu that we are investigating" (Emerson 1997:220). He adds, "The plans of the larger Mississippian temple towns, with their central precincts, can be seen as composite dualistic sets . . . while the presence of a similar site organization in the countryside indicates the pervasiveness of this theme" (Emerson 1997:220–222). Pauketat and Emerson have even been able to demonstrate persuasively this penchant toward dualism in the decorative designs of some Mississippian ceramic wares (Pauketat and Emerson 1991).

Archaeology also makes it evident that the role dualism played in Mississippian societies came as a natural result of the underlying kin systems and social organization of those societies, for they were all, regardless of ethnic composition, two-class social systems, distinguishing a powerful ruling elite from the rest of the population (see, especially, Emerson 1997, Pauketat 1994). On an abstract level, such overriding, opposing dualisms occur only in kin systems of the types we have defined as *IIN* and *IIB* in the introduction. Thus the archaeological record implies such kin systems, specifically *IIB*, for all of the variant Mississippian societies.

As indicated earlier, the ethnic/linguistic groups participating in the Mississippian tradition were the Caddoan peoples to the west of the Mississippi and perhaps in the upper Mississippi Valley, the Natchez, Tunica, and (peripherally in the Plaquemine culture) the Chitimacha in the lower valley, probably Iroquoian peoples in western Tennessee, and the Muskogean peoples to the east of the river in the interior and coastal Southeast. The Caddoan peoples today still have varieties of type *IIB* kinship systems, as do the Iroquoian Cherokee, and the Natchez, Tunica, and Muskogean peoples of the A.D. 900–1400 time level can also be demonstrated to have had the same type of systems (see Murdock 1949:323–352 for the reconstructive methods). That is, regardless of the fact that at least five different ethnolinguistic populations are known to have been part of the Mississippian tradition, they were all characterized by dualistic *IIB* kin systems at this time level. This commonality in underlying social philosophy and action would have contributed greatly to the ease with which Mississippian organizational, political, socioreligious, economic, and even artifactual and architectural traits spread from one ethnic group to the other throughout the Mississippi River Valley and adjacent regions.

Such pervasive dualism can only have originated in a dualistic *IIN* or *IIB* society or in a society heavily influenced by such a system, which, in turn, served as the initial carrying mechanism for the adoption, modification, and spread of traits that came to be called Mississippian. It is suggested that the Caddoan peoples may have been at least the major carriers and modifiers, if not the originators, of the basic elements of the tradition, for Caddoan artifactual traits are the most widespread of all Mississippian traits—from Cahokia in the north to Spiro in the west to Moundville in the south. Even today general Caddoan culture traits are more reminiscent of Mississippian patterns than are those of any other extant culture of the region—pervasive dualism, a *IIB* kin system, an elite social class itself dualistically divided into political and religious-ceremonial leaders.

By A.D. 900 the results of such probably Caddoan-inspired dualism in action were communities that exhibited most of the social traits that would later become typical of the Classic Mississippian societies of A.D. 1200–1400. Startlingly similar to the cities of the distant dualistic Classic Maya, the typical settlement was large, consisting of a carefully planned civic center core with imposing pyramidal platform mounds clustered around a spacious central plaza, all enclosed by palisaded earthworks. Radiating from these centers, often for many miles, were smaller surrounding rural farmstead communities, some with mounds but most without. The impression is not unlike that of a modern American city center and its sprawling suburbs. By the 1200s groups of such towns seem to have been linked together to form regional power bases, reminiscent again of Maya kingdoms.

It is equally apparent from the archaeological evidence that all communities that shared the Mississippian tradition had not only dualistic kin systems but also strongly hierarchical social systems that emphasized the role of the individual in society, particularly the role of members of the elite class. Special luxury goods are archaeologically abundant, and warfare-related artifacts are present. Special burial areas were also reserved for the elite. While the ordinary man was usually interred near his own rural farmstead with few if any burial goods, others, whom we infer were of higher social rank, were interred with elaborate ceremonial objects in or near the civic center complex of mounds.

It has also been suggested on ethnohistoric grounds that there was not only a ruling political elite in Mississippian societies but also an organized priesthood, which maintained the community's temples and cemeteries and was responsible for the rituals that kept the social system intact (Knight 1986: 681). Thus, just as society in general was segmented into two classes, so the elite class itself was segmented into a political elite on the one hand and a socioreligious elite on the other.

All of the larger Mississippian communities participated in widespread trading networks for the exchange of both raw materials and artifactual goods. Many of the goods spread by trade were highly imaginative modeled ceramic wares and stone images as well as equally creative and artistic engravings on shell and copper. These were clearly a reflection of a distinction not only between general everyday goods and luxury goods but also between utilitarian and ceremonial artifacts, emphasizing the most salient of the shared cultural traits of the Mississippian tradition, the religious system. Referred to nowadays as the Southern Cult or the Southeastern Ceremonial Complex, this full constellation of traits reached its apogee between A.D. 1200 and approximately 1400.

The building of platform mounds, indisputably the most distinguishing characteristic of Mississippian towns, did not originate with that cultural tradition. It began many millennia earlier in the Poverty Point culture of the lower Mississippi Valley. The Poverty Point site itself is located on a bayou overlooking the Mississippi River floodplain at the confluence of six rivers in northeastern Louisiana, and similar sites extended all along the river from the area of present-day St. Louis south to New Orleans, encompassing much of what would later become the heartland of Mississippian culture. Around 2200 B.C. the people occupying these sites began to build earthworks and platform mounds, and diagnostic artifact types, differing somewhat from one site complex to another, begin to appear throughout the Mississippi Valley, up into the Ohio River region and the Midwest, throughout the Southeast, and as far away as the southwest Gulf Coast of Florida (Bense 1994:99–104).

While we still know almost nothing about the social organization of the Poverty Point culture or the variant ethnic and linguistic groups that seem to have participated in it, many of us, including the writer, suspect that it was itself a Tunican society (personal communication, Jon Gibson, 2003). Regardless of our paucity of information on Poverty Point social structure, it is abundantly clear from the far-flung archaeological evidence that it was a highly organized and sophisticated trading culture, both manufacturing and exporting its own products and importing and moving raw materials from one section of the American Midwest and Southeast to another (Gibson 1980).

The specific use of the earthwork structures and mounds at Poverty Point sites cannot be conclusively defined, though it would seem that the long earthworks formed protective barriers against outside intrusion, while platform mounds show evidence of having been erected over mass cremated burials at successive intervals over long periods of time. What can be said for a certainty, however, is that the building of platform mounds occurs earliest and most typically not in North America proper but much farther south in the Olmec region of Mexico's Gulf Coast and on into Mayan Central America. It accordingly seems both highly possible and probable, at least to this writer, that the concept of mound building was diffused from that point of origin northward over a very long period of time, probably through prehistoric native trade networks, which often, as we have seen in our discussion of the Aztec and Maya, covered and linked wide geographical areas and spread concepts as well as the material artifacts and raw materials of commerce (Ford 1969). Or, as likely, perhaps in tandem with trading networks, the concepts may simply have gradually spread naturally from one adjacent society and community to another toward the north, around the western coast of the Gulf of Mexico, into the Caddoan hinterlands, and from there on into the Mississippi River Valley and the heartland of North America through what Irving Rouse has called *transculturation* (Rouse 1986).

Perhaps the most interesting and rather detailed similarity between the Maya world and that of the Mississippi Valley lies in the realm of the supernatural, for Maya religious beliefs and practices and those of the Mississippian tradition are strikingly parallel. For the rituals and beliefs of the Classic Maya, we rely heavily both on a series of hieroglyphic texts on ceramic wares—the so-called Maya *Book of the Dead,* referred to in the last chapter—as well as the *Popol Vuh,* a religious text of the Quiché Maya. While we have no equivalent Mississippian texts, we do have detailed knowledge of Muskogean religious beliefs associated with the surviving elements of the Southeastern Ceremonial Complex. Vernon Knight has given us a comprehensive analysis of that information and correlated it with Mississippian archaeological data (Knight 1981, 1986), and Thomas Emerson has provided us with a perceptive comparison between Southern Cult ethnographic data and stone and ceramic ceremonial artifacts from the Cahokia site (Emerson 1997:193–248).

In both mythologies the world is segmented dualistically into an Upper World and an Under World. The latter is the world of death, monsters, danger, and evil, while the former is the world of life and light. In both mythologies the Under World is also associated with water and fertility. In both mythologies a goddess gives birth to a set of twins who perform a series of miraculous exploits to become culture heroes. In both there is a belief in reincarnation, that the souls of the dead are born again in children. In both there is an emphasis on renewal and fertility, which, of course, is rather generic to many religious systems. The parallels, however, are so numerous, that, though it is always possible that they are fortuitous, taken together with the other Mississippian culture traits of possible Middle American origin, it seems likely that through transculturation over a period of perhaps as much as 3,000 years, many of the Mississippian tradition–Middle American cultural similarities and, at times, near identities may indeed be indicative of ultimate Middle American origin. As will be seen in the following chapter on the Pueblo peoples, we know that those peoples were the recipients of artifactual items of Mexican origin, probably through the Aztec *pochteca* trading network or the trading network of the Chontal Putún Maya. From Pueblo lands in the American Southwest to the Caddoan region of the lower Plains is but a short distance.

Whatever the origin of earthwork and mound-building traits and the accompanying sociopolitical, socioreligious dualism they demonstrate so clearly, those characteristics of the Poverty Point sites of 2200–500 B.C. are evident the length of the Mississippi River Valley and continue throughout the subsequent Woodland period (1000 B.C.–A.D. 1000) with the increasingly urbanized Adena, Hopewell, and Hopewellian cultures of the American Midwest and the upper Mississippi Valley. These progressively more urban settlement patterns and their accompanying specialized structures clearly reflect social systems in which both individualism and rank distinctions were of increasing importance.

The growth of the developing Mississippian tradition from Poverty Point origins is also evidenced in the most frequently traded artifacts and goods. These were personal decorative ornaments, often found in association with burials throughout the Southeast and Midwest. Most seem to have been status markers—another indication of the importance of individualism.

It is, in short, apparent that the constellation of primary social traits that ultimately came to characterize Mississippian towns and cities—dualism, an emphasis on individualism, and an accompanying emphasis on differential social rank—had its origins perhaps in Middle America and its North American beginnings in Poverty Point times and cultures. It is also apparent that it was elaborated on and carried through the subsequent Woodland cultures of the Mississippi Valley to give rise to the Classic Mississippian cultures of A.D. 1000–1500 (Jenkins and Krause 1986:119–123).

By the late A.D. 900s and early 1000s the total social-cultural pattern that we call Mississippian had coalesced to become a full-fledged socioreligious cultural tradition, melded with, as Knight has said, the other cultural attributes of the individual dualistic ethnic groups which accepted the Mississippian assemblage (Knight 1986:681). Its final shape was determined by molding, alteration, addition, and deletion of traits from cultural sources in the Caddoan, Tunican, Natchez, and Muskogean worlds during the millennia-long period of its development.

One of the earliest large Mississippian civic center cities was at Ocmulgee, near Macon, Georgia, dating to the late 900s and early 1000s. Its main ceremonial lodge and in-ground raptorial bird image are two of the most striking of early Mississippian Southern Cult manifestations. The largest and most impressive city from the A.D. 1000–1050 period, however, was located much farther north, on the extensive floodplain bottomlands at the confluence of the Missouri and Mississippi rivers in what is now St. Louis, Missouri, and East St. Louis, Illinois. This was the city-state of Cahokia, which lasted as the most highly organized and influential of Mississippian polities from its founding around A.D. 1000 until its ultimate abandonment as an urban center sometime around 1350 (see Emerson 1997, Pauketat 1994 for thorough coverages).

While Cahokia was indisputably the most lasting and powerful of the Mississippian city-states, there were others that shared its social pattern. The Moundville site near Tuscaloosa in Alabama was one of these. The largest city-state site in the Southeast, it flourished between approximately A.D. 1200 and 1400 and was abandoned sometime just before 1500. It was situated high on a bluff above the extremely fertile floodplain of the Black Warrior River (see Peebles 1970 for thorough coverage). The Spiro site in Oklahoma, on the floodplain of the Arkansas River, the Lake Jackson site near Tallahassee, and the Etowah site near Atlanta were all major city-states dating from approximately the same time period.

These cities and their satellite settlements, however, had been gone for several centuries, in some cases more, by the time Europeans began to explore the Mississippi River Valley in the late 1600s. When the Frenchman La Salle descended the river in 1682, the sole surviving post-Mississippian chiefdom was that of the Natchez, located near the present city of that name in Mississippi. While much of the social structure of Mississippian times, including the presence of a hereditary ruler, was still largely in place, and the basic rituals of the Southern Ceremonial Complex seem still to have been practiced, the Natchez towns could not be compared to those of earlier times. Under European pressure even this survival succumbed in the early 1700s.

What led to the dissolution of the Mississippian cities and towns? Like the

Classic Maya Old Kingdom, they seem to have dissolved over a relatively short period of time. Even the vast and powerful metropolis of Cahokia and its regional city-state were reduced from an estimated population of some 15,000 souls at their high point in the 1100s to probably fewer than 2,000 only a century later (Emerson 1997:253). Farther south in Alabama, Moundville suffered the same fate several centuries later.

The fact that most of the larger Mississippian settlements were fortified with stockades and earthworks from earliest times clearly suggests that intercommunity warfare was a prevalent feature of the cultural tradition. The added fact that most Mississippian cemeteries had special areas reserved for the burial of warriors, accompanied in death with war paraphernalia, reinforces the suggestion. It may thus be presumed, as with the Classic Maya in the Petén region of Guatemala, that fairly constant internecine strife and shifting alliances of power—a classic feature of most dualistic societies— must have played a large part in the dissolution. It is also possible that an increasing demographic base over the period from A.D. 1000 to 1350/1400 may have overstressed the individual cities' agricultural potential, in spite of the extremely fertile bottomlands on or near which most cities were situated. As with the Maya, we can only make educated assumptions based on our archaeological data.

Had the Mississippian cities survived until the time of European arrival, the European settlement of the valley might have gone quite differently. The native American population of this section of North America might have survived in much the same manner as the Yucatec Maya, through retreat to less sought after lands and accompanied by cultural retreat from European society, perhaps accompanied by now-successful/now-not guerrilla warfare with the newcomers. This we will never know.

II

The Pueblo Towns

In the American Southwest the Spanish word *pueblo,* town, is used with a capital *p*—Pueblo, to refer both to the settlements and the inhabitants of the native American towns that line the Rio Grande in central New Mexico and the adjacent mesas of eastern Arizona, and which in earlier centuries were found in all the Four Corners region where Utah, Colorado, Arizona, and New Mexico come together. When the Spanish first arrived in 1540 there were over 120 Pueblo towns. Of these, thirty-six have survived to the present.

Though culturally similar in most respects, the communities represent four different historically unrelated social and language groups which have lived neighboring one another for at least several millennia: the Hopi, with ten communities and a single language; the Zuni, with seven communities and a single language; the Keresan peoples, with seven communities and five closely related languages; and the Tanoan peoples, with twelve communities and five closely related languages. Over the centuries these originally diverse peoples have together forged an urban way of life congruent with and well adapted to the geography of the region. Their communities still form one of the most remarkable and representative of surviving native American polities.

The cohesiveness and overriding similarities of the variant cultural groups making up the Pueblos and the long-term success of their peoples in living peacefully side by side for so many centuries is in large part owing to a common underlying social philosophy that pervades all of their cultures, a philosophy that has kept them closely united as a single, multifaceted confederation for at least the past 320 years, since the formal founding of an All-Pueblo Council in 1680. Though each Pueblo has its own government, they are all members of this unifying council, which since 1965 has had a formal constitution enabling it to act on behalf of all of the Pueblos. It has served to bind

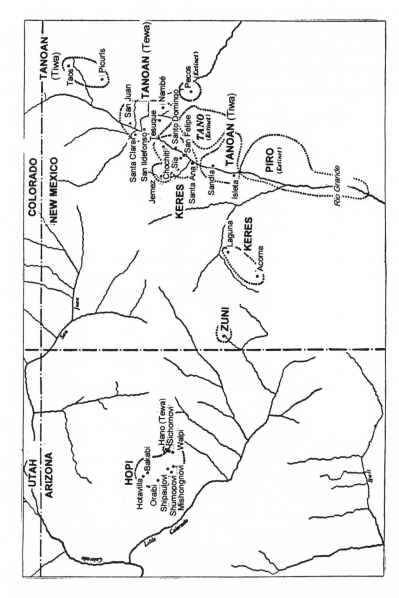

Figure 16. Pueblo Towns in 1492

the individual towns together and override their social and cultural differences, and, though not an official body before 1680, similar decision-making mechanisms were in place long before the arrival of Francisco Vásquez de Coronado in 1540. The Pueblo peoples have become the perfect example of *E Pluribus Unum,* melded into one by the superposition of a uniform set of goals and modes of action.

When the Spanish first arrived, the 120-some Pueblo settlements of New Mexico and Arizona, though then and now impressive and attractive towns, were what remained from yet more spectacular times, when large Pueblo cities and settlements dominated the entire Four Corners area. The earlier people were called the *Anasazi* by the Navajo, a word meaning literally "The Enemy Ancestors." While the name does not sit lightly with the present Pueblo peoples, whose ancestors the Anasazi were, it has stuck, for better or worse. Today it is taken to mean simply a polite "The Ancient Ones," and this is the usage it is given here.

The Anasazi occupied the Four Corners region from at least the B.C.–A.D. dividing line, and there has been cultural continuity from that time to the present. While it is impossible to say which of the four present Pueblo stocks —Zuni, Hopi, Keresan, or Tanoan—was in the region first or which language-cultural stocks were the builders and inhabitants of specific earlier cities, there is no question but that Anasazi ruins are the handiwork of the ancestral Pueblo.

The pinnacle of Anasazi glory came in A.D. 950 to 1300, particularly from 1000 to 1300. By far the most brilliant expression is that of the 300-plus sites in the Chaco Canyon and Aztec Ruins area of northwestern New Mexico, in the Ánimas and San Juan River drainage region. In all, 125 large Anasazi pueblos have been found, explored, and excavated in Chaco Canyon alone, along with literally thousands of smaller settlements. Almost rivaling the Chaco Canyon pueblos were those of the Mesa Verde region to the north in neighboring Colorado and those in the Canyon de Chelly to the east in Arizona.

Most of the large Anasazi towns were built between 950 and 1100 and were voluntarily abandoned about 1300. The abandonment seems to have been the result of a number of factors, the most important of which was a series of devastating droughts between 1275 and 1300. Inasmuch as Anasazi economy was largely agricultural, like that of the Pueblos today, such prolonged conditions could be ruinous. To judge from tree-ring dating techniques, periods of drought became increasingly frequent from 1050 through the early 1300s, often lasting two or three years at a time. Given the already fragile desert environment, such a long-term scarcity of water could have been sufficient in itself to cause the Anasazi to move toward more permanent sources of water. This they found to the south and east in the Rio Grande Valley and the high mesa country south of Chaco Canyon, where the Pueblo peoples live today.

It is possible that depredations of nomadic tribes—the Navajo and Apache peoples were moving into the area during this period—also contributed to the decision to abandon the regions of earlier Anasazi settlement, for the very locations of the Anasazi pueblos were such as to indicate a concern for protection from at least as early as 1100, and most of the large pueblos were clearly constructed with defense at least partly in mind. They were built as single complexes, similar to but in most cases infinitely larger than our modern apartment buildings, surrounded by high walls with access only by ladder.

In the Mesa Verde and Canyon de Chelly regions, in southwestern Colorado and northeastern Arizona, this same period saw the abandonment of mesa-top pueblos and the construction of the famous cliff dwellings, which were themselves abandoned toward the end of the Great Drought of 1275–1300. The most interesting of these was the Cliff Palace at Mesa Verde. Tucked under the overhangs of large cavernous openings into the cliffs, which jut up from the desert floor, the structures are truly remarkable feats of engineering. They are not small, crudely built isolated dwellings but large, extremely solid minicities, with all the comforts found in the mesa-top towns. Access to them was by wooden ladders and steps cut into the rock faces of the cliff.

The most urbanized of the Anasazi cultural provinces was certainly Chaco Canyon. Of the 300-some major settlements in that region, a dozen are large towns of solid masonry construction. Pueblo Bonito, located in the approximate center of Chaco Canyon, is the largest. It contained 800 large rooms, built in a D-shaped semicircle around a large enclosed plaza. Its estimated population was at least 12,000, likely more. In the central plaza was a series of circular *kivas*, partly underground religious structures. The main part of the dwelling units rose to four stories, five in some sections. It is the best example of a Pueblo town of the early days not only because it was typical but also because it shows all the major attributes of Anasazi culture at its flourishing best. It was probably built about 1100 and finally abandoned sometime shortly after 1300. Several other Chaco pueblos, such as Chetro Ketl, were almost as large and as impressive.

Pueblo Bonito and its outlying towns and hamlets were linked to one another by over 300 miles of roadways, carefully engineered even to the presence of curbing. A number of these roads also led outside the canyon, primarily toward the area of the Aztec and Mesa Verde towns to the northwest. That this was a purposefully constructed highway system is very evident, for it does not simply follow the natural terrain. When a highway changes direction, it does so at right angles, and the paths are straight and direct. At times the roadway is as wide as thirty feet. Cliffs and other natural obstacles were not bypassed. Rock steps were simply cut into the face of cliffs to connect roadways of different levels. Aerial photographs indicate both that the entire highway system was greater in extent than the sections so far explored and that the roadways didn't just go toward the north and northwest but radiated out in all directions from Chaco Canyon.

While such a highway system was certainly partly for general communication and the transport of various kinds of products within the San Juan River drainage area, it seems clear from archaeological data that it was also part of a far-ranging trade network. It may have articulated with the poorly known northern routes of the Aztec *pochteca* and the other professional trading classes of Middle America, such as the Chontal Putún Maya, as well as with the American Southeast. In the latter region the Tunica and Natchez peoples created the equally far-flung Poverty Point Trade Network, continued in later years—1000–1400—by the Caddoan and other Mississippian peoples of mid-America, just to the east of the Pueblo region. We do not have any actual proof that this was the case, but we do know that Southwestern turquoise found its way in great quantities to the México Empire and other parts of Middle America, and the frequent presence in Anasazi sites of Pacific and Gulf of Mexico seashells, often beautifully incised or inlaid with turquoise and other stones, indicates trade well outside the local area. Whether the Pueblo peoples themselves had a professional trading class remains unknown, but the size and sophistication of the Chaco–San Juan River drainage towns and the dimensions of the Pueblo roadway system would make this a definite probability.

An additional characteristic of Chaco–San Juan Anasazi culture was the use of finely made irrigation networks for the growing of crops. Rainwater from the tops of the mesas was diverted by canals to a headgate on lower land. From there it was channeled to walled-in garden plots. Given the desert nature of the region, this system of irrigation made highly intensive gardening both possible and fruitful.

When the Big Drought of 1275–1300 hit with its full force, abandonment of the Chaco, Mesa Verde, and Canyon de Chelly cities and towns began. When Coronado arrived in 1540, he found Pueblo towns located only on the

Hopi Mesas of eastern Arizona and along the length of the Rio Grande from the present Colorado border south toward the Mexican border. These had all been established in the 1300s and 1400s, following the south and eastward movement of the Pueblo peoples from the San Juan River drainage. As we have said, approximately 36 of these settlements remain, the exact number depending upon whether one counts all the smaller communities, with a total population today of about 40,000 (see Cordell 1979, Eggan 1979, Plog 1979, Simmons 1979a, 1979b for general coverage of Pueblo history and prehistory).

For 140 years the Pueblo people tolerated Spanish attempts to Hispanicize their social institutions, particularly their religion. The citizens of each pueblo, in good compromising fashion—for the Zuni and Hopi both have trinary type *III* kin systems, and the type *IIB* Keresans and type *IIN* Tanoans early on learned that compromise led to survival—practiced Catholic rites in public and their own ceremonies under the cover of night. Then, in 1680, having taken all they could, they consolidated their forces and rebelled. In a matter of hours the well-coordinated plot exterminated the Spanish clerical and secular presence in New Mexico and Arizona. True to the tenets of their trinary social philosophy, the Pueblo people allowed the survivors to leave for Mexico unharmed and then returned to their own nonforceful way of life. This lasted until 1692, when the Spanish returned (see Sando 1979 for more information on the Pueblo Revolt).

Though the Spanish reconquest was successful this time, the Pueblo people steadfastly refused both European culture and the uncompromising absolutism of Christianity, a refusal they have largely maintained to this day. Because of the historical lessons received from the Spanish, later the Mexicans, and yet later the Anglo-Americans, the Pueblo people have learned to share as little as possible of their thoughts and their cultural philosophy with their European neighbors. They have understandably, for their own protection, become a secretive people. This is the manner in which they have managed to survive intact as a confederated society to the present.

Of the native American Big Six, only the Pueblo towns still exist and flourish much as they did when Columbus arrived in the New World in 1492. Of all the native American polities, the Pueblos alone retain a way of life only superficially influenced by European customs and beliefs.

If the other native American polities discussed in this volume have either vanished or their peoples been forced into cultural and political retreat, how have the Pueblos survived over the past 500 years, still living on their ancestral lands and still with most of their native culture and social system intact? The answer lies partly in the cloak of reserve and secrecy they have maintained over the centuries since 1680, but it lies even more in their underlying philosophy of life, the philosophy that enabled the formation of the cooperative All-Pueblo Council, for regardless of their diverse historical origins and external cultural differences, all four of the Pueblo cultures are united by the same fundamental social theme. That theme is what we referred to as the *trinary theme* in the introduction. Even the dualistic type *IIN* Tanoans and the dualistic type *IIB* Keresan peoples have over the past ten centuries adapted and modified their kin systems toward the trinary norm. All of the Pueblos, in fact, show this social philosophy in perhaps its purest form.

This all-pervading social theme of dividing everything into threes, with emphasis on the middle, compromising ground, shows itself in every aspect of Pueblo culture, whether trinary Hopi and Zuni or modified dualistic Keresan and Tanoan. It is perhaps seen most clearly and directly in the method that the Pueblo peoples use for naming, describing, and interacting with their relatives. Though the description here simplifies the situation somewhat, in essence direct-line relatives—parents, brothers and sisters, and children—are called by one set of terms; relatives on the father's side of the family—what we would call paternal uncles, aunts, and their children—are called by a different set of terms; and relatives on the mother's side of the family—what we would call maternal uncles, aunts, and their children—are called by yet a third set of terms. Each of the three sets of relatives is looked on and treated in a separate, distinctive manner.

While in our society we accord the greatest attention, affection, and respect to our direct-line relatives—parents, siblings, and children—in Pueblo societies it is the relatives on the mother's side of the family who receive the greatest amount of respect, particularly mother's brothers. One looks, for instance, more to one's mother's brother for "fatherly" advice than to one's own biological father. When one marries, one lives first with and then near one's wife's mother's family. In some instances, though it is rare, if a family uses an English family name in addition to its native name—for interaction with the surrounding, English-speaking world—a man who marries will take his wife's English family name, precisely the reverse of the system in male-oriented dualistic cultures such as our own.

None of this implies a female-dominated society in which men play a subservient role. Rather it simply indicates that Pueblo societies are organized along lines that assign particular importance to the role that women play in life, though, as in all human societies, specific roles are assigned to both sexes.

Kin-naming terms and the treatment accorded the three kin classes are but one example of the emphasis on three-ness which so pervades all of Pueblo social norms and action. The world and all existence is traditionally divided into three categories: the Natural Human World, the Natural Nonhuman World, and the Supernatural World. Both the Human and Nonhuman Natural Worlds are also subdivided into three categories each—the nonhuman categories are usually referred to as Hot, Cold, and Of the Middle, each containing specific kinds of plants and animals; the human categories, which have different names from one Pueblo group to another, might be called the Common Men, Political Leaders, and Ritual Leaders. The members of each human category have their own special duties, their uniform purpose being to see that the unity and solidarity of the community are maintained in the realm to which they belong. Each group has a reciprocal relationship of responsibilities to the other two groups, and members of the middle group, the Political Leaders, serve as general mediators and compromisers in making community decisions (see Ortiz 1969 for a thorough and fascinating coverage of this philosophy of life).

The Supernatural World is also divided into three categories, which mirror the three categories of humanity. Thus the souls of the Common Men occupy one part of the Supernatural World, the souls of Political Leaders occupy a second part, and the souls of Ritual Leaders occupy a third, along with spirits that were never born into the Natural World but continue to inhabit the Supernatural World. The most important of the third category of spirits that were never born into the Natural World are called *kachinas* in Hopi and by equivalent terms in Zuni, Keresan, and Tanoan. While the first two types of Supernaturals are always present, they do not return to the Natural World. The kachinas, however, come back annually to the Natural World from the Supernatural World in the form of masked impersonators in a series of often spectacular rituals and ceremonies, such as the Zuni *Shalako* and Hopi *Soyal* ceremonies. Such Supernaturals may be approached at any one of three locations: certain bodies of water, such as lakes and ponds; specific shrines; and what are referred to as "earth navels," which are natural or artificial openings into the earth at specific points within each town and the adjacent lands. These "navels," *sipapu* in Hopi, are seen as literally leading to the center of the earth and the dwelling place, in three levels, of the three categories of Supernaturals.

In many of the Pueblos three Political Leaders are chosen from each of the tribal subdivisions of Common Men and serve the community for a period of one year. There are three classes of Political Leaders: the Governor, the Lieutenant Governor (sometimes more than one), and the *Fiscal,* whose duties are limited to coordinating activities with the Catholic Church. These officers serve both the Common Men of the community and the Ritual Leaders and act as mediators between all segments of the society, as well as the outside world, in the case of potential conflict or problem.

The Ritual Leaders dedicate their lives to scheduling, controlling, and directing the community's ritual and ceremonial activities, and they are the real powers behind maintenance of overall social cohesion. They plan the annual cycle of ritual involving the Supernaturals, who appear in masked form at specific times of the ritual year. The Political Leaders are in charge of seeing that the rituals are performed, and the Common Men are enjoined to take part in them as planned and executed by the other two groups.

A full description of the trinary groups in Pueblo society, community by community, could occupy a hefty volume all its own, and while the complexities and details of these three-way groupings have not been given here, the principle is, I imagine, clear.

In addition to the principle of three-ness, Pueblo society is characterized, as indicated earlier, by a strong principle of *compromise*. This principle, as seen from the discussion of trinary societies in Chapter 6, is typical of such social systems. Among the Pueblo peoples it shows most obviously in their handling of conflict, whether between individuals within the Pueblo community or with the outside world. In the earlier chapters in this section, we spent a considerable number of pages discussing the conquests and ways of warfare of the Tawantinsuyu Inca, the México Aztecs, and the Classic Period and Yucatec Maya. By contrast, almost nothing need be said regarding Pueblo methods of defense. This is because, unlike their dualistic cousins, who use force as a first line of defense, or their unitary cousins, who alternately either attack when confronted or who simply retreat from potential confrontation, trinary cultures habitually use physical force only as a last resort, only when pushed to the wall—as in the 1680 Pueblo Revolt. Instead they use compromise as the basic means for solving all problems.

In times of potential conflict, trinary societies resolve differences of opinion by seeing that both sides gain a little and that each side also sacrifices enough to keep the other happy—no one wins, no one loses, or, one might say, everyone wins. Trinary states are thus by nature peacemakers, and they invariably prefer diplomacy and compromise to physical force. "Live and let live" has been the mainstay of Pueblo social and political success for over 2,000 years. That accomplishment could, indeed, and should provide a lesson for the statesman.

The only known instance of out-and-out violence against others was the

Pueblo Revolt of 1680. The Pueblo peoples' open-arms reception of the Spanish in the 1540s was based on the Pueblo belief that all reasonable people will give a little, even if they take a little. They did not realize that Spanish dualism left no room for such compromise and that their new visitors considered themselves not another society among equals but, rather, conquerors, nor did they at first realize that the Spanish stance required them to abandon their lifeways for those of European absolutism. After 140 years of coercive treatment from the Spanish, and with no seeming compromising alternative that the Spanish would accept, the Pueblos banded together and drove the oppressor out. While there were deaths, it is noteworthy that the successful Pueblo people neither slaughtered nor enslaved the survivors but allowed them to leave peaceably toward the south and their colonial confrères in Mexico.

Thus to this day the Pueblos maintain their customs and social philosophy, little touched by alien culture. The externals have some Hispanic and Anglo-American veneer, but the inner structure of native belief and action remains untouched. Survival has been ensured by steadfast refusal to admit outsiders into the fold, and many Pueblo towns still do not allow Hispanics or Anglos to live within the town limits or to attend either Pueblo political meetings or the ceremonials of Holy Days. These have become closed societies in which the lessons of the past have made the outsider no longer welcome. Toleration, moderation, and compromise are still the internal norm, but they realize that such norms extend no farther than the limits of each pueblo. More than any other native American group, the Pueblos have retained their social system and its underlying philosophy in almost pristine form. In this increasingly intolerant age, they could well serve as a model for most other societies.

12

The Taíno Kingdoms

If the trinary confederation of the Pueblo towns of the American Southwest has been the most durable of all the native American Big Six, the trinary Taíno Kingdoms of the Greater Antilles were the least durable, for they no longer exist in remnant population or even the slightest vestige of everyday cultural belief or modern-day artifact. This striking contrast has, of course, historical reason behind it, but it is all the more arresting in the loss that was created.

The Taíno peoples of the Caribbean, speakers of an Arawak language of ultimate origin in the Guianas region of northeastern South America, were the first native Americans to be confronted by Europeans. When Columbus set foot in the New World on October 12, 1492, it was on the island of Guanahaní in the Bahamas, where he was met by the Lucayan people, first cousins to the Taíno of the Greater Antilles, just to the south on the islands of Cuba, Hispaniola, and Puerto Rico. After journeying through the Bahamas and along the Cuban coast, Columbus landed on the north shore of the island of Hispaniola on Christmas Day 1492 and began to establish the first European settlement in the New World, La Navidad. The town was built by local Indians, forcefully recruited as corvée labor. The harsh treatment accorded these unsuspectingly cooperative workers was returned the following year when the Indians destroyed the town. Not to be deterred, however, the Europeans went on to establish La Isabela and other settlements in the years immediately following, and within a short time all of the native population of Hispaniola was under the permanent and rigid yoke of Spanish political and clerical rule.

In contrast to our abundant knowledge of the Inca, Aztec, Maya, and Pueblo and their forebears, our reliable data on the Taíno both before and at the time of Columbus's arrival is surprisingly meager. Archaeologists are gradually piecing together the prehistoric backgrounds and migrations of the native peoples of the Caribbean, but even that picture is in a state of flux today. The official Spanish accounts of the time, preserved in the Archives of the Indies in Seville, with few exceptions discuss only the Indies' potential for wealth and the conversion of the native peoples to Christianity. Almost the only interest shown in the people per se was as a source of unpaid, baptized labor. There is some information of ethnographic interest in these early accounts but regrettably little.

Economic disruption and forcible reeducation were the tools of Spanish expansion in Hispaniola and the other islands of the Greater Antilles. In Chapter 1 we mentioned that Spanish clerics of the 1500s routinely read what were called "requirements" to their new charges, stating unambiguously that the Pope had given the Indian lands to the Spanish monarchs and that they, the friars, *demanded* that the Indians accept Christianity and acknowledge the sovereignty of the King and Queen of Spain. The good friars carried out their directive with dispatch and to the letter in the years immediately following 1492.

A few men with heart did soon take interest, but they were few, and by the time their pleas for leniency reached the Spanish Crown and were halfheartedly acted upon there was no longer a Taíno society or a Taíno people to be saved. It all happened in a period of less than fifty years. Fortunately, those few who did see the Taíno as other human beings rather than mere chattels have left us enough details on their way of life to make at least some general statements possible. Archaeology and linguistics add further clarification.

Spanish control over the native people was facilitated by a system referred to as *repartimiento* and *encomienda*. The former referred to the parceling out and resettlement of local inhabitants, by force when necessary, to specific areas of the island and to specific work tasks. *Encomienda* referred to the assignment of individuals to the overlordship of a specific Spanish settler—in effect, nonindentured slave labor. These methods were backed by the Spanish Crown and strictly enforced by the Spanish settlers who quickly followed Columbus in the early years of the sixteenth century.

As frequently happens in the settlement of a new area, the settlers came either from the upper reaches of society, the junior nobility of Spain, or from the absolute bottom. Those of the upper echelons were used to enforcing their desires rigidly back home and, of course, saw nothing amiss in doing so with their New World charges. By somewhat the same token, those on the bottom of the social ladder had been used to harsh treatment at home and so saw nothing wrong in inflicting the same treatment on the native inhabitants of Hispaniola. The social picture was a cruel and violent one from the start.

Confronted by this situation, the leaders of the Taíno kingdoms at first permitted such treatment to be meted out by their Spanish visitors and, in true compromising, trinary fashion, attempted to adjust as much as they could to Spanish demands. But adjustment was not what the Europeans were after. They would settle for nothing less than complete subjugation.

By far the most fruitful and important Spanish chronicles from the early days of colonization are the works of Fr. Ramón Pané and Fr. Bartolomé de Las Casas, both of whom lived among the Taíno and knew them firsthand in the years immediately after 1492, before the work of subjugation became complete. These two clerics knew each other, and both saw the consequences of Spanish policy on the native cultures. Pané arrived in 1494 and lived both among the non-Taíno Macorix people in northern Hispaniola and the Taíno people farther south. He was commissioned by Columbus to learn the native languages and discover what he could about the customs of the people. His account of Taíno religion is the only description we have of the Taíno philosophy of life and reveals a culture thoroughly imbued with a live-and-let-live modus operandi.

Fr. Las Casas came to Hispaniola in 1502 as a young man and participated in the settlement of both Hispaniola and Cuba. What he saw so alienated him from his fellow adventurers that he returned to Spain to train for the priesthood. When he returned in 1516, he turned his attention to describing the plight of the native people. His outspoken works were so controversial that they were not published until many years after his death, some not until the twentieth century, and they remain something of a bête noire to Spanish-speakers throughout the world because of the grimly uncompromising picture painted of Taíno treatment at the hands of the colonizers. For many years Las Casas was accused of inventing most of what he wrote and of providing an artificially negative picture of Spanish colonial policy—*La Leyenda Negra,* the Black Legend. Though his work is still viewed with suspicion and disbelief in some quarters, all the later documentary evidence supports the veracity of his reports. He may, in fact, have been overly kind and moderate to his compatriots in much of what he had to say.

It is in the original accounts of these and other firsthand observers that we find the only ethnographic material we have on the Taíno, for by the mid-1500s there was no Taíno society left and very few pure-blooded Taíno men and women. The picture delineated by Pané, Las Casas, and the few other reliable writers of the time indicates that there were three partly independent non-Taíno, non-Arawak kingdoms in the northern sections of Hispaniola, representing the earlier population of the island before the ancestral Taíno arrived about the time of the birth of Christ. These were the kingdoms of the Lower Macorix, the Upper Macorix, and the Ciguayo peoples. Five independent Taíno kingdoms controlled the remainder of the island, each kingdom under the jurisdiction of a powerful paramount king. The kingdoms themselves were divided into provinces, each controlled by a Lesser King. A sixth, new Taíno kingdom was in the process of formation on the eastern end of Cuba at the time the Spanish arrived, but its formation was effectively halted by the advance of the Europeans to that island. A confederation of chiefdoms, apparently under a single paramount ruler, existed on the island of Puerto Rico.

The Taíno developed a distinctive culture and society on Hispaniola during the 1,500-year period between the time of their arrival and Spanish settlement in 1492. From archaeological data, it is evident that they reached their full flowering between A.D. 1000 and 1400, drawing both from ancestral mainland South American Arawak culture and from the cultures of the earlier Ciguayo and Macorix peoples of Hispaniola. By the time of Spanish intervention, Taíno society had reached the final stages of amalgamation, blending culture traits from all three sources into a uniquely local Taíno culture.

The first Taíno kingdom, the Kingdom of Marién, under King Guacanagarí, included most of what is now northern and central Haiti. The region had been populated by Macorix people until movement of Taíno-speaking people into the area several centuries before the Spanish arrived. In keeping with the trinary social norms of Taíno society, the Taíno newcomers did not obliterate or subjugate the Macorix peoples they encountered but allowed them to continue full expression of their own social customs. The Taíno simply became the ruling class of Marién. The culture of the people of Marién Kingdom at the time the Spanish arrived was, however, still noticeably different from that of the other Taíno kingdoms as a result of its large Macorix population.

The second Taíno kingdom, under the leadership of King Guarionex, was the Kingdom of Maguá, which occupied the bulk of northern Hispaniola to the east of Marién as well as a goodly portion of what is now the central Dominican Republic. The third kingdom, under King Cayacoa, was the Kingdom of Higüey, in eastern Hispaniola. The fourth was the Kingdom of Maguana, which ran from the south-central coast of the island northward to and including the vast Vega Real or central plain as well as the mountainous regions on its northern border with the Maguá kingdom. King Caonabó, the Golden One, ruled Maguana kingdom along with his equally famous wife,

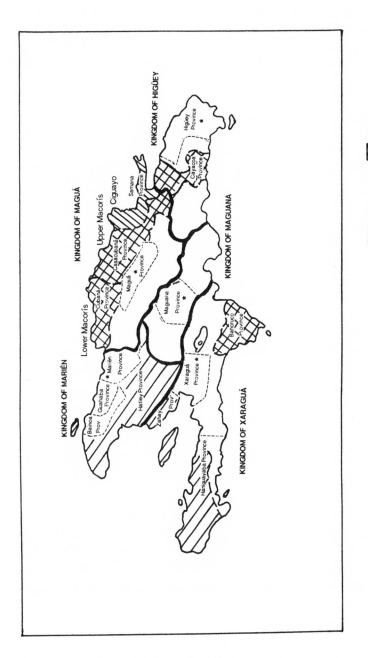

Figure 17. Taíno Kingdoms of Hispaniola in 1492

Anacaona, the Golden Lady. Maguana was the major gold-producing kingdom of the island and hence came in for the most devastating confrontation
with the Europeans. Caonabó and Anacaona met tragic, early, and ignomini-
ous deaths at the hands of the conquerors, a fate shared by all of the leading
rulers of Hispaniola.

The fifth, and largest, of the Taíno kingdoms, occupying all of central and
southern Haiti as well as a large part of the southwest Dominican Republic,
was the Kingdom of Xaraguá (pronounced *Hah-rah-WA,* with emphasis on
the last syllable). Xaraguá, which means "Lake District," was ruled by King
Behequio, the brother of Anacaona, and was the shining gem of the Taíno
kingdoms, considered by both Taíno and Spanish alike as the most civilized
and cultivated of the kingdoms. The customs and language of Xaraguá, Las
Casas tells us, were models for the rest of the Hispaniolan world. It is largely
from accounts of the culture of Xaraguá that we know what we do about
Taíno society.

The major town of Xaraguá was one of the largest in Hispaniola, and all
the rulers of the other four kingdoms looked to the ruler of Xaraguá as something of an Over-King. The kingdom was the island's major producer of cotton, and the Camín River had been diverted for purposes of irrigating the vast
conucos or agricultural fields devoted to the cultivation of cotton, manioc, and
other crops. Even the Spanish were impressed by the civility of the citizens of
Xaraguá and its rulers. We have, for example, a lengthy description of a formal
reception given by King Behequio and his sister Queen Anacaona of Maguana for Bartolomé Colón. All of this, however, did not prevent the decimation of Xaraguá, the execution of its rulers, and the enslavement of its people
under the *repartimiento* and *encomienda* system.

The island of Puerto Rico contained a number of small kingdoms, each
with its own ruler. There was, however, a single paramount king. The only
two about whom we know anything were both named Agüeíbana, and their
major settlement was located near the modern city of Guayanilla. Though
Puerto Rican kingdoms were smaller than those of Hispaniola, their bril-
liance is well attested by the quality of workmanship of the artifacts of the
time that have survived. Many of the Puerto Rican sites are very large and
indicate the presence of considerable sophisticated urbanization.

Cuba did not see a Taíno presence until approximately 1425, according to
Las Casas and the other chroniclers. At that time, Taíno from the Kingdom
of Marién crossed the straits between western Haiti and eastern Cuba and
established themselves in several large towns in Oriente Province. By far the
largest influx of migrants, however, came after the arrival of the Spanish, as a

result of European pressures and depredations in their Hispaniolan homeland. We know that the Taíno ruler in Oriente Province in Cuba was Hatüey, Lesser King of Guahaba province in the Kingdom of Marién. He fled to Cuba with most of his subjects as a direct result of the Spanish invasion of Marién. He was, of course, rewarded for his flight by being burned at the stake when the Spanish crossed the straits between Hispaniola and Cuba and began their inexorable march through eastern Cuba. In honesty, it should be said that he was offered a choice of conversion to Christianity or death at the stake. When he asked if Spaniards and Christians went to heaven and was given a positive response, he replied that he would rather be burned than go to a Spanish or Christian heaven!

Other than their attempts to please and appease their Spanish visitors rather than do battle directly with them, we know only from indirect evidence that the Taíno were a trinary people. The evidence, however, is so compelling that it leaves no doubt but that such was the case.

We know, for example, that the citizens of Taíno states were divided into three classes: the *caciques* or Political Leaders, the *behiques* or Ritual Leaders, and the *naboría* or Common Men. From the previous chapter on the Pueblo peoples, we learned that this is also the three-way division of individuals in those societies. It is, in fact, a social division common to most, though not all, trinary societies in any part of the world.

The *caciques* or Political Leaders were themselves of three different kinds. The *matuheri* or Great Lords were highest in rank, and they were the rulers of the five large Taíno kingdoms—Caonabó of Maguana, Guacanagarí of Marién, Guarionex of Maguá, Cayacoa of Higüey, and Behequio of Xaraguá. Second in rank were the *bahari,* the Lesser Lords, who ruled the subkingdoms or provinces into which each kingdom was divided—Hatüey of Guahaba Province in Marién kingdom, for example. The third rank of *caciques* were the *waoheri,* the Gentlemen, who filled lesser orders of political office within each kingdom and province.

We do not have any details on varying classes of Ritual Leaders, the *behiques,* or on subclasses of the Common Man, the *naboría.* We know that the *naboría* (the word literally means "my home people" or "neighbors") devoted their lives to agricultural and other types of labor for their communities. The Spanish erroneously thought that the term was derogatory and that it implied a servile, servant status. Las Casas, however, makes it clear that the status of *naboría* held no stigma and that it simply meant that one performed the ordinary daily work duties that most people perform in all societies.

The role that females played in Taíno society was significant. We know, for example, that certain kinds of property, such as *duhos* or ceremonial stools, were inherited only in the female line. We know, too, that the line of succession to the kingships of the Taíno states, while usually from male to male, did not normally go from a male ruler to his son but, rather, to his sister's son. This is a clear indication that Taíno society was matri- or female-oriented. The feeling is further reinforced by our knowledge that when King Caonabó of Maguana kingdom died, his wife, Anacaona, became the ruler of Maguana, and that when her brother, King Behequio of Xaraguá, was executed by the Spanish, she became the ruler of that kingdom as well. A beautiful woman whose hand was sought by many Taíno and Spanish leaders after her husband's death, Anacaona was an accomplished ruler and diplomat. Regardless of the brutal manner in which her husband Caonabó had been captured and thrown aboard a ship for Spain, a journey on which he died, she managed to keep relationships between her people and the Spanish on a less than violent level for some time. She was, of course, ultimately taken by the Spanish authorities and burned at the stake in Santo Domingo City, becoming a martyr to her people as well as to later generations. There is today a moving statue of her in Santo Domingo, a tribute to the memory of a beautiful, accomplished, and valorous lady.

Such an emphasis on the role of women in society, on the use of compromise as a bargaining tool, and on a three-way division of social classes normally occurs only in societies that have a trinary kin-naming system, and while we do not have information on this topic from the Spanish, it seems a fair assumption that the Taíno did, indeed, have such a system.

While many Taíno sites have been excavated by archaeologists, we know surprisingly little about their overall nature. We have lists of the larger towns in each of the kingdoms of Hispaniola but almost nothing in the way of full descriptions of what they were like and how they were laid out. The only exception is the site of San Juan de Maguana, which is assumed to have been the location of Caonabó's principal town. The problem of defining the nature of Taíno towns is further complicated by the fact that buildings were constructed from perishable materials. There were no stone buildings, as in Inca Tawantinsuyu, Aztec Tenochtitlán, the Maya cities, or the Pueblo towns, and there was very little monumental use of stone. From Columbus himself as well as the later chroniclers, we know that many towns had as many as 300 to 400 houses and that some had in excess of 1,000. This information enables us to estimate the population of Taíno towns as varying between 1,000 and 3,000 or more souls.

One of the less reliable chroniclers, Gonzalo Fernández de Oviedo y Valdés, tells us that most towns had a central plaza and that the house of the town *cacique,* whether a *matuheri, baheri,* or *waoheri,* was located there. Such houses were called *caney* and were large and circular in form, in contrast to the dwellings of the *naboría,* which were rectangular. Both types of structures were built of thatch with sturdy wooden wall posts, beams, and rafters. The chroniclers make it clear that they were not shoddily built.

Each town also had either a circular or rectangular court for playing *batey,* a ball game played with a rubber ball. *Batey* seems to have been as much a national mania with the Taíno as soccer is in Europe and Latin America or baseball and football are in the United States today. Such courts are found throughout both Hispaniola and Puerto Rico. The largest known court, at Caonabó's main town of San Juan de Maguana, is 2,270 feet in circumference, though the most thoroughly excavated and best known of the courts are those at Utuado in Puerto Rico. In addition to their use as ball courts, the *batey* enclosures were also used for ceremonial dances, called *areitos.*

The Taíno were an agricultural people, and their primary staple crop was manioc, which was called *yuca* in Taíno, used for making cassava bread. Many other vegetable and fruit crops were also raised as food sources, and both hunting and fishing provided more than adequate sources of protein. Important nonfood agricultural crops were tobacco, extensively used for ceremonial purposes, and cotton for the making of fabrics.

A sea-oriented people, the Taíno made large oceangoing canoes, and it is known both from the accounts of the Spanish chroniclers and from archaeologically recovered artifacts that commodities of all types were traded not only among the islands of the Greater Antilles but also further afield. A trading settlement from Cuba called Abaibo, "First Distant Home," for example, was made on the southwest coast of Florida for trade with the Calusa Indians. Artifacts made from Greater Antillean jadeite have been found throughout the Antilles and the Bahamas.

Taíno art, as in most trinary cultures—Islamic art or Pueblo art, for example—is inextricably linked to religious and ritual concepts. Ceremonial artifacts of jadeite, stone, gold, shell, wood, and fabric, all beautifully and skillfully executed, have survived the holocaust of the Spanish conquest. The most intriguing and important are images of Taíno supernatural beings, called *zemi,* which are almost the exact counterpart of the Pueblo *kachinas*—images of spirits from the Supernatural World. Unlike the Pueblo *kachinas,* however, which usually took human form, the *zemis* were invariably shown in animal form, usually, from our point of view, very grotesque animal form. In spite of this—*zemi* means "sweet" or "delicate"—these spirits were held in general affection, and their images had to be fed and, like their living counterparts, kept in good health and natural balance.

Like the Pueblo peoples, and in common with many other cultures, the Taíno believed that man came to the Natural World from a supernatural underground world, inhabited by the *zemi* spirits, which come to the upper world on special ceremonial occasions. Entrance to the Supernatural World was, also as with the Pueblo peoples, through openings in the earth. Unlike the Pueblo, whose *sipapu* openings might be either natural or man-made, openings to the Taíno underground were only through natural caves, which consequently had a holiness that other parts of the earth did not. Many ceremonial artifacts have been recovered from caves throughout the Taíno region, indicating the use and importance of such holy places in Taíno ritual.

Life was thought to have emerged from the underground through a number of specific caves—*caciques* or Political Leaders and *behiques* or Ritual Leaders were thought to have emerged from a cave called *Cacibagiuagua,* and the Common Man, the *naboría,* were thought to have emerged from a cave called *Amaiauba.*

The Taíno had no concept of an omniscient and omnipotent personal deity. Rather the world was governed by an all-encompassing force which they called *Yaya* or, more frequently, *Yucahú,* the spirit of *yuca,* manioc. A male force, it was neither worshipped nor supplicated for help. It was an inactive, invisible, and impersonal force that dwelled in the heavens above and manifested itself only in dreams.

All living things had a soul, called *guaíza,* which lasted after death as a spirit called *opía.* Both wandered at will, though the spirits of the dead, nocturnal in their movement, lived in a land called *Coaibai,* deep in the forests. Their lives were much the same as those of living beings, except always in a state of order and balance. Their world was governed by the same three-way social distinction among ruler, ritual leader, and commoner that prevailed in the world of the living. In their wanderings, the *opía* most often took the form of a bat, and this motif is the most striking and frequent of all sculptural designs on ceramic wares and on stone and wooden artifacts. The bat was a particularly revered supernatural animal, representing one's ancestors and the shape one's own *guaíza* would take one day.

As in the Pueblo world, the primary social directive was maintenance of the natural order and prevention of any kind of social imbalance. While all three social classes were responsible for maintaining such stability, the *caciques* were responsible for keeping such order in the Natural World, and the *behiques* were charged with seeing to it that the balance between the Natural World and the Supernatural World remained positive. The *naboría* or Common Man played his part by participating in ritual ceremonies called *areitos.*

The *behiques* ensured ongoing harmony between the upper and underground worlds through ritual contact with the *zemis* in trancelike states induced by the use of smoke from *cahoba,* an extremely powerful and potent tobacco. Through such trances, the *behique* would provide omens of action that should be taken by an individual or by society at large to maintain the order of nature.

The *behique*'s oracular rituals were not public, but the entire community took part in the periodic ceremonial *areitos,* held for the purpose both of pleasing the *zemi* spirits and ensuring continuing social stability. Las Casas and Oviedo give us vivid descriptions of *areitos.* The term itself means both "song" and "dance," and we are told that as many as 300 to 400 men and women danced in a long line in the town plaza, accompanied by singing and musical instruments. The overall effect was apparently both pleasing and very moving.

The impression given by our scanty information on Taíno society of the late 1400s is what one would expect from a trinary culture—a generally peaceable society with a live-and-let-live attitude enmeshed in a philosophy of maintenance of the order and balance of nature. When confronted by the inexorable force of an economically motivated and proselytizing dualistic society, it simply crumbled. By the mid-1500s Taíno society and culture had ceased to exist.

Part IV
THE FUTURE OF THE PAST

At this stage in our discussion of native American societies we need to know with the highest degree of probability what the New World would be like today if Columbus had not arrived and if none of his comrades from other European or African lands had set foot in the Americas.

It is also this stage of our discussion that will draw the greatest number of raised eyebrows from both general and academic readers, for we are treading on ground not touched before. We are in the genuine realm of *future-cast* and suggesting circumstances and consequences that can be neither confirmed nor rejected. We could, of course, simply use our imaginations and fantasize, but this was not the goal. The goal was forecasting on the basis of verified data. Thus, being without a crystal ball and not wishing to make overactive use of personal imagination, the outcomes suggested here come only from known information. One must hasten to add, however, that this does not mean that other equally probable, parallel sets of future consequences could not have grown from the same array of verified data. They might. *The Americas That Might Have Been* depiction here is but one of many, and it should be taken for what it is—a professional opinion of what might well have transpired in an un-Europeanized twenty-first-century America.

One will notice, I trust, that nowhere in the following future-cast are specific events suggested. This is purposeful. Only possible and probable societal links are considered, based on known commonalities and differences among the cultures under discussion. Thus, if cause and effect is indeed a viable theory of time and behavior, then the picture outlined here *could*, positively, have existed. Let the reader decide.

13

Hemispheric-Internal Relationships in the Twenty-first Century
The Inner Design

The Broad Perspective

If anthropologists are correct, it is unlikely that any major alterations would have occurred in New World social systems during the past five centuries. Every example of substantial social change elsewhere has taken seven to ten centuries to establish itself, and then only if accompanied by significant long-term contact with other societies (Kryukov 1998, Murdock 1949:330–331).

In the case of the Inca, Aztec, Maya, and Pueblo peoples we know that no major alterations have in fact occurred. The social fabric of those societies is fundamentally the same today as it was in the late 1400s and early 1500s, though on a reduced and nonurban demographic base and with reduced social self-determination. The Taíno, we also know, did not survive even as a tribal entity.

Only the ethnically pluralistic Mississippian social systems saw significant modification. From archaeological evidence we know that the Mississippian Caddoan, Natchez, Tunica, and early Muskogean peoples of the era A.D. 1000–1400 all had highly individualistic, hierarchical, *IIB* dualistic social systems in which rank was based on genealogical lineage and membership in dual social groups (moieties). With emphasis on the social role of the female strongly implied by the numerous archaeologically recovered stone ceremonial figurines of females, it is clear, too, that those societies were matri-oriented (see, for example, Emerson 1997:193–223). When we look at the social systems of these peoples today, however, we see that while all are still matri-oriented and some of the Caddoan peoples still retain a dualistic *IIB* social system, other Caddoan groups, as well as the historically known Natchez and all of the Muskogean peoples, are now characterized by a type *III* trinary social system.

By the mid-1500s the large dualistic urban settlements of the Classic Mississippian period had long been abandoned, replaced by smaller, less highly organized settlements typified by the towns of the Natchez and the Muskogean peoples. The replacement of dualistic social systems by trinary systems implies the end point of gradual, ongoing modulation over a very long period of time. The precise nature of such long-term change in this case is not known, though it may well be attributed to gradual alteration in rules of marital residence and the concomitant nature of family households, which do seem to be reflected in changes through time in domestic household types as seen archaeologically (Rogers and Smith 1995).

The Americas' unitary, dualistic, and trinary societies today are shown in the map in Figure 18. The relationships that link and separate them from one another form the discussion of the remainder of this chapter.

Trinary Societies

Though the twenty-first-century New World would be dominated demographically and in area by unitary societies, as Figure 18 indicates, the more politically accommodating trinary societies would account for a large share of the New World population north of Mexico. As in the 1500s, they would continue to dominate the North American midlands, the Southeast, and significant portions of the Southwest. Many would be small independent tribal groups, but some, through confederation, as suggested below, would show considerable areal spread, demographic size, and concomitant power. In Central and South America, other than the Taíno in the Caribbean and in Amazonian Brazil, trinary groups have always been fewer.

The most well known native American trinary polity is certainly that of the Pueblos of New Mexico and Arizona. These ethnically diverse societies joined together in a kind of confederacy for self-protection against their Navajo and Apache neighbors sometime in the 1400s. That this polity would have lasted regardless of a European or Anglo-American presence is indisputable, and the United Pueblos would have been one of the major trinary policy makers in a twenty-first-century America.

The largest and most dominant trinary polity in the hemisphere today, however, would unquestionably be that governed by the Muskogean peoples of the Southeast. In the 1500s the Muskogean-speaking Coosa chiefdom of northwest Georgia and northeast Alabama—inheritors of the social, political, and religious beliefs and practices of the Classic Mississippian tradition—had

Figure 18. New World Polities and Alliances, 2004

already forged a politically and ceremonially powerful confederation of Creek-speaking towns and was on its way to controlling a significant geographical area (Hudson 1990:214–230, Hudson et al. 1985, Smith 1987:129–142, Smith 2001, Swanton 1946:124–126, 153–154). Given the political and cultural prestige of the Coosa towns during the sixteenth century, it seems probable that they would have continued to spearhead a Mississippian revival. Had this taken place, it would have attracted the allegiance not only of other culturally related, trinary Muskogean tribes such as the Hitchiti, Alabama, Koasati, and perhaps Chickasaw and Choctaw but also the trinary Timucua and Tunica-related Calusa of Florida, creating a true multiethnic trinary Southeastern Confederacy reminiscent of the days of Mississippian dominance in mid- and southeastern North America.

In similar manner the smaller yet still powerful Natchez and Tunica peoples of west-central Mississippi and adjacent northeast central Louisiana, also trinary in social structure by the 1500s, continued the practices of much of the Mississippian tradition in modified form and remained an influential force to reckon with. The primary goal of the Natchez ruler, referred to splendiferously as *The Sun*, was not territorial conquest but the acquisition of prestige and economic goods through control of his neighbors. Possibly aligned with the Natchez in lower coastal Louisiana would be the Chitimacha and their Atakapa and Karankawa neighbors to the west along the Louisiana and Texas coasts.

Whether the trinary Siouan and Caddoan peoples of the Midwest would have formed their own confederation is difficult to say. While the southernmost Caddoan peoples of Oklahoma had been participants in the Mississippian cultural tradition in the period 1000 to 1300—the vast Mississippian Spiro site in Oklahoma was certainly a Caddoan city—they did not continue an urban tradition after the breakup of the Mississippian cities, and there is no indication that they would have returned to that way of life. Their Siouan neighbors, to the north through the American midlands and beyond the present Canadian border, had never embarked on the road to urbanization, nor is there reason to think that they would have done so in later years. Nonetheless, it is not impossible to imagine that the Siouan and Caddoan peoples, with their vast territorial holdings, might have aligned themselves for protection, if only informally, with the already multiethnic Southeastern Confederacy, centered in Georgia.

The Taíno Kingdoms of Hispaniola, Puerto Rico, and Cuba would be the sole twenty-first-century trinary urban polities south of North America. They would certainly have remained a growing, thriving, and peaceable society. Still expanding through the island of Cuba in the late 1400s, there seems little reason to doubt that the Taíno would have successfully survived to the present and, as consummate seafarers, contributed to the creation and maintenance of trade networks both within the Caribbean Basin and between North and South America.

Though at the time of European intervention the Taíno were divided into a large number of local groups under the control of five kingdoms, it is likely, considering the ongoing expansion of Taíno settlement and the increasing power of the Kingdom of Xaraguá, that all of the separate kingdoms would ultimately have consolidated into a single state, each of its subparts retaining considerable local autonomy.

With the penchant of trinary societies to align themselves with one another, particularly against dualistic aggressors or expanding unitary states, it is also likely that the Southeastern Confederation, the Natchez and Tunica, the United Pueblos, the Taíno State or unified Kingdom of Xaraguá, and, most likely, the many independent Siouan and Caddoan societies in the North American midlands would have joined together in a kind of hemispheric *Great Alliance* of nonaligned trinary powers to protect their own territorial and economic interests from the always present potential of aggression from the México Empire and Tawantinsuyu, the two most powerful polities in the New World. There would be less danger from the dualistic Maya and Iroquois, or from other dualistic states, simply because of the geographical distances that separated them from one another. The demographic power and consequent protection that a Great Alliance could provide would be both considerable and of great importance when it came to maintaining hemispheric peace.

Unitary Societies

Unitary societies in the New World (Figure 18) have always been concentrated across the northern regions of North America, along the Pacific coasts of both North and South America, and in Mexico. Such was their distribution in 1492, and it remains their distribution today. The widespread Algonquian peoples spanned North America from far western Canada to the Atlantic and dipped deep into the middle heartland of the continent. In the Far West, unitary Uto-Aztecan societies—the Shoshone, Ute, Paiute, Comanche, and others—occur in Washington, Oregon, California, and the interior West. Other unitary tribal groups—non-Algonquian—are found in far western Canada, in Mexico and, sporadically, on through Central America into Pacific South America, where they dominated in 1492 and now. None of the unitary peoples of North America had become organized urban entities by the fifteenth century.

Because of their close linguistic and ethnic similarities and interests, the Uto-Aztecan peoples of far western North America would surely have joined forces to solve problems mutually affecting them all. Given the seminomadic way of life of all of those tribes, however, it seems doubtful that such a *Ute Confederation* would have become urban. The Algonquian peoples, spanning almost the entire breadth of northern North America, may also have joined forces to create a single, probably rather loosely organized *Algonquian Alliance,* though it is not likely that the people of such an enormous territory would be closely united in a single confederation. More probable would be the formation of five separate, smaller Algonquian confederations: a *Western Confederation* in the far western provinces of Canada and adjacent lands in what is now the United States, probably centered on the Blackfoot and Cheyenne tribes; a *Northern Confederation* spanning all of northern Canada from Saskatchewan through maritime Quebec, centered on the Cree and Ojibwa peoples; a *Central Confederation* dipping down into the Great Lakes region, Wisconsin, Michigan, Illinois, and Indiana; a *New England Confederation* in New England; and a *Delaware Confederation* in the maritime states from the Hudson River region as far south as Virginia and coastal North Carolina, centered on the Mahican and Delaware peoples. Such a scenario is conjectural and would likely be dependent upon the appearance of motivated, farsighted sociopolitical leaders, who, like an Aztec Tlacaelel or an Inca Pachacuti, could form and guide such unions.

The Northern Athabaskan peoples of interior Alaska and much of northwestern Canada are in somewhat the same category in that they were and still remain independent unitary tribes. With no archaeological or ethnohistorical evidence of a trend toward urbanism, it is unlikely that they would have moved toward either urbanism or political unification.

The Tlingit, Haida, Tsimshian, Kwakiutl, Wakashan, Chimakuan, and Salishan towns of the northwest coast of North America, all well-organized, semiurban unitary groups up through the late 1700s, might, unlike the Northern Athabaskans, have consolidated their ranks during the 1800s and 1900s. With a highly complex political, economic, and religious-ceremonial system as well as large permanent settlements, the trend toward areal consolidation and cooperation already existed in the 1700s and probably would have moved on toward the creation of a confederated polity.

The only unitary peoples of native America who had already established large urban centers and territorial states by the time of European intervention were, as we have seen, the Aztecs of Mexico, their Mixtec neighbors, and the Inca of Peru. Both the Aztecs and Inca were still extending their borders rapidly in 1492 and would undoubtedly have continued to spread. It is likely, in fact, that all of modern Mexico, except the dualistic Tarascan Kingdom and Maya Yucatán, as well as parts of northern Central America, would today be either part of the Aztec México Empire or closely allied with it. It is equally probable that all of Andean South America would have become part of an expanded Inca Tawantinsuyu.

The boundaries of the Aztec state in 1519 included almost all of the unitary tribal groups of central Mexico except the Mixtec, and it is probable that they, too, would ultimately have been brought into the Aztec fold as close allies, likely retaining their own independence. Nor is it beyond reason to suggest that the México Empire would, in its inexorable spread, have come into contact with the Pueblo peoples of the American Southwest on its northern borders and with at least the outer reaches of colonial Tawantinsuyu on its southern flank. From archaeological evidence, we know, for example, that Aztec *pochtecas* and the Chontal Putún Maya traded with the Pueblos to the north and southern Central America to the south, and that the South American traders of Colombia traded as far north as northern Central America. These extremes, far from the central heartland of the empire in the Valley of Mexico, would likely have sapped the resources of the military machine and, barring the improbable but not impossible individualistic megalomania of a Hitler in a unitary state—as happened in Milošević's unitary Serbian Yugoslavia as well as in Mao's modern China—it is probable that Aztec energies would have contained themselves within the framework of Mexico's unitary groups and parts of non-Maya northern Central America.

Tawantinsuyu, largely bypassing the dualistic societies of central and eastern Colombia, would with almost equal likelihood have expanded along the Pacific coast of Colombia into the southern reaches of Central America, where it would have absorbed the unitary Cuna and Chocó peoples. Perhaps it would have come within reaching distance of the southernmost extensions of the Aztec state. Like Aztec Mexico, these border realms, far from Cuzco and the norms of Andean societies, would undoubtedly have remained only the outer shield of empire rather than a driving wedge for movement farther north into Middle America.

Already well entrenched along the Chilean coast in easily conquered trinary Mapuché lands, all of Chile except the lands of the dualistic Araucanian peoples would sooner or later have been added to the territory of Tawantinsuyu's southernmost province of Collasuyu. What is less certain is the spread of Tawantinsuyu eastward, across the Andes into the lowlands of Amazonia and the Argentine Pampas. Expansion into the latter realm had already begun by the late 1400s, and it probably would have continued until the Atlantic coast of present-day Uruguay and Argentina was reached. That large area was then and is now occupied by kindred unitary peoples. Certainly the Guaraní towns of Paraguay, also unitary in social pattern, semiurban in nature, and politically well defined, would have succumbed to or at least joined Inca might. Expansion into Amazonia, however, seems never to have been an Inca goal, and sparsely settled Amazonia, like the Central Plains of North America, would undoubtedly have remained a stronghold for diverse dualistic type *IIB* peoples and smaller nonaligned trinary tribal groups.

As pointed out before, in both Aztec Mexico and Inca Tawantinsuyu, confrontation with nonunitary societies, particularly dualistic societies, seems to have been avoided. The Aztec, for example, made no attempt to conquer the neighboring Tarascan Kingdom, a large, powerful, and highly sophisticated dualistic *IIB* society to the west of Tenochtitlán, and Inca Tawantinsuyu avoided clashes with the dualistic *IIN* Chibchan Muisca people of central Colombia and the related *IIB* Tairona people of northeastern Colombia, both of whom had well-developed urban centers at the time of Spanish intervention in the region. In 1519 the southernmost territory controlled by the Aztec Empire was Xoconochco Province in present-day El Salvador. Inca control stretched only as far as northern Ecuador, which was part of Chinchaysuyu Province. Between these two centers of power in lower Central America, Colombia and northern Ecuador, was a region known today by anthropologists as the *Intermediate Area*. With the urbanized dualistic Muisca and Tairona towns at its center, it formed a political buffer between Aztec might to the north and Inca supremacy to the south.

Dualistic Societies

New World *IIN* dualistic societies have always been few in number and are concentrated across the far northern reaches of North America and at the southernmost regions of South America. There are other *IIN* societies interspersed between these two extremes. Most except the Maya and Tarascans are small (Figure 18). In the far north the *IIN* Aleut and the Inuit, Inupiaq, and Yupik Eskimo peoples are relative newcomers to the Americas, having settled Alaska from their Siberian homeland around 3,000 B.C., the split between the Yupik and Inuit-Inupiaq languages and their social norms coming sometime during the first century after Christ (Woodbury 1984:61). Dualistic *IIB* cultures (Figure 18) occur with much greater frequency and are widely spread across both continents.

The only organized, urban dualistic polities in the Americas in 1492, however, were the Tarascan Kingdom in Mexico, the Maya Kingdoms of Middle America, the Chibchan Muisca and Tairona chiefdoms and towns of Colombia in South America, and in North America the formerly dualistic *IIB* Natchez and the Muskogean societies, part of the Mississippian cultural tradition from A.D. 1000 to the 1400s, which had, as discussed earlier, become trinary systems by the late 1400s or early 1500s. The Navajo of Arizona and New Mexico, along with their Apache cousins in the same region, all with type *IIB* social systems, had not yet embarked on the road toward political self-determination but began to walk that path in the late 1800s and on into the mid-1900s. The present Navajo political entity, *Dinétah,* "The People's Land," would surely have come into existence without provocation from Anglo-Americans, since the Navajo and Apache peoples are surrounded by a combination of unitary and trinary societies. Dinétah will consequently be figured into the scenario of the twenty-first century. The Yuman peoples of western Arizona, also *IIB* in social philosophy, are surrounded by unitary neighbors. Their tribes would, accordingly, like the Navajo, probably have joined forces for self-protection. The same is true of the Tanoan Pueblo peoples, who are linked by language and social system. The eastern Tanoans, the Kiowa people of Oklahoma and Kansas, were then seminomadic, but the western Tanoans of Taos and other pueblos in New Mexico were part of the urban tradition of the Pueblo people. Though dualistic, they had joined forces in pre-European times with their trinary Pueblo neighbors, and it seems likely that they would have formed, in effect, a small, dualistic *Tanoan Towns* group within the otherwise trinary United Pueblos, as, in fact, they have done since the 1400s.

The Maya Kingdoms, however, were far and away the most highly urbanized and politically secure dualistic polity in the pre-Columbian Americas. Firmly and narrowly dualistic in nature, they would certainly still control the core of Middle America—Yucatán, Belize, Guatemala, and large parts of Honduras and El Salvador. It is also likely that they would be in off-again-on-again conflict with each other and with the neighboring Aztec. Though dualists and unitarians tend to avoid each other, when they are neighbors conflicts are frequent, for, as we have seen, these two systems of social philosophy are polar opposites.

Unlike the expanding realms of Tawantinsuyu and the Aztec México Empire, the Maya Kingdoms rarely waged war simply to acquire territory but more to gain controlling power over neighboring cities, their rulers, and their economic assets—a situation analogous to medieval European fiefdoms. Such wars were particularly waged because conquest reflected positively on the prestige of the winner.

The dualistic *IIB* Tarascan Kingdom of west-central Mexico was Mexico's only large dualistic polity. Urban and independent, the Tarascans, unlike most dualists, never attempted to spread their base of power by territorial acquisition, and Aztec power in nearby Tenochtitlán did not attempt to conquer them. They remained independent and aloof, and Tarascan culture and towns have remained relatively intact through the centuries, still located and inhabited where they have been since at least the 1300s. Had the Spanish never come, there is good reason to think that a Tarascan state would have lasted comfortably into the present (Beals 1969).

In South America, the most powerful dualistic entities were the Chibchan-speaking Muisca and Tairona peoples of central and northeastern Colombia, located in the *Intermediate Area* buffer zone between the Aztec to the north and the Inca to the south. The Chibchan Muisca were located in the area around the present city of Bogotá, and the Tairona were located far to the northeast in the Sierra Nevada de Santa Marta mountains fronting Colombia's Caribbean coast. Both societies were urban, politically independent, and economically more than self-sufficient. Both specialized in commerce, with luxury goods in gold being their stock-in-trade. At the time of Spanish contact in the early 1500s, the Tairona population was estimated at well over 300,000, and a number of towns had in excess of 1,000 dwellings. Smaller villages were politically allied to larger towns, which were ruled by a chief, and each cluster was organized in such a manner that we would call it a political state (Feldman and Moseley 1978:170). Like the Tarascans in Mexico, the Tairona traditionally resisted efforts to control them, retreating far up into the Sierra Nevadas, where, as the Cágaba people, they have lasted to the present, their culture largely intact today. The dualistic *IIN* Muisca in the Bogotá region, as urban and self-reliant as the Tairona, would likely have lasted to the present, for the Inca, as pointed out, like the Aztec, studiously avoided confrontation and conflict with all but closely neighboring dualistic ethnic groups.

Two other native American dualistic societies were to embark on the road to statehood as well, but this came, with one exception, only well after. These were the dualistic *IIN* Inuit Eskimo peoples of far northern North America and Greenland and the *IIB* Iroquoian peoples of New York State.

The Five Nations of the New York State Iroquois—the Seneca, Cayuga, Onondaga, Oneida, and Mohawk—later joined by the Tuscarora, who had migrated north from their North Carolina homeland, constituted a well-organized, though nonurban, political confederacy by the 1630s. Tribal tradition places its formation "six generations before white people came," sometime in the 1400s, and there is no reason to question this assertion. Tribal tradition also states that it was created in an effort to halt the constant intertribal warfare that wracked the region, and it was referred to as the Great

Peace (Tooker 1978:418–441). The confederacy began as a meeting in council the fifty chiefs of the individual tribes of the Five Nations, striving for consensus handling intertribal problems, and that method of discussion to forestall and resolve potential conflicts has continued through the centuries to the present. The League, governed by the tribal chiefs and a roster of officers, was perpetuated through an oral constitution and appropriate ceremonies. Its effect was beneficent with regard both to intertribal decision making and to decisions involving extraconfederacy relations.

Had Europeans not been present, it is likely that the effective intertribal government created by the New York Iroquois would have spread to include the other Iroquois groups of the region—the Huron, Wenro, Neutral, Petun (or Wyandot), and Erie to the north and west, the Susquehannock of Pennsylvania, as well as the smaller Iroquois tribes of Virginia and North Carolina. Contact among all of these Iroquois groups through trade is known to have been normal in pre-European times, and their ultimate political linkage through the League therefore more likely than not. A true confederacy in the dictionary sense of the word, with wide governing powers left to the individual tribes rather than rule through a single-minded federal government—such a confederacy would not have been a literal territorial state. It might also have eventually brought in the Iroquois-speaking Cherokee people of western North Carolina, northwestern Georgia, and southeastern Tennessee, linking a large area of inland northeastern North America into a pan-Iroquois Confederacy.

The Inuit of Canada and Greenland, with type *IIN* social systems, have gained self-determination and at least home rule, if not out-and-out sovereignty, only within the past several decades. The fight for home rule by the Greenland Inuit people was long but largely peaceful, and, beginning with an act of the Danish Parliament in 1953, the island was gradually prepared for home rule, which was granted in 1978 and became effective on May 1, 1979. The island adopted its Inuit name, *Kalaallit Nunaat,* and Inuit became the official language along with Danish (Kleivan 1984). Only on April 1, 1999, were Inuit lands in northern Canada granted internal home rule by the Canadian Parliament under the name *Nunavut,* "Our Land." There, too, the struggle for self-determination was long and protracted but, as in Kalaallit Nunaat, largely peaceful (Vallee, Smith, and Cooper 1984). The related Yupik and Inupiaq peoples of Alaska have not consolidated their efforts toward more complete self-determination than that allowed to date by the U.S. government.

It is difficult to say if the Inuit would have reached toward greater self-determination on their own had Europeans not intruded on their lands—the Norse in Greenland around 985, and the British in maritime Canada in 1576. There are no archaeological indications of trends either toward urbanization or toward permanent territorial acquisitions on the part of either group.

Interpolity Politics

The relationships of native New World societies to one another when discovered by Europe were based on the similarities and differences in their social philosophies, as intersocietal relationships have always been in all parts of the world. There is no new, startling rationale underlying the attraction that, for example, pulled the ethnically variant Mississippian together around the year 1000. All with dualistic *IIB* social systems, language and cosmetic cultural differences did not keep them apart. They voluntarily linked themselves into a continuum of city-states because of their fundamental samenesses. Thus an examination of the probable interpolity relationships in a non-Europeanized twenty-first-century native America should, and would, be based on the same universal principle.

The most obvious comparison between New World polities then and now and their Old World counterparts is, I think, the striking parallel between the unitary Chinese and the dualistic Japanese on the far side of the Pacific and the unitary Aztec and dualistic Maya on this side. Aztec and Chinese share many unitary core cultural traits, as do the dualistic Maya and Japanese. On both sides of the ocean cultural interplay has been extensive and largely one-sided—Chinese to Japanese in the Far East and Maya to Aztec in Middle America. This interchange of cultural ideas and artifacts has lasted for many centuries in both areas and, since in both regions the powers are close neighbors to one another, has led to outbursts of incredible violence from time to time since at least the late 1200s and the rise of Yüan power in China and since the early 900s and the Toltec invasions of Yucatán in Middle America. In both instances the unitary power has been demographically and geographically the larger of the pair. In both instances it has also been the major areal aggressor, except for minor periods in the Pacific arena, when it has been the dualistic power that has filled that role. Just as the pattern of confrontation has continued in the Far East to the present, so it is likely that it would have continued to the present in Middle America had Spanish intervention not altered the cultural balance.

It is doubtful that the trinary Pueblo, Taíno Xaraguá, or even the vast Southeastern Confederacy would have spread their domains far from their original homelands, since trinary societies expand only for the sake of trade or of consolidating their natural homelands, never simply for the acquisition of new territory. The Pueblo Confederacy of towns would certainly still be centered around the Four Corners area of Utah, Colorado, Arizona, and New Mexico, though trade routes would surely have been extended. The Taíno as well would have extended their economic control over the remainder of Cuba, and it would be expected, as supported by sporadic archaeological evidence in southeastern and southwestern Florida, that the seagoing routes of Taíno trade would ultimately have spanned the gap from northern South America to at least the southeastern United States.

The dualistic newcomers of Kalaallit Nunaat and Nunavut, the two Eskimo nations in the far North, would, one suspects, because of size and isolation, live uneasily with their unitary Algonquian neighbors bordering them on the south across the entire breadth of North America. Their closest philosophical kin would be the Iroquois far to the south and the geographically far, far distant Maya kingdoms. While an alliance might be formed among these three, it would certainly be only a paper alliance.

Would the México Empire and the empire of Tawantinsuyu eventually have turned the Americas into a two-state realm, the Aztecs controlling North America and the Incas South America, with a meeting of the two somewhere in mid- or lower Central America? Probably not, if the overall hemisphere balance of a Great Alliance of trinary states and tribal groups materialized, which it surely would, in the same manner that the trinary nations of the Middle East and Central Asia have joined ranks. We know, judging from the confines of their empires in the early 1500s, that both Aztecs and Incas avoided extended contact with dissimilar, nonunitary cultures. The expenditure of national energy was simply too great for the meager economic rewards. They settled, instead, for trade connections, such as those between the Aztecs and the Pueblos of the American Southwest or the Incas and the Chibchan peoples of Colombia and the peoples of lowland Amazonia across the Andes.

It seems more likely that the Great Alliance of trinary states would be too formidable a stumbling block for the creation of a two-state New World. Always ready to compromise, its member states and tribal groups would know when to give in and when not to, how to satisfy both Aztec and Inca without losing their own independence and freedom. Neither does it seem likely that any of these states themselves would attempt to consolidate their own individual power through subjugation and conquest, since that is not the essence of protection through compromise.

The Final View

The "final view" of interhemisphere polities, confederations, and their probable alliances with one another is suggested in Figure 18.

Our scenario envisions three groups of polities, some highly urban, others not, and their interrelationships with one another based on similarities and differences among their social systems as the realization of their life philosophies. The entire view of this suggested future reconstruction stems from the obvious—that people tend to interact more readily, more frequently, and more successfully with others who have similar values and beliefs and who express them in similar ways than with those whose ideational world differs from their own. The greater the distance between belief systems, the greater the difficulty of understanding and interacting. Likes, in other words, attract; unlikes do not—they conflict and, at the extreme, they repel.

On this basis, there would be three major unitary hemisphere political alliances: the *Algonquian Alliance* of northern North America, probably expressing itself through Western, Northern, Central, New England, and Delaware subgroups; the important *México Alliance* in Middle America, consisting of the México Empire and the Mixtec Kingdoms; and the *Andean Alliance* in South America, consisting of the vast empire of Tawantinsuyu and at least the towns of the neighboring Guaraní. Of lesser size but still an important entity would be the *Northwest Coast Towns,* probably expressing their joint desires through some type of confederation. The Northern Athabaskan peoples of far northwest Canada and interior Alaska and the Ute peoples occupying vast sections of the North American Great Plains have never evinced an interest in broader unification, but it is not beyond question that they might, by the twenty-first century, have formed their own separate loose-jointed unions.

There would also be three major dualistic hemispheric political alliances: the *League of the Iroquois* in New York State, Pennsylvania, and probably all down the ridge of the Appalachian Mountains into northern Georgia, likely including the North Carolina Cherokee; the *Inuit Alliance* in northern Canada, with the nation of Nunavut, and in Greenland, with the nation of Kalaallit Nunaat; and the *Chibchan Alliance* in Colombia, South America, including the Muisca Towns and the Tairona Towns. Of equal importance would be the *Maya Kingdoms* of Yucatán, Belize, Guatemala, and Honduras; the *Tarascan Kingdom* neighboring the Aztecs in west-central Mexico; and *Dinétah,* the Navajo nation in Arizona and New Mexico. It is also likely that the Yuman towns of Baja California and southwestern Arizona would have organized into some kind of political union for protection against their largely unitary neighbors.

It is suggested that there would be a single trinary New World alliance, spanning both North America and the Caribbean. It would surely be dominated by the *Southeastern Confederation* of the *Muskogean Tribes* and their Florida allies, the *Timucua* and *Calusa* peoples. Closely allied to them would be the *Natchez* and *Tunica* of Louisiana, together with their *Chitimacha, Atakapa,* and *Karankawa* neighbors along the coast from the mouth of the Mississippi River to the central Texas Gulf coast. The *Taíno Kingdoms,* or *Greater Xaraguá Kingdom,* of the Great Antilles would undoubtedly have allied themselves with the Southeastern Confederation for mutual protection and decision making. In the North American Southwest, the *United Pueblos* would beyond doubt still be in existence, and they, like the Taíno, would likely have joined their cultural cousins in the Southeast as part of the *Great Alliance* of trinary polities. Whether the Siouan and Caddoan peoples of the Great Plains, also trinary in social philosophy, would have thrown their lot in with the New World's other trinary states is difficult to assess. They have shown no indication in their long histories of linking themselves in a federation, nor have they moved toward urbanization.

This is the most likely scenario for a twenty-first-century New World future. One may, of course, rightly call these suggestions historical fiction or fictional history, and either assessment would, of course, be correct. The difference, however, between this particular resolution of "the fallacy of historical questions" (Fischer 1970:15–21) and other resolutions is that this one is based on archaeological, ethnographic, and historical data. This may or may not lend more credence to the outcome suggested than to other postulated outcomes. What this view does provide, though, is rational data for thought, data for looking at native American peoples and societies not as time-warped curiosities—still the usual approach of Europeans and Euro-Americans—but as human beings with their own beliefs and innermost convictions, human beings acting out their lives on an always complex stage.

This is the New World that would be interacting with the Old World today.

14

Commerce and Discovery of the Old World

If Europeans had never ventured westward across the Atlantic, would native America have ventured east and discovered Europe? If the picture we have sketched is anywhere close to the mark, the answer has to be "very likely." If so, then what kinds of interaction would have taken place?

To answer these questions and to understand why certain patterns of interaction would have developed, one must look at the differing motivations for intersociety contact of unitary, dualistic, and trinary peoples and the methods, peaceable or otherwise, that each of those societal types normally uses to implement such contact.

Inter-American Trade and Commerce

The most frequent and universal form of social interaction is certainly peaceable commerce. In the pre-Columbian New World there is ample evidence that there, as elsewhere in the world, commercial interchange played a major role in the development of native lifeways and the alignment of one people with another. In the North American Southeast, for example, this is abundantly attested by the archaeological record from at least as early as 4,500 years ago. Artifacts occur in locales often hundreds or even thousands of miles away from the closest source of the raw materials from which they were made. At times it is evident that the finished artifacts themselves were traded from a distant area of origin. At other times we find unworked raw materials of alien origin, ready to be formed by local craftsmen into a finished product (Ford 1969, Sassaman 1993, Sears 1964, and many others). By 2,000 B.C. there were two major trade complexes in the Southeast: the Poverty Point network, emanating from probable Tunica and Natchez sources on the lower Mississippi, and, at least in the view of this writer and a number of other archaeologists and linguists, the Timucua network, stemming from the Atlantic coast of Georgia and North Florida, though with ultimate origins traceable linguistically as well as archaeologically to northern South America, again in the opinion of at least a minority of professional researchers (Granberry 1993: 41–60, 1995:158–169). Both networks were in the hands of professional, experienced merchants who knew who wanted what, when, and where. The geographical area covered by these two trading systems was enormous—from southwest Florida to the Great Lakes and from the southeast Atlantic coast at least to Caddoan Oklahoma in the west. Both networks remained viable through Mississippian times and were still largely intact at the time Europeans arrived in the New World.

The Pueblo peoples of the Southwest also participated in their own widespread trade network, articulating not only with the trading systems of the Southeast, the Mississippi River Valley, and the Caddoan Midwest but also with the precursors of what was to become the Mexican *pochteca* system of the Aztecs and the vast sea-trading network of the Chontal Putún Maya, who operated from the Aztec port of Xicallanco in southern Campeche. Commodities of undisputed lowland tropical Mesoamerican origin, such as macaw feathers, for example, occur in Pueblo archaeological sites (Lange 1979:201–205, Parmentier 1979:617, Plog 1979:127–128).

The Aztec *pochteca* and their Chontal Putún Maya counterparts were both hereditary merchant classes with special social position and privileges, and they traded not only northward into the American Southwest but also far to the south, deep into Central America and northern South America (Borhegyi 1959, Coe 1960, Fagan 1984:203–209, Thompson 1970). In South America a similar hereditary class, the *mindala*, filled the same role. The *mindala*, which meant *The Great Lords,* were at least a society apart from all others and probably a separate multiethnic, nontribal group drawn from diverse sources within the Vaupés region of southeast Colombia and adjacent Venezuelan and Brazilian Amazonia (Feldman and Moseley 1978:143, Granberry 1993:48, Salomon 1977–1978:236). This unique group, with its own form of speech creolized from diverse Colombian, Venezuelan, and Amazonian sources, traveled from the heart of Amazonia to Peru, Colombia, Ecuador, and up into Central America as far as Guatemala (Borhegyi 1959, Coe 1960, Gómez-Imbert 1991, Gómez-Imbert and Kenstowicz 2000, Granberry 1993:41–50, Jackson 1982). In the view of an increasingly sizeable minority of archaeologists, they also very likely traded by sea from their Central American entrepôts as far as both the southwest coast of Florida and the Savannah River region of the Atlantic coast of Georgia sometime during the second millennium B.C. and were possibly responsible for the introduction of pottery-making techniques to North America by way of the Georgia coast and the river systems of the American Southeast (Ford 1969, Granberry 1993:50–60, Meggers and Evans 1978, Sears 1964, 1982:20, 24, 191–192).

The Kwakiutl, Haida, Tlingit, Nootka, and other tribal groups of the Northwest Coast of North America were also noted traders, covering the northern Pacific coast from southern Alaska to northern California in their large seaworthy canoes. The primary commodities traded were furs and the dentalium shell, which was widely used by most of the tribal groups along the Pacific coast of North America (Cole and Darling 1990).

These are but some of the known long-distance trading networks in native America at various time periods. There were others in almost any region one wishes to explore—the Shipibo of Peru, for example, thought nothing of traveling several thousand miles down the Amazon and back for trading purposes (Lathrap 1973:161–162). Intertribal and interregional trade networks were the norm rather than the exception in native America from the earliest times.

Patterns of Contact

Each of the three social types—unitary, dualistic, and trinary—has specific motivations for making political, economic, and general social contacts with the world beyond its borders. Each type also distinguishes between peaceful commercial exchange on the one hand and bellicose territorial expansion on the other. It is fair to say, in fact, that most societies partake of both kinds of contact with other societies at one time or another in their histories. Though the majority of contacts between societies are for the purpose of commercial exchange and are usually peaceable, at times, for philosophical reasons deeply embedded in the mores of a specific society, contacts become confrontational and aggressive. The latter is particularly so with unitary and dualistic societies, less so with trinary societies.

It may also be pointed out that the axiom "likes attract, unlikes repel" applies full force in this situation. Contacts between two unitary, dualistic, or trinary societies are generally peaceful, while unitary-dualistic, unitary-trinary, dualistic-trinary contacts are likely to become strained or even bellicose, no matter which side initiates the contact. The situation most fraught with serious potential for aggression is that between unitarian and dualist—China and Japan, Toltec and Maya, Serbia-Montenegro and Croatia or Slovenia, for example. By the same token, unless dualists and unitarians live close to one another they tend to steer clear of any interaction with each other except commercial. In this chapter we are considering peaceable commercial contacts alone. Possible confrontational situations are discussed in the following chapter on international alliances.

The Unitary Contact Pattern

The political and economic contacts initiated by unitary societies usually stem from real or imagined pressures from within—the need for land to ensure a proper food supply for a growing population or the perceived need for new or different economic products and markets. Unitary traders frequently explore markets far afield from their homelands and are astute in determining the economic needs and wishes of other societies. This type of contact is invariably peaceful, with no desire on the part of the unitary initiators to alter the beliefs or actions of the societies with which they come into contact. The vast trading network of the Aztec *pochteca* is a classic example of unitary commercial contact in the New World, as are China's commercial ventures today.

If, however, contact takes the form of territorial expansion, through the perceived need for more land or to reclaim lands deemed its own, a unitary state will often use stringent, uncompromising military force. In such expansions the subjugated peoples are seen as expendable. If they acquiesce, they are invariably either enslaved, indentured, or, at best, treated as second-class citizens, even if they conform to the norms of the conquering society. If they rebel or do not acquiesce, they are obliterated through what has come to be known today as "ethnic cleansing." Prime examples are the Chinese takeover of Tibet in the 1950s and the Serbian wars in Bosnia-Herzegovina and Kosovo in the 1990s.

The Dualistic Contact Pattern

Dualistic societies—the majority of European, sub-Saharan African, and Euro-American societies—on the other hand, though frequently involving themselves in contacts with other societies for the sake of peaceable trade, rarely content themselves with commercial exchange alone. The implicit social philosophy of dualists—part of those societies' Freudian Unconscious—is that one's own view of the world is the only proper and correct view and that all other views are by nature of lesser or no validity. Thus contact initiated for economic reasons alone quickly adds a dimension of social conversion. What the American corporate world refers to as *Airport Culture* is the prime example—everywhere European and Euro-American business spreads it brings with it the same modus operandi and the same underlying set of rules and behavioral norms. The insistence of the United States and Great Britain in 2003 and 2004 that the people of Iraq *must* democratize their government and overall way of life is another example. The enforced Anglicization of India during the eighteenth and nineteenth centuries by the British is yet another.

Even trade between dualist nations is interwoven with this "do-it-my-way" theme. So, for example, in the dealings between members of the North American Free Trade Agreement (NAFTA), each agreed to economic exchange but, it turns out, if and only if the underlying beliefs of their particular society becomes part of the contract. Since the NAFTA treaty went into effect in 1994, such inabilities to reach consensus have continued to undermine the effectiveness of the original economic proposal.

In some cases dualistic societies make contact solely for the purpose of social conversion—the European Crusades into the Near East from 1095 to 1244, for example. In other instances conversion comes first and the economic motive follows, often accompanied by territorial expansion—the territorial spread of the Alexandrian Greeks, the Romans, Britain, the Austro-Hungarian Empire, Russia, Spain, Portugal, the Dutch, Germany, Japan, and the United States.

When met with resistance to their attempts at social conversion, dualistic societies, as we have seen, usually provide themselves with what to them are comfortable, reasonable, and logical rationales for physical attack as the preferred method for accomplishing their goals. Generally the survivors of such action are left largely unharmed, so long as they subscribe to the new way of life. If they do not, they become, as one expects in dualistic systems, "the enemy," to be methodically routed out and expunged, again with a variety of rationales. To judge from the record, these same contact rationales and devices were those employed by the Maya Kingdoms and the Mississippian cities in native pre-Columbian America.

The Trinary Contact Pattern

Trinary societies show yet a third method of handling intersociety contact. Normally contact is made for economic gain alone, to find new markets, new raw materials, and new products. This type of contact is invariably peaceful. In instances, however, contact occurs to regain territory, sometimes of vast geographical extent, considered, with real or imagined justification, the rightful property of the initiator of the relationship. In the latter instance, warfare is not uncommon, though violence is normally kept to a minimum. In neither type of trinary contact is there a perceived need to convert the other party to one's own way of life or beliefs. The Mongol expansion and empire of the 1200s, the Arab expansion and empires of 700–1500, and the Ottoman

Turkish Empire of the 1300s–1900s are examples of the latter, while the Phoenician-Carthaginian trading empires of the period 1200–146 B.C. are an example of the former. All of the Semitic peoples, in fact, have been particularly noteworthy as peaceable traders since the time of the 2,500 B.C. Dilmun civilization of Arabia.

Thus when trinary contact occurs for purposes of what is considered homeland recovery, the conquered people are allowed to continue their normal daily lives much as they had before, with as little disruption as possible. While replacing the political structure of the conquered societies, a trinary conqueror normally attempts to preserve the economic status quo, for a great part of the rationale for conquest is trade and economic profit. The Muslim conquest of Spain in 711 is certainly an outstanding example—no one was expected to convert to Islam, no one was required to speak Arabic, no one was expected to become Arabicized unless he wished, and the economic and cultural lives of the new communities were allowed to continue as usual. This philosophy remained staunchly in effect for 800 years, until dualistic Spain retook the Muslim lands and expelled both Muslim and Jewish citizens. The same social modus operandi was used by the trinary Turks when they overcame the last outposts of the Byzantine Empire and took the city of Constantinople in May 1453. In the pre-Columbian Americas the trading networks of the Florida/Georgia Timucua, the Tunica-Natchez of the lower Mississippi Valley, and the Pueblo trading region of the Southwest provide examples of this philosophy of societal interaction.

First European Contacts

One might expect that initial New World–Old World trade would have begun in the far North, since the Norse had begun to explore and settle both uninhabited Iceland and Inuit-inhabited Greenland. One might then surmise that the Inuit Eskimo people would have ventured eastward to Iceland and perhaps onward, under Norse influence, to Scandinavia. Because Norse and Inuit have differing underlying social philosophies—the Inuit dualistic, the Norse unitary type *IB*—contact might have been difficult, as indeed in fact it was when the Norse settled southern Greenland in 985. We know, however, that neither extensive nor ongoing trade between the two ethnic groups became reality. This lack of interchange was almost certainly the result of the decimation of the Norse population of Greenland and Iceland by the devastating plague of 1349, which killed, it is estimated, one out of every three in Northern Europe and its Arctic colonies. European ties to Iceland and Greenland were temporarily severed, and by the end of the 1400s, the 3,000-strong population of Viking Greenland had vanished entirely, a mystery still largely unsolved (Gad 1984:556–576, Kleivan 1984:549–555).

Since, however, the only aspect of known European history we are attempting to turn back is discovery of the New World, we will assume that what happened in Iceland and Greenland as a result of the Black Death of 1349 did, indeed, happen. In that case, it does not seem likely that the Inuit would have pushed farther eastward until considerably later, not until internal social pressures caused by continuing interaction with their unitary Algonquian neighbors in what is now northern Canada forced them toward union as Kalaallit Nunaat and Nunavut. Given the wide dispersal of such a small population in such a large geographical area, that may well not have happened until sometime in the 1600 or 1700s, perhaps even later.

In short, in spite of initial Inuit-Norse contact in the 1000s–1300s, it seems unlikely that American-European commerce would have begun in the North Atlantic region. Rather we must turn to those native American polities that were already of some size and urban sophistication and whose commerce was handled by professional merchants during that time period. This would suggest, likely sometime in the 1400s, what was then the fledgling Aztec Empire through its growing *pochteca* merchant class, the already well established Chontal Putún Maya of Campeche and Tabasco, the Mississippian merchants of the North American Southeast—inheritors of the Poverty Point and Timucua trade networks—and the tribally and polity unaffiliated *mindala* of Colombia, north of Tawantinsuyu. Of these the most likely to have ventured outside the normal New World trade routes would have been the Putún Maya and the Colombian *mindala,* both of whom were engaged in widespread exploration and movement of economic goods by sea, the *mindala* as early as 2,000 B.C. (Salomon 1977–1978), the Putún by at least A.D. 1000 (Thompson 1970). Unlike the *pochteca* and Mississippian merchants, who specialized in riverine and land trade, both *mindala* and Putún were consummate seafarers, comparable to the Polynesians in the Pacific. Thompson (1970), in fact, calls the Putún the Phoenicians of the New World. Though we do not have any details on the nature of the vessels used by the *mindala,* we know that Putún canoes were large, rugged, and very seaworthy (Thompson 1970).

Both classes of trader seem to have operated on their own, without close affiliation to any single ethnic tribe or state. Both were, perhaps for this reason, primarily interested in their own welfare and enrichment and in the hunt for new products and new raw materials. They were both not only merchants but also explorers in the classic sense of the word. This would be in keeping with the tenets of both dualistic (the Putún) and trinary groups (the *mindala*).

We know that the Putún traded with the Ciboney Taíno peoples of Cuba (Thompson 1970). They did not hesitate to venture out into the open seas. In like manner, both archaeological and linguistic evidence indicates to many, though not all, that the *mindala* succeeded in navigating by way of the Caribbean currents and the Gulf Stream from northern Colombia to the Central American coast and on to both Southwest Florida and the St. Johns and Savannah River regions of the North American Southeast (Ford 1969, Granberry 1993:49–60, Meggers and Evans 1978, Sears 1964, 1982:20, 24, 191–192). Thus, ventures by sea yet farther afield cannot be ruled out. Of the two, *mindala* and Putún, it is the latter who would philosophically be the most likely to have spearheaded exploration out into the open sea to the east, for the majority of the world's explorers have come from dualistic societies. The trinary *mindala* would have been more likely to have followed the leadership of the Putún, once the sea route was known. The unitary *pochteca* and the Aztec and Inca empires, however, would ultimately have been the main suppliers of goods, as the unitary nations of the Far East are today.

The Development of American–Old World Trade

Though Columbus's faith in the round-earth hypothesis is certainly what led him to his insightful first voyage, his successful landfall on the Lucayan Island of Guanahaní on October 12, 1492, was as much a fortuitous function of the Atlantic steering currents as it was a function of his convictions. In like manner, with no conviction at all other than that there might be land "out there," Putún, and perhaps *mindala,* mercantile explorers venturing out into the Gulf Stream could, sooner or later, have as fortuitously been carried to Western Europe (see Figure 19).

It is not possible to say with any degree of certainty when such a voyage might first have occurred. Since trading networks were well in place from at least 4,500 B.C. throughout most of the Americas (Ford 1969), such an event might have taken place at any time thereafter. We know, of course, that in fact no ongoing contact did take place between that early time and European arrival in 1492. There may well have been sporadic contacts, but, if so, they did not lead to ongoing commercial and cultural interchange (see Jett 1978 for thorough coverage of possible pre-Columbian transoceanic contacts). Once New World urban polities began to emerge in the centuries around the time of the birth of Christ and thereafter, however, hemispheric-internal trade

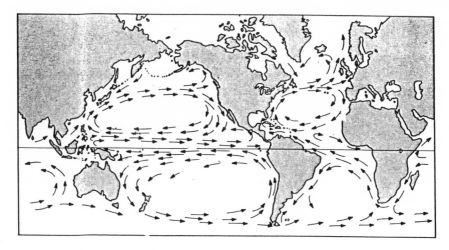

Figure 19. Major Surface Ocean Steering Currents

became significant and far-reaching. Had these emerging nation-states been able to continue their growth and political and social-cultural expansion beyond the late 1400s, it seems not amiss to suggest that the kind of fortuitous initial contacts discussed above would have become reality, just as that same time period proved intellectually optimal for the genesis of westward movement for the emerging national states of Western Europe. On both sides of the Atlantic the 1300s–1500s were Renaissance times, which consciously harked back to a revered and envied Classic past in both hemispheres—Greek and Roman in Europe, Toltec, Classic Maya, Tiahuanaco, Classic Pueblo, and Mississippian in the Americas—and at the same time was reaching ahead to forge successful national futures. It seems most likely that ongoing commercial contact, first initiated without intent by Putún traders, would thus have occurred between A.D. 1400 and 1600.

Once such contact was made and maintained, word of the world to the east would certainly have spread to other New World polities by way of the many interlocking trade networks that linked all but the most out-of-the-way areas of the hemisphere.

The vast trinary trading complex of the confederated post-Mississippian peoples of southeastern North America, the Southeastern Confederation, and its connections through the postulated trinary Great Alliance, would have gotten wind of the new lands, and contacts with the Pueblo trade network would have spread the word to the American Southwest. The Mexican *pochteca* would already have learned of the discovery, since *pochteca* and Putún

Maya came together at the Aztec port of Xicallanco on the Laguna de los Términos. The Putún also traded with the Greater Antilles, and the Taíno peoples of the Caribbean would soon have known of this faraway discovery, as would the Incas of Tawantinsuyu and the other tribal groups of South America through the connections of the *mindala* trading system. It would not have taken long for the word to spread, just as the news of Columbus's discovery electrified all of fifteenth-century Europe in less than a year.

How long would it have taken to build a firm commercial connection between the two hemispheres? We are certainly talking only of years, not centuries. Unitary Aztec *pochteca,* dualistic Putún Maya merchants, and trinary traders from all areas of North and South America would surely have realized the vast potential of a European market for their goods and the equally vast potential of new goods from Europe. By shortly after 1500 it should have been common knowledge to native Americans and native Europeans alike that new and different peoples, markets, and products existed on both sides of the Atlantic.

Because of the distances involved, and because the motive for transAtlantic voyages was solely commercial, it seems unlikely that any New World polity would have attempted European colonization other than the establishment of small trading entrepôts. Because the major spearheaders of a European connection, the seafaring Putún Maya, were dualists, as were the nations of Western Europe, contact would likely remain peaceable and strictly commercial for a long period of time.

While the world's largest number of global trading connections have been those created and maintained by dualistic societies—Britain, Germany, the United States, Japan, Korea—it is the world's unitary societies that have always been the world's major suppliers of general consumer goods of all kinds. So today's major exporters to the rest of the world are China, Taiwan, Thailand, and other unitary Far Eastern polities. Unitary states are also traditionally among the world's largest consumers of manufactured goods. It might thus be expected that Aztec Mexico and Inca Tawantinsuyu would become the major suppliers of American goods to Europe and to have become the major importers of European artifacts by the twenty-first century. Unitary societies have shown a genius for accurately reading the economic needs of the societies with which they trade, and European needs would have been carefully defined and fulfilled by the Aztec *pochteca* and the merchants of Inca Tawantinsuyu once the Putún and *mindala* merchants had established the trade routes and created the mechanisms for their maintenance.

With both Old and New Worlds moving outward in search of economic resources by the 1500s, then, the reply to the question "Would native America have discovered Europe?" has to be a rather definite "yes."

Would similar ventures have led to Africa and to Asia? Africa, for a certainty, given its geographical proximity to European markets. It would, as indeed it actually did, have become part of such a growing international commercial network. Considering the trade that had developed between medieval Europe and the Near and Far East in the 1200s–1400s, certainly word of that part of the Old World would also have reached the New, and once the concept of a globular world dawned on both New and Old World societies, trans-Pacific trade should also have been initiated sometime between the fifteenth century and the present. The Haida and Tlingit of the North American Northwest Coast, seafaring traders, as we have said, along the Pacific coast from Alaska to California, would surely have extended their routes on to Siberia and south into Manchuria, Korea, Japan, and China once the word of the new lands had spread to that part of native America.

Cultural Exchange

Would an American discovery of the Old World have led to more than just commercial interchange? Would there also be an exchange of ideas, philosophies, and technical information? These possibilities are more difficult to assess. Certainly the natural outcome of trade and economic interchange since time immemorial has been a concomitant exchange of ideas. Concepts alien to one side might be rejected through a lack of understanding, or simply because they did not fit well with the recipient's social philosophy, but surely many ideas would be of interest to both sides of an economic-intellectual exchange and would be passed on from one culture to another.

Among the most fertile ideas exchanged, one suspects, would be scientific concepts. It is not difficult to envision Maya dualistic mathematical and astronomical concepts merging with the equally dualistic scientific concepts of Europe, which represented an integration of Hindu and Greek science through the filter of the medieval Spanish Islamic world. What other intellectual exchanges might have taken place across the oceans it is difficult to say. One could certainly see European philosophers evincing an interest in the concepts of Aztec philosophy as so ably expressed in our surviving Náhuatl texts from the last days of the México Empire, and one could as well see Aztec philosophers perusing the works of Plato, Socrates, and Aristotle. Such a meeting of minds would, indeed, be interesting, and the results might be both fruitful and practical. Intellectual exchanges between the native American world and the cultures of the Old World might have drastically altered our understanding and use of both the Graeco-Roman tradition, so important in modern European cultures, and the Judeo-Christian tradition, of equal or greater importance to the European world today.

These interchanges would most likely have been between kindred cultures—between American dualists, such as the Putún and the other Maya kingdoms, and European dualists; between the trinary American Great Alliance and the trinary Near East; and between the unitary Aztec and Inca and at least Far Eastern unitary China. While some intellectual exchange would certainly have taken place between Europe and the unitary Aztec and Inca, such as the philosophical exchange suggested above, it would likely have been limited, for the only unitary societies in Europe are the Southern Slavs of Serbia-Montenegro and the Scandinavian descendants of the Norse Vikings. The underlying social philosophies of dominant dualistic Europe and the unitary New World cultures are so vastly different and at odds with one another that extensive borrowing of culture traits would have been doubtful, just as Europe has never borrowed cultural concepts from China and the Asian unitary societies. Exchange between dissimilar cultures is usually limited to the exchange of utilitarian consumer goods, while exchange between like or similar cultures frequently involves the less physical and more directly ideational aspects of culture.

The Twenty-first Century View

If commercial contacts were first made in the late 1400s and substantial trade became the norm by perhaps the early 1600s, the twenty-first-century world would see flourishing international trade between the Americas and Europe, with the manufacture and exchange of technical utilitarian goods the primary job of the dualists on both sides of the Atlantic as well as of the dualist states of the Far East. Such goods would surely include heavy machinery, machines of transportation such as automobiles, aircraft, and ships, and scientific machinery of all sorts. It would be expected that the major countries of Europe, Japan, Korea, Australia, New Zealand, India, some of the countries of sub-Saharan Africa, the Maya Kingdoms, the Iroquois Confederation, Inuit Nunavut and Kalaallit Nunaat in the far north, and probably the Chibchan Muisca and Tairona cities of northern South America would form some type of International Trade Alliance to regulate the manufacture, pricing, and distribution of such goods (Figure 20).

Other than what was manufactured by the dualist nations, general merchandise of all kinds, with emphasis on style and economy of cost, would come from the unitarian states of the Americas and the Far East, with distri-

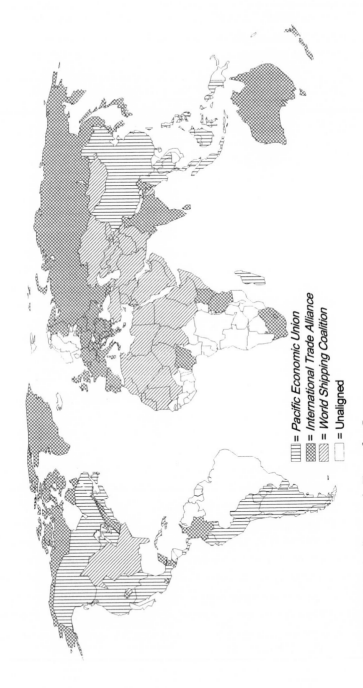

Figure 20. World Trade Alliances in the Twenty-first Century

= Pacific Economic Union
= International Trade Alliance
= World Shipping Coalition
= Unaligned

bution worldwide. Again it would be likely that a loose-jointed, consortium-like Pan-Pacific Economic Union might be formed, consisting primarily of China, Taiwan, much of Southeast Asia, the Northwest coast towns of North America, Aztec Mexico, and Tawantinsuyu. In keeping with the norms of unitary societies, such a union would probably not be as rigidly structured nor as tightly organized as the dualistic nations' trade association.

Trinary states, including members of the American Great Alliance and the North African, Near Eastern, and Central Asian republics, would, as the last three segments do today, constitute a third commercial group. Their specialty would be not so much the manufacture of finished goods as it would be the entrepreneurial side of commerce. Something like a World Shipping Coalition of entrepreneurs from all of the trinary countries would likely be formed to effect the movement of both raw materials and manufactured goods to their final worldwide destinations. Such a commercial coalition would, in typical trinary manner, act as the third party in business transactions. Its members would act as facilitators, transporters, and middlemen between manufacturer and consumer, both for the companies of the unitary Pan-Pacific Economic Union countries and those of the dualist countries of an International Trade Alliance.

Social Change

What changes would such commercial enterprise have brought about in native American societies? The lessons from history indicate that the innermost tenets of all societies are highly resistant to change resulting from contact. The differences in worldview are simply too great, particularly between unitary and dualistic societies. Dualistic philosophies are, as said earlier, rigid and absolutist, while unitary philosophies are relativist and highly pragmatic. Both types of social system will accept cosmetic, artifactual innovations—the dualist if the innovation seems to have long-term value and be in accordance with his norms, the unitarian if the innovation has practical value at the moment. Thus the unitary societies of the Americas would, as China has done in the Orient, accept and use most artifactual innovations introduced from dualist sources, but their values would not change. American dualists, however, would accept and use only those cosmetic, artifactual innovations that were clearly in accord with their concepts of what society needed on a long-term basis. Both social systems would remain essentially unchanged in terms of their underlying philosophies of life.

American trinary societies, like all trinary societies, would be the most adaptable, accepting and modifying artifacts from both dualist and unitarian sources. While, as with all three basic societal types, the inner core of trinary societies would remain unchanged, the very nature of middle-ground culture trait acceptance that characterizes these social systems would indicate that members of the American Great Alliance would take full advantage of the artifactual innovations of the modern world.

International Alliances and Interaction in the Twenty-first Century
The Outer Scheme

The most vital form of interchange between a native American New World and the nations of the Old World would have been economic, but, to solidify old economic ties and forge new ones, this would surely have been followed by diplomatic and political interaction. This interaction, as in all such interchanges, would have taken the form of ambassadorial exchanges and international alliances and, inevitably, military confrontations and incursions of one kind or another, from time to time. In this chapter we will concentrate on natural political alliances, inasmuch as predictions of specific cases of out-and-out warfare, with one exception, would be even more highly speculative than the already speculative picture we are considering. The single instance in which hostility would be a distinct possibility will be briefly described later in the chapter.

We have on several prior occasions reiterated the axiom "like tends to attract like," which verbalizes the obvious universal principle that one tends to side with people who think in like manner, who have the same goals, and who approve of reaching them in the same way. One's relationships with those of similar though differing philosophy are, on the other hand, considerably more cautious and strained, and one's relationships with those of diametrically opposed opinion and philosophy are frequently if not usually downright hostile.

In reality, of course, such relationships form a continuum, from those of totally like mind to those of totally alien mind. With the first we develop cordial, friendly, even intimate relations. For the middle ground, with only partially common interests, we develop varying degrees of acquaintance and friendship with accompanying tactics of politeness, diplomacy, and tact. With our opposites we generally use total avoidance, communication through a third party, or, if direct contact is unavoidable, either stubborn insistence

upon adherence to one's own norms or open attack. The statement is as valid
for relationships between nations as it is for those between individuals, as
even a cursory look at political-economic alliances today or at any time in the
past amply testifies.

Today there is no single contingent of unitary states. The obvious reason is
that China is at present the world's only large unitary nation. Other nations
with predominantly unitary populations are either small and scattered or
are dominated politically by a nonunitary minority—Peru, Ecuador, Bolivia,
Serbia-Montenegro, Madagascar, Nigeria, Benin, Burma, Indonesia, Malaysia,
and Thailand. Nonetheless, China, because of its extremely large population
—over one-quarter of the world's people—and its large geographical size,
constitutes one primary segment of the world's twenty-first-century alliances.

We commented earlier on the differences between China's unitary communism and the artificial, dictatorially imposed state Marxist-Leninist "communism" of the former Soviet Union. These differences have been evident since
the advent of the Bolshevik Revolution in the first decade of the twentieth
century. From the outset China rightfully handled its link to European "communism" with suspicion of its tenets, motives, and actions. Russia, that artificial experiment with unitary norms in a dualistic society, has, of course,
failed, and China finds herself largely alone as the world's only large unitary
state.

Until recently there were two dualistic alliances: the Western Alliance of
Western Europe, essentially NATO, Euro-America, Japan, and South Korea,
and the Eastern Alliance, essentially the former Warsaw Pact, consisting of the
USSR and the nations of Central and Eastern Europe. Socially, however, were
it not for a long series of historical accidents, these should have been a single
system, for both are culturally dualistic—Western and Central Europe largely
IIN, Eastern and Southern Europe largely *IIB*. That there were in fact for
many years two dualistic European alliances comes from the attempt to graft
Marxist Communism unnaturally onto a dualistic base. While many political
theorists felt that the graft might take, it is now clear that what the anthropologists had been saying all along is true—one can not alter a society's fundamental cultural norms in any way less than something approaching a millennium, and even that is rare. Unitary Serbia-Montenegro, as Yugoslavia, and
trinary Albania long ago broke away from the Russian system, and in the later
months of 1989 not only did the remaining Eastern and Central European
nations begin the same grass-roots process, but even non-Russian, internal
republics of the USSR did so. The result of this return to cultural normalcy
has been the dissolution of the Soviet Union and the Warsaw Pact and the

gradual merging of Eastern and Central Europe with its natural allies in the Western Alliance—a conclusion long ago expected and forecast by many in the business of political prediction.

In addition to these two distinctly different social coalitions—the Unitary Alliance, presently consisting only of China, on the one hand, and the Dualistic Alliance of all of Europe, European America, Japan, and South Korea on the other—there is a third, somewhat fragmented but nonetheless largely cohesive international alliance. It consists, of course, of what Europeans and Euro-Americans refer to as Third World countries, by far the greatest majority of which are trinary in social philosophy. The dominant members of this Trinary Alliance are the countries of Central Asia and the Arabic-speaking countries of Africa and the Middle East, as well as, by extension, most of the Islamic countries of the world, including the demographically important Southeast Asian countries of Indonesia and Malaysia.

That is, patterns of international alliance today are already formed along unitary-dualistic-trinary lines. Since the percentages of worldwide social types would not change appreciably with the inclusion of the non-Europeanized native American polities, there is no reason to suspect that such an inclusion would have altered the twenty-first-century alliances we presently see. The American Great Alliance that we have postulated for the majority of the trinary ethnopolitical units of the Americas would beyond doubt have joined hands with what we call the Third World Alliance. American dualists— certainly Nunavut, Kalaallit Nunaat, the Iroquois Confederacy, the Maya Kingdoms, and the Chibchan federation of the Muisca and Tairona would by nature have joined the Western or Dualistic Alliance; and the unitary Aztec, Mixtec, and Inca of Tawantinsuyu would as surely have joined forces with China as part of a worldwide Unitary Alliance. On cultural grounds alone, this seems assured.

In 2004, there are 194 independent world nations. If one does not include the present-day Euro-American countries, which in our scenario would not exist, and adds in the native American polities that were flourishing in 1492 prior to European intervention, the total becomes 178. Of this number, trinary societies would account for 108, or 60 percent, of the world's nations and for approximately 45 percent of the world's population. Unitary states would number only 12, or 7 percent, of the world's nations but about 25 percent of its population. Dualistic states would number 58, or 33 percent, of its nations and only 30 percent of its population.

The Trinary World, centered in the Americas, Africa, the Middle East, and Central and Southern Asia, would, in other words, represent a majority of

108 nations of the 178 and would include almost half of the world's population. On these grounds, unlike today, trinary societies in alliance would clearly be something for the Dualistic and Unitary Alliances to reckon with. Even without a United Nations, these ethnopolitical groups could, if they wanted, coerce the rest of the world toward its decisions.

Third World countries today do not push to take an upper hand in the world balance of power but remain as an international alliance of nonaligned powers. The addition of the native American trinary states and confederated tribal groups would strengthen such a nonaligned base. Such a World Trinary Alliance would continue to effect compromise where possible and to throw its weight now behind one balance of power disrupter, now behind another, in an attempt to maintain a nonpolarized world.

In drawing up a list of international political and economic allies in such a revised twenty-first century, it seems unquestioned that both the México Empire of the Aztecs and the Inca Empire of Tawantinsuyu would ultimately align themselves with each other and, on the world scene, would face west across the Pacific to join hands with their distant Chinese and Southeast Asian kin, for social and philosophical compatibilities would be great.

The relations of dualistic Europe and Asia with the México-Tawantinsuyu-China axis would be much the same as those today between the dualistic powers and China—constantly strained and with considerable misunderstanding of motives and goals on both sides. This is to be expected, since the two social types are the flip sides of the same coin. Unitary and dualistic cultures are, as pointed out, always at odds with one another, the former with a bias against both individual competition and individual privileges and rights, the latter biased strongly in favor of the same traits. It is not surprising that meetings of the minds are rare and difficult both to achieve and to maintain, particularly since neither social type considers compromise a virtue: to the dualist it is a distinct weakness, to the unitarian simply unnecessary. This pattern would certainly still persist, with the added weight of its native American adherents.

The Dualistic Alliance would include, as indicated earlier, not only all of Europe, most of sub-Saharan Africa, Japan and Korea in the Far East, and at least Nunavut, Kalaallit Nunaat, the Iroquois Confederacy, the Maya Kingdoms, and the Chibcha towns of Colombia in the Americas. This areally fragmented power base—unlike the Circum-Pacific base of the Unitary Alliance, and the Middle Eastern base of the Trinary Alliance—would not have, except in Europe, a single geographical focus, making it difficult to achieve absolute consensus on many matters. The inability of dualists to see eye to eye, even among themselves, is almost proverbial—we used the example of NAFTA earlier—and a worldwide, geographically fragmented Dualistic Alliance would, indeed, render genuine ongoing cooperation in a solid front both difficult and questionable.

By the twenty-first century we would thus have an overall world balance of power quite at variance with what we see today. If the Trinary Alliance prevailed, with its sense of achieving international solution by compromise, as it currently does through the United Nations, it might possibly be a more tolerant, less colonialist world. With equal certainty, however, if ultimate battle lines were drawn—and, so long as the world contains unitary vs. dualistic states, they *would* be drawn—they would be drawn as they are today between members of the Circum-Pacific Unitary Alliance and the members of the largely European Dualistic Alliance. In that event, the dualists would clearly lose, since the more tolerant Trinary Alliance members, when push came to shove, would throw their weight behind the culturally more similar, more pragmatic Circum-Pacific unitary states. A combination of Trinary and Unitary states would dominate both in population—70 percent of the world's people—and in number of individual states—120 nations of the world's 178. The largely European Dualistic Alliance would become the new power minority.

This prognostication of war is the only specific event that can be uttered with certainty in our 1492–2004 scenario. It can be said so definitely not from a crystal ball and not from personal opinion but from the evidence of human history. In any instance in the past when a unitary and dualistic society, or conglomerates of unitary and dualistic societies, have lived neighboring one another or have come into close contact as a result of trade, commerce, and cultural interchange, the result has been devastating conflict, expressed through unusually brutal and destructive war. The examples are many: the conquest of unitary Ming China by dualistic Manchuria in 1644, the Sino-Japanese war of 1895, the Boxer Rebellion of 1898–1900, the Sino-Japanese wars of the early 1930s, the Sino-Japanese theater of World War II, the expansion of the unitary Toltec of central Mexico into the lands of the dualistic Maya around A.D. 900, the expansion of the unitary Quechua-speaking Inca throughout the Andes region of South America in the 1400s.

In like manner, as pointed out earlier in the chapter, the imposition of the communal system of social organization so typical of unitary states, even when imposed only as an ideal if not in real day-to-day practice, does not sit lightly on dualists. When superficially imposed on the remains of the dualistic Russian Empire in the years following World War I, it could be predicted that

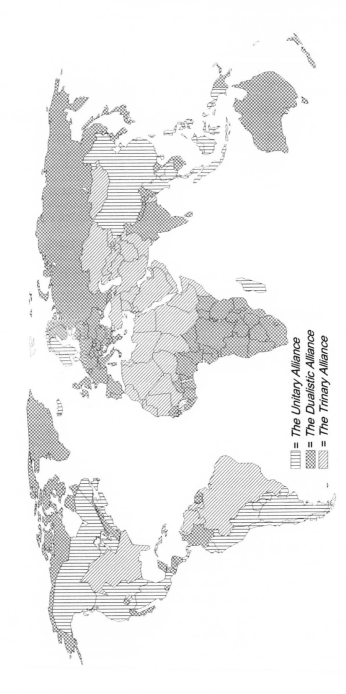

= The Unitary Alliance

= The Dualistic Alliance

= The Trinary Alliance

Figure 21. International Alliances of New World Polities in the Twenty-first Century

it would not last, as it has not. In like manner, the imposition of the artificial Soviet unitary system on dualistic Eastern Europe after World War II should not have lasted, as it, too, has not. The most obvious instance of such an artificial unification of unitarians and dualists came in the Balkans with the creation of Yugoslavia on December 1, 1918. With dualistic Slovenia, Croatia, and Macedonia, trinary Bosnia, Herzegovina, and Kosovo, and unitary Montenegro and Serbia, such a union was socially impractical from the beginning, particularly when political control was from the start in the hands of the unitarian Serbs. That it would not last was thus evident from the time of its founding, and, after almost eighty years of constant infighting, it has not lasted, each socially distinct segment declaring its own independence with violent conflict. Any instance of unitary-dualistic confrontation one wishes to describe in history has ultimately and invariably resulted in war. Thus such a confrontation in the future, which we are describing here, is, for better or worse, to be considered both socially routine and expected.

If the dominating Trinary Alliance took a strong and successfully compromising position at the conclusion of such a dualist-unitarian holocaust, a combined Unitary/Trinary Alliance might well end up, if not ruling, at least controlling the earth. This would certainly mean a Chinese/Aztec/Inca presence in the remainder of the Americas, in Europe, Africa, and Asia, a scenario difficult if not impossible for Europeans and Euro-Americans to imagine. Dualists would be the Have-Nots, and Europe would lose its present worldwide hold. Political decisions would be based on compromise and what was pragmatically the optimal solution for the problem of the time. Concepts of rigid absolutes would lose their pertinence, and both individuals and societies that did not learn to bend with the situation would increasingly lose political and economic power. Competitive individualism, while perhaps not totally a thing of the past, would not ensure one a position of respect or power. Only those who demonstrated a proven ability to govern in order to serve would be elected to positions of control, and they would be quickly replaced if they did not live up to the rules of pragmatic, relative compromise.

The world would, indeed, be quite a different place than it is today, with the world balance of power thrown considerably toward a way of life as alien to Europe and Euro-America today as it was to the Spanish when they entered Cuzco and Tenochtitlán almost five centuries ago. The dominant culture would be totally foreign to and at odds with the Mediterranean, Graeco-Roman/Judeo-Christian heritage we are so used to today. The Americas That Might Have Been—indeed. The World That Might Have Been!

Epilogue
The First Baktun

From a cultural point of view, the European conquest of the Americas was likely the most amazing event in human history. With respect to the enormity, gravity, and permanence of the extinction it brought, it compares favorably, if that is the right word, to the disappearance of the dinosaurs. It altered the lifestyles of a larger percentage of humankind than ever before or since. The entire course of world history was irrevocably altered.

Restitution cannot be made, however, for historical "wrongs" without the risk of creating yet greater dislocations. The Palestinian problem is a case in point: The 2,000-year gap between the original Israeli occupation of the land and all that has happened since cannot simply be nullified, much as some might wish. History does not turn itself back. In similar vein with regard to the Americas, it can only be said that the lesson of history since 1492 is that the nature of the future depends on the ability of the present to understand and profit from the unkindnesses of the past, not to hope for their reversal.

If, indeed, Columbus had not set forth from Palos and the Europeans had not come—but, in fact, it did all happen, and the dream is over. The Americas *are* a European land, and only a fragmented native heritage survives in hard-to-find enclaves far from the haunts of Euro- and Afro-American man. The attempt of the majority to understand this fragmented minority is still a feeble one, and the myth of the incapable childlike Noble Savage persists now as it did in the beginning.

There is, however, always that hope which springs eternal. The Maya calendar was graduated in Great Cycles of approximately 5,126 years, each of which contained thirteen smaller calendar counts of approximately 394 years called *baktuns*. It was understood that at the end of each Great Cycle of thirteen baktuns the world was destroyed, perhaps literally, perhaps figuratively, in preparation for a New Beginning. To the Maya mind a new world, a new chance, began with the start of Baktun 1 of each new Great Cycle. By our calendar, Baktun 13 of the current Great Cycle, which began in 3114 B.C., will end in December of 2012. The old order of the past 5,126 years will go, and with the first day of Baktun 1 of the new Great Cycle a new order will begin. This will be the day before Christian Christmas in the year of Our Lord 2012.

This is perhaps prophetic, and perhaps the upcoming new Baktun 1 *will* bring a brighter future for Native America, the land, its 70 million people, and its traditions. Right now this may be difficult to envision, with all the plunder the last two baktuns have brought. There may be a way, however, though such a future is likely to come at the expense of the inner man. The way will require both an immersion in the Euro-American mainstream to ensure physical survival and a forging of new ways to retain the traditions of the past yet blend them with new ways of the future. In a few places—the Pueblos, Navajo Dinétah, parts of the Maya world, Kalaallit Nunaat and Nunavut, among the Guaraní of Paraguay, and in the old lands of Tawantinsuyu—real survival and revival of a core for such a New Beginning may already be waiting. Otherwise, *The Americas That Might Have Been* are truly that, part of a past to be appreciated, marveled at, and hopefully understood—but part of a world no more.

References

While all the references cited in the text are listed below, there are a number that may be of particular interest to the reader on individual topics. These are listed here, with full references cited below.

Introduction (Kinship Studies): Godelier, Trautmann, and Tjon Sie Fat 1998; Murdock 1949.

Chapter 1 (Men Out of Asia): Coe, Snow, and Benson 1986; Crosby 1972; Dobyns 1983; Fitzhugh 1984; Ramenofsky 1987; Thomas 1989–90.

Chapter 2 (Americas 1492): Jennings 1978a, 1978b.

Chapter 3 (Native Philosophies of Life): Benedict 1934; Geertz 1973; Hall 1959, 1966, 1976; Hofstede 1984; Kardiner 1963.

Chapter 4 (Unitary Norms): Kapp 1983.

Chapter 5 (The Dualistic View): Benedict 1945; Gastil 1975; Mead 1942.

Chapter 6 (The Trinary Compromise): Hitti 1939.

Chapter 7 (The Inca): Davies 2000b; Hyams and Ordish 1963; Moseley 2001.

Chapter 8 (The Aztec): Coe 1999b; Davies 2000a; Fagan 1984.

Chapter 9 (The Maya): Coe 1999b; Hammond 2000; Jones 1989; Martin and Grube 2000; Schele and Friedl 1990.

Chapter 10 (The Mississippians): Emerson 1997; Lewis and Stout 1998; Pauketat 1994.

Chapter 11 (The Pueblos): Eggan 1950, 1979; Fox 1967; Ortíz 1969.

Chapter 12 (The Taíno): Las Casas 1971; Lovén 1935; Olsen 1974; Rouse 1992; Stevens-Arroyo 1988; Wilson 1997.

There are also three multiple-volume *Handbooks* to assist the reader in acquiring vast amounts of pertinent data on all native American societies: the *Handbook of South American Indians,* ed. Steward (1946–1959); the *Handbook of Middle*

American Indians, ed. Wauchope (1964–1976); and the *Handbook of North American Indians,* by Sturtevant (1978 to date).

Aberle, Sophie D.
  1948 *The Pueblo Indians of New Mexico: Their Land, Economy, and Civil Organization.* American Anthropological Association, Memoir No. 70.
Adams, Richard E. W.
  1977 *Prehistoric Mesoamerica.* Little, Brown and Company, Boston.
Alegría, Ricardo E.
  1983 *Ball Courts and Ceremonial Plazas in the West Indies.* Yale University Publications in Anthropology, No. 79. Yale University Press, New Haven.
Anghiera, Pietro Martire d'
  1970 *De Orbe Novo: The Eight Decades of Peter Martyr D'Anghera.* Translated by Francis Augustus McNutt, 1912; reprinted by Nutt Franklin, New York.
Anonymous
  1930 [1563–1564] *Relación del Primer Descubrimiento del Perú* [1563–1564]. Edited by T. Medina. Lima.
Asch, Michael
  1998 Kinship and Dravidianate Logic: Some Implications for Understanding Power, Focus, and Social Life in a Northern Dene Community. In *Transformations of Kinship,* edited by Maurice Godelier, Thomas R. Trautmann, and Franklin E. Tjon Sie Fat, pp. 140–149. Smithsonian Institution Press, Washington.
Austin, Paul Britten
  1946 *The Swedes: How They Live and Work.* International Thomson Publishing Company, New York.
Barry, Herbert III, and Alice Schlegel (editors)
  1975 *Cross-Cultural Samples and Codes.* University of Pittsburgh Press, Pittsburgh.
Beals, Ralph
  1969 The Tarascans. In *Handbook of Middle American Indians,* vol. 8, *Ethnology* pt. 2, pp. 725–776. University of Texas Press, Austin.
Bellwood, Peter
  1979 *Man's Conquest of the Pacific: The Prehistory of Southeast Asia and Oceania.* Oxford University Press, New York.
Benedict, Ruth F.
  1934 *Patterns of Culture.* Houghton Mifflin, New York.

1945   *The Chrysanthemum and the Sword: Patterns of Japanese Culture.*
       Houghton Mifflin, New York.

Bense, Judith A.
1994   *Archaeology of the Southeastern United States: Paleoindian to World War I.*
       Academic Press, New York.

Betanzos, J. D.
1996   *Narrative of the Incas* [1557]. University of Texas Press, Austin.

Billard, Jules (editor)
1993   *The World of the American Indian.* National Geographic Society, Wash-
       ington.

Binford, Lewis R.
1972   *An Archaeological Perspective.* Seminar Press, New York.

Blitz, John H.
1993   *Ancient Chiefdoms of the Tombigbee.* University of Alabama Press, Tus-
       caloosa.

Borhegyi, Stephen F.
1959   Pre-Columbian Cultural Connections Between Mesoamerica and
       Ecuador. *Middle American Research Records* 2:6:141–155.

Brose, David S., C. Wesley Cowan, and Robert C. Mainfort, Jr. (editors)
2001   *Societies in Eclipse: Archaeology of the Eastern Woodland Indians,
       A.D. 1400–1700.* Smithsonian Institution Press, Washington.

Castillo, Edward D.
1978   The Impact of Euro-American Exploration and Settlement. In *Hand-
       book of North American Indians,* vol. 8, *California,* edited by Robert F.
       Heizer, pp. 99–127. Smithsonian Institution, Washington.

Chambers, James
1979   *The Devil's Horsemen.* Atheneum, New York.

Childe, V. Gordon
1951   *Social Evolution.* Schuman, New York.

Chomsky, Noam
1965   *Aspects of the Theory of Syntax.* MIT Press, Cambridge.

Cieza de León, Pedro de
1973   *La Crónica del Perú.* Promoción Editorial S.A., Lima.
1976   *The Incas of Pedro Cieza de León.* Translated by Harriet de Onís. Uni-
       versity of Oklahoma Press, Norman.

Coe, Michael D.
1960   Archaeological Linkages with North and South America at La Victo-
       ria, Guatemala. *American Anthropologist* 62:363–393.
1984   *Mexico.* 3d edition. Thames & Hudson, New York.

1999a *Breaking the Maya Code.* Revised edition. Thames & Hudson, New York.

1999b *The Maya.* 6th edition. Thames & Hudson, New York.

Coe, Michael D., and Mark Van Stone

2001 *Reading the Maya Glyphs.* Thames & Hudson, New York.

Coe, Michael D., Dean Snow, and Elizabeth Benson

1986 *Atlas of Ancient America.* Facts on File, Inc., New York.

Cole, Douglas and David Darling

1990 History of the Early Period. In *Handbook of North American Indians,* vol. 7, *Northwest Coast,* edited by Wayne Suttles, pp. 119–134. Smithsonian Institution, Washington.

Columbus, Christopher

1987 *The Log of Christopher Columbus,* edited by Robert E. Fuson. International Marine Publishing Company, Camden, Maine.

Cordell, Linda

1979 Prehistory: Eastern Anasazi. In *Handbook of North American Indians,* vol. 9, *Southwest,* edited by Alfonso Ortiz, pp. 131–151. Smithsonian Institution, Washington.

Cronon, William

1983 *Changes in the Land: Indians, Colonials, and the Ecology of New England.* Hill and Wang, New York.

Crosby, Alfred W.

1972 *The Columbian Exchange: Biological and Cultural Consequences of 1492.* Greenwood Press, Westport, Connecticut.

Curtsinger, Bill, and Richard Schlecht

1985 Discovery in Labrador: A 16th Century Basque Whaling Port and Its Sunken Fleet. *National Geographic* 168(1):40–49.

Davies, Nigel

2000a *The Aztecs.* The Folio Society, London.

2000b *The Incas.* The Folio Society, London.

Díaz del Castillo, Bernal

1963 *The Conquest of New Spain.* Translated by J. M. Cohen. Pelican Books, Baltimore.

Dobyns, Henry F.

1983 *Their Number Become Thinned: Native American Population Dynamics in Eastern North America.* University of Tennessee Press, Knoxville.

Dunn, Oliver, and James E. Kelley, Jr.

1989 *The Diario of Christopher Columbus's First Voyage to America, Abstracted by Fray Bartolomé de Las Casas.* University of Oklahoma Press, Norman.

Durán, Diego
  1964   *The Aztecs: The History of the Indies of New Spain.* Translated by Doris Heyden and Fernando Horcasitas. University of Oklahoma Press, Norman.
  1971   *Book of the Gods and Rites* and *The Ancient Calendar.* Translated by Doris Heyden and Fernando Horcasitas. University of Oklahoma Press, Norman.

Eggan, Fred
  1950   *Social Organization of the Western Pueblos.* University of Chicago Press, Chicago.
  1979   Pueblos: Introduction. In *Handbook of North American Indians,* vol. 9, *Southwest,* edited by Alfonso Ortiz, pp. 224–235. Smithsonian Institution, Washington.

Emerson, Thomas E.
  1997   *Cahokia and the Archaeology of Power.* University of Alabama Press, Tuscaloosa.

Ewen, Charles R.
  2001   Historical Archaeology in the Colonial Spanish Caribbean. In *Island Lives: Historical Archaeology of the Caribbean,* edited by Paul Farnsworth, pp. 1–20. University of Alabama Press, Tuscaloosa.

Fagan, Brian M.
  1984   *The Aztecs.* W. H. Freeman and Company, San Francisco.

Feldman, Robert A., and Michael E. Moseley
  1978   The Northern Andes. In *Ancient South Americans,* edited by Jesse D. Jennings, pp. 139–178. W. H. Freeman and Company, San Francisco.

Fenton, William
  1978   Northern Iroquoian Culture Patterns. In *Handbook of North American Indians,* vol. 15, *Northeast,* edited by Bruce G. Trigger, pp. 296–321. Smithsonian Institution, Washington.

Fischer, David Hackett
  1970   *Historians' Fallacies: Toward a Logic of Historical Thought.* Harper & Row, New York.

Fitzhugh, William
  1984   *Cultures in Contact.* Smithsonian Institution Press, Washington.

Fitzhugh, William W., and Elisabeth I. Ward (editors)
  2000   *Vikings: The North Atlantic Saga.* Smithsonian Institution Press in association with the National Museum of Natural History.

Fletcher, Richard

1992   *Moorish Spain.* Henry Holt and Company, New York.

Ford, James A.

1969   *A Comparison of Formative Cultures in the Americas.* Smithsonian
       Contributions to Anthropology 11. Smithsonian Institution, Wash-
       ington.

Fox, Robin

1967   *The Keresan Bridge: A Problem in Pueblo Ethnology.* Athlone Press,
       London.

Fuson, Robert E.

1987   *The Log of Christopher Columbus.* International Marine Publish-
       ing Co., Camden, Maine.

Gad, Finn

1984   History of Colonial Greenland. In *Handbook of North American Indi-
       ans,* vol. 5, *Arctic,* edited by David Damas, pp. 556–576. Smithsonian
       Institution, Washington.

Garibay, Ángel María

1971   *Historia de la Literatura Náhuatl.* Editorial Porrúa, Mexico City.

Gastil, Raymond D.

1975   *Cultural Regions of the United States.* University of Washington Press,
       Seattle.

Geertz, Clifford

1973   *Interpretation of Cultures.* Basic Books, New York.

Gibson, Charles

1988   Spanish Indian Policies. In *Handbook of North American Indians,*
       vol. 4, *History of Indian-White Relations,* edited by Wilcomb E. Wash-
       burn, pp. 96–102. Smithsonian Institution, Washington.

Gibson, Jon L.

1980   Speculations on the Origin and Development of Poverty Point Cul-
       ture. In *Caddoan and Poverty Point Archaeology,* edited by Jon L. Gib-
       son, pp. 321–348. Bulletin of the Louisiana Archaeological Society
       No. 6.

Gillmor, Frances

1983   *Flute of the Smoking Mirror: A Portrait of Nezahualcoyotl, Poet-King of
       the Aztecs.* University of Utah Press, Salt Lake City.

Godelier, Maurice

1998   Afterword: Transformations and Lines of Evolution. In *Transforma-
       tions of Kinship,* edited by Maurice Godelier, Thomas R. Trautmann,

and Franklin E. Tjon Sie Fat, pp. 386–413. Smithsonian Institution Press, Washington.

Godelier, Maurice, Thomas R. Trautmann, and Franklin Tjon Sie Fat, editors
1998 *Transformations of Kinship.* Smithsonian Institution Press, Washington.

Gómez-Imbert, Elsa
1991 Forces des Langues Vernaculaires en Situation d'Exogamie Linguistique: Le Cas du Vaupés Colombien (Nord-Ouest Amazonien). *Cahiers des Sciences Humaines* 27:535–559.

Gómez-Imbert, Elsa, and Michael Kenstowicz
2000 Barasana Tone and Accent. *International Journal of American Linguistics* 66(4):419–463.

Granberry, Julian
1993 *A Grammar and Dictionary of the Timucua Language.* University of Alabama Press, Tuscaloosa.
1995 The Position of the Calusa Language in Florida Prehistory: A Working Hypothesis. *Florida Anthropologist* 48(3):156–173.

Grenier, Robert
1985 Excavating a 400-Year-Old Basque Galleon. *National Geographic* 168(1):58–68.

Hall, Edward T.
1959 *The Silent Language.* Doubleday, New York.
1966 *The Hidden Dimension.* Doubleday, New York.
1976 *Beyond Culture.* Doubleday, New York.

Hammond, Norman
2000 *The Maya.* The Folio Society, London.

Hanke, Lewis
1938 The "Requerimiento" and Its Interpreters. *Revista de Historia de América* (Mexico City) 1:25–34.

Hitti, Philip K.
1939 *History of the Arabs from Earliest Times to the Present.* Macmillan, London.

Hofstede, Geert
1984 *Culture's Consequences.* Sage Publications, Beverly Hills.

Hudson, Charles M., Jr.
1990 Conversations with the High Priest of Coosa. In *Lamar Archaeology: Mississippian Chiefdoms in the Deep South,* edited by Mark Williams and Gary Shapiro, pp. 214–230. University of Alabama Press, Tuscaloosa.

Hudson, Charles M., Jr., Marvin T. Smith, David J. Hally, Richard Polhemus, and Chester B. DePratter

1985 Coosa: A Chiefdom in the Sixteenth-Century Southeastern United States. *American Antiquity* 50:723–737.

Hyams, Edward, and George Ordish

1963 *The Last of the Incas: The Rise and Fall of an American Empire.* Barnes & Noble, New York.

Jackson, Jean

1982 *The Fish People: Linguistic Exogamy and Tukanoan Identity in North-West Amazonia.* Cambridge University Press, Cambridge.

Jane, Cecil (translator)

1960 *The Journal of Christopher Columbus.* Clarkson N. Potter, New York.

Jenkins, Ned J., and Richard A. Krause

1986 *The Tombigbee Watershed in Southeastern Prehistory.* University of Alabama Press, Tuscaloosa.

Jennings, Jesse D.

1978a *Ancient North Americans.* W. H. Freeman and Company, San Francisco.

1978b *Ancient South Americans.* W. H. Freeman and Company, San Francisco.

Jett, Stephen C.

1978 Precolumbian Transoceanic Contacts. In *Ancient South Americans,* edited by Jesse D. Jennings, pp. 337–394. W. H. Freeman and Company, San Francisco.

Jones, Grant D.

1989 *Maya Resistance to Spanish Rule: Time and History on a Colonial Frontier.* University of New Mexico Press, Albuquerque.

Kapp, Robert A. (editor)

1983 *Communicating with China.* Intercultural Press, Chicago.

Kardiner, Abram, Ralph Linton, and Cora Du Bois

1963 *Psychological Frontiers of Society.* Columbia University Press, New York.

Kirchoff, Paul

1955 The Principles of Clanship in Human Society. *Davidson Journal of Anthropology* 1(1):1–10.

Kleivan, Inge

1984 History of Norse Greenland. In *Handbook of North American Indians,* vol. 5, *Arctic,* edited by David Damas, pp. 549–555. Smithsonian Institution, Washington.

Knight, Vernon J., Jr.

1981 Mississippian Ritual. Unpublished Ph.D. dissertation, Department of Anthropology, University of Florida, Gainesville.

1986   The Institutional Organization of Mississippian Religion. *American Antiquity* 51(4):675–687.

Kroeber, Alfred

1909   Classificatory Systems of Relationship. *Journal of the Royal Anthropological Institute* 39:77–84.

Kryukov, M. V.

1972   *The Chinese Kinship System* [*Sistema Rodstva Kitaitsev*]. Nauka, Moscow.

1998   The Synchro-Diachronic Method and the Multidirectionality of Kinship Transformations. In *Transformations of Kinship,* edited by Maurice Godelier, Thomas R. Trautmann, and Franklin E. Tjon Sie Fat, pp. 294–313. Smithsonian Institution Press, Washington.

Lange, Charles H.

1959   *Cochiti: A New Mexico Pueblo, Past and Present.* University of Texas Press, Austin.

1979   Relations of the Southwest with the Plains and Great Basin. In *Handbook of North American Indians,* vol. 9, *Southwest,* edited by Alfonso Ortiz, pp. 201–205. Smithsonian Institution, Washington.

Las Casas, Bartolomé de

1971   *Bartolomé de Las Casas: History of the Indies.* Edited and translated by Andree M. Collard. Harper and Row, New York.

Lathrap, Donald Ward

1973   The Antiquity and Importance of Long-Distance Trade Relationships in the Moist Tropics of Pre-Columbian South America. *World Archaeology* 5(2):170–186.

Lavrovski, P. A.

1867   *The Original Meaning of Slavic Kinship Terms* [*Korennoye Znachenie v nazvaniyakh Rodstva u Slavyan*]. Tip. Imp. Akademii Nauk, St. Petersburg.

Laxalt, Robert

1985   The Indomitable Basques. *National Geographic* 168(1):69–71.

León-Portilla, Miguel

1963   *Aztec Thought and Culture: A Study of the Ancient Náhuatl Mind.* Translated by Jack Emory Davis. University of Oklahoma Press, Norman.

1979   *La Filosofía Náhuatl Estudiada en sus Fuentes.* Prólogo de Ángel María Garibay K. Universidad Nacional Autónoma de México, Instituto de Investigaciones Históricas. Mexico City.

León-Portilla, Miguel (editor)

  1962   *The Broken Spears: The Aztec Account of the Conquest of Mexico.*
         Beacon Press, Boston.

Lévi-Strauss, Claude

  1949   *The Elementary Structures of Kinship.* Beacon Press, Boston.

Lewis, R. Barry, and Charles Stout (editors)

  1998   *Mississippian Towns and Sacred Places: Searching for an Architectural
         Grammar.* University of Alabama Press, Tuscaloosa.

Lounsbury, Floyd G.

  1956   A Semantic Analysis of the Pawnee Kinship Usage. *Language*
         32:158–194.

  1964a The Structural Analysis of Kinship Semantics. In *Proceedings of the
         Ninth International Congress of Linguistics,* pp. 1073–1093. Mouton,
         The Hague.

  1964b A Formal Account of the Crow and Omaha-Type Kinship Terminolo-
         gies. In *Explorations in Cultural Anthropology: Essays in Honor of
         George Peter Murdock,* edited by Ward H. Goodenough, pp. 351–393.
         McGraw-Hill, New York.

Lovén, Sven

  1935   *Origins of the Tainan Culture, West Indies.* Elanders Boktryckeri Aktie-
         bolag, Göteborg.

Lowie, Robert

  1928   A Note on Relationship Terminologies. *American Anthropologist*
         30:263–267.

Magnusson, Magnus

  1980   *Vikings!* E. P. Dutton, New York.

Mahon, John K.

  1988   Indian–United States Military Situation, 1775–1848. In *Handbook of
         North American Indians,* vol. 4, *History of Indian-White Relations,* ed-
         ited by Wilcomb E. Washburn, pp. 144–162. Smithsonian Institution,
         Washington.

Markoe, Glenn E.

  2000   *Phoenicians.* University of California Press, Berkeley.

Martin, Simon, and Nikolai Grube

  2000   *Chronicle of the Maya Kings and Queens: Deciphering the Dynasties of
         the Ancient Maya.* Thames & Hudson, London.

Mead, Margaret

  1942   *And Keep Your Powder Dry: An Anthropologist Looks at America.* Inter-
         national Institute of International Studies, New York.

Meggers, Betty J., and Clifford Evans

1978   Lowland South America and the Antilles. In *Ancient South Americans,* edited by Jesse D. Jennings, pp. 287–335. W. H. Freeman and Company, San Francisco.

Merrill, William L., and Ives Goddard (editors)

2002   *Anthropology, History, and American Indians: Essays in Honor of William Curtis Sturtevant.* Smithsonian Institution Press, Washington.

Milanich, Jerald T., and Susan Milbrath, editors

1989   *First Encounters: Spanish Explorations in the Caribbean and the United States, 1492–1570.* University of Florida Press/Florida Museum of Natural History, Gainesville.

Molina, Alonso de

1977   [1571] *Vocabulario en Lengua Castellana y Mexicana y Mexicana y Castellana.* Edited by Miguel León-Portilla. Editorial Porrúa, México.

Morgan, David

1986   *The Mongols.* Basil Blackwell, New York.

Morison, Samuel Eliot

1963   *Journals and Other Documents on the Life and Voyages of Christopher Columbus.* Heritage Press, New York.

1971   *The European Discovery of America: The Northern Voyages, A.D. 500–1600.* Oxford University Press, New York.

1974   *The European Discovery of America: The Southern Voyages, A.D. 1492–1616.* Oxford University Press, New York.

Moseley, Michael E.

1983   Central Andean Civilization. In *Ancient South Americans,* edited by Jesse D. Jennings, pp. 179–240. W. H. Freeman and Company, San Francisco.

2001   *The Incas and Their Ancestors.* Revised edition. Thames & Hudson, New York.

Motolinia, Toribio

1951   [1536–43] *History of the Indians of New Spain.* Translated by Francis Borgia Steck. Academy of American Franciscan History, Washington, D.C.

Murdock, George Peter

1949   *Social Structure.* Macmillan Publishing Company, New York.

Nash, Manning

1989   *The Cauldron of Ethnicity in the Modern World.* University of Chicago Press, Chicago.

Olsen, Fred
  1974   *On the Trail of the Arawak.* University of Oklahoma Press, Norman.
Ortiz, Alfonso
  1969   *The Tewa World: Space, Time, Being, and Becoming in a Pueblo Society.* University of Chicago Press, Chicago.
Parmentier, Richard J.
  1979   The Pueblo Mythological Triangle: Poseyemu, Montezuma, and Jesus in the Pueblos. In *Handbook of North American Indians,* vol. 9, *Southwest,* edited by Alfonso Ortiz, pp. 609–622. Smithsonian Institution, Washington.
Parsons, Elsie Clews
  1939   *Pueblo Indian Religion.* 2 vols. University of Chicago Press, Chicago.
Pauketat, Timothy R.
  1994   *The Ascent of Chiefs: Chaokia and Mississippian Politics in Native North America.* University of Alabama Press, Tuscaloosa.
Pauketat, Timothy R., and Thomas E. Emerson (editors)
  1991   The Ideology of Authority and the Power of the Pot. *American Anthropologist* 93:919–941.
Peebles, Christopher
  1970   Moundville and Beyond: Some Observations on the Changing Social Organization in the Southeastern United States. Paper presented at the 69th Annual Meeting of the American Anthropological Association, San Diego.
Plog, Fred
  1979   Prehistory: Western Anasazi. In *Handbook of North American Indians,* vol. 9, *Southwest,* edited by Alfonso Ortiz, pp. 108–130. Smithsonian Institution, Washington.
Proskouriakoff, Tatiana
  1946   *An Album of Maya Architecture.* Carnegie Institution of Washington Publication 558. Carnegie Institution of Washington, Washington.
  1960   Historical Implication of a Pattern of Dates at Piedras Negras, Guatemala. *American Antiquity* 25(4):454–475.
Rainey, Froelich G.
  1940   *Porto Rican Archaeology.* Scientific Survey of Porto Rico and the Virgin Islands, vol. 18, pt. 1. New York Academy of Sciences, New York.
Ramenofsky, Ann F.
  1987   *Vectors of Death: The Archaeology of European Contact.* University of New Mexico Press, Albuquerque.

Robicsek, Francis, and Donald M. Hales
  1981   *The Maya Book of the Dead: The Ceramic Codex.* University of Virginia Art Museum, Charlottesville.
Rogers, J. Daniel, and Bruce D. Smith (editors)
  1995   *Mississippian Communities and Households.* University of Alabama Press, Tuscaloosa.
Rouse, Irving
  1952   *Porto Rican Prehistory.* Scientific Survey of Porto Rico and the Virgin Islands, vol. 18, pts. 3–4. New York Academy of Sciences, New York.
  1986   *Migrations in Prehistory: Inferring Population Movement from Cultural Remains.* Yale University Press, New Haven.
  1992   *Tainos: Rise and Decline of the People Who Greeted Columbus.* Yale University Press, New Haven.
Roys, Ralph
  1939   *The Titles of Ebtún.* Carnegie Institution of Washington Publication 505. Carnegie Institution of Washington, Washington.
Sahagún, Fray Bernardo de
  1950– *General History of the Things of New Spain (The Florentine Codex).*
  1970   13 volumes. Translated, with notes, by Arthur J. O. Anderson and Charles E. Dibble. School of American Research and University of Utah, Santa Fe.
Salomon, Frank
  1977– Pochteca and Mindala: A Comparison of Long-Distance Traders in
  1978   Ecuador and Mesoamerica. *Journal of the Steward Anthropological Society* 9(1–2):231–246.
Sando, Joe S.
  1979   The Pueblo Revolt. In *Handbook of North American Indians,* vol. 9, *Southwest,* edited by Alfonso Ortiz, pp. 194–197. Smithsonian Institution, Washington.
Sassaman, Kenneth E.
  1993   *Early Pottery in the Southeast: Tradition and Innovation in Cooking Technology.* University of Alabama Press, Tuscaloosa.
Schele, Linda, and David Friedl
  1990   *A Forest of Kings: The Untold Story of the Ancient Maya.* William Morrow, New York.
Schele, Linda, and Mary Ellen Miller
  1986   *The Blood of Kings; Dynasty and Ritual in Maya Art.* George Braziller, Inc., New York.

Sears, William H.

   1964   Southeastern United States. In *Prehistoric Man in the New World,* ed-
          ited by Jesse D. Jennings and Edward Norbeck, pp. 259–290. Univer-
          sity of Chicago Press, Chicago.

   1982   *Fort Center: An Archaeological Site in the Lake Okeechobee Basin.* Uni-
          versity Presses of Florida, Gainesville.

Service, Elman R.

   1962   *Primitive Social Organization.* Random House, New York.

   1975   *Origins of the State and Civilization.* Norton, New York.

Simmons, Marc

   1979a History of Pueblo-Spanish Relations to 1821. In *Handbook of North
          American Indians,* vol. 9, *Southwest,* edited by Alfonso Ortiz, pp. 178–
          193. Smithsonian Institution, Washington.

   1979b History of the Pueblos Since 1821. In *Handbook of North American
          Indians,* vol. 9, *Southwest,* edited by Alfonso Ortiz, pp. 206–223.
          Smithsonian Institution, Washington.

Smith, Marvin T.

   1987   *Archaeology of Aboriginal Culture Change in the Interior Southeast: De-
          population during the Early Historic Period.* University of Florida Press,
          Gainesville.

   2001   The Rise and Fall of Coosa, A.D. 1350–1700. In *Societies in Eclipse:
          Archaeology of the Eastern Woodlands Indians, A.D. 1400–1700,* edited
          by David S. Brose, C. Wesley Cowan, and Robert C. Mainfort, Jr.,
          pp. 143–156. Smithsonian Institution Press, Washington.

Stevens-Arroyo, Antonio M.

   1988   *Cave of the Jagua: The Mythological World of the Taínos.* University of
          New Mexico Press, Albuquerque.

Steward, Julian H. (editor)

   1946– *Handbook of South American Indians.* 7 vols. Bureau of American
   1959   Ethnology Bulletin 143, Smithsonian Institution, Washington. [This
          excellent though somewhat outdated series is complete but difficult to
          find except in large public or university libraries.]

Sturtevant, William C. (editor)

   1978– *Handbook of North American Indians.* 20 vols. Smithsonian Institu-
   2001   tion, Washington. [This highly recommended series is in progress,
          with 12 volumes published to date.]

Swanton, John R.

   1946   *Indians of the Southeastern United States.* Bureau of American Eth-
          nology Bulletin No. 137. Smithsonian Institution, Washington.

Thomas, David H. (editor)
  1989– *Columbian Consequences* 2 vols. Smithsonian Institution Press, Wash-
  1990   ington.
Thompson, J. Eric S.
  1970   *Maya History and Religion.* University of Oklahoma Press, Norman.
Thornton, Russell
  1987   *American Indian Holocaust and Survival.* University of Oklahoma
          Press, Norman.
Tjon Sie Fat, Franklin
  1990   *Representing Kinship: Simple Models of Elementary Structures.* Faculty of
          Social Sciences, Leiden University, Leiden.
  1995   Rewriting the Rules: Operator Algebras and the Structural Analysis of
          Kinship Semantics. Unpublished paper.
  1998   On the Formal Analysis of "Dravidian," "Iroquois," and "Genera-
          tional" Varieties as Nearly Associative Combinations. In *Transforma-
          tions of Kinship,* edited by Maurice Godelier, Thomas R. Trautmann,
          and Franklin E. Tjon Sie Fat, pp. 59–93. Smithsonian Institution
          Press, Washington.
Todorov, Tzvetan
  1984   *The Conquest of America.* Harper and Row, New York.
Tooker, Elisabeth
  1978   The League of the Iroquois: Its History, Politics, and Ritual. In *Hand-
          book of North American Indians,* vol. 15, *Northeast,* edited by Bruce G.
          Trigger, pp. 418–441. Smithsonian Institution, Washington.
Toynbee, Arnold
  1972   *A Study of History,* revised and abridged, with Jane Caplan. Weather-
          vane Books, New York.
Trigger, Bruce G.
  1978   Early Iroquoian Contacts with Europeans. In *Handbook of North
          American Indians,* vol. 15, *Northeast,* edited by Bruce G. Trigger,
          pp. 344–356. Smithsonian Institution, Washington.
Tuck, James A.
  1985   Unearthing Red Bay's Whaling History. *National Geographic*
          168(1):50–57.
Utley, Robert M.
  1988   Indian–United States Military Situation, 1848–1891. In *Handbook of
          North American Indians,* vol. 4, *History of Indian-White Relations,* ed-
          ited by Wilcomb E. Washburn, pp. 163–184. Smithsonian Institution,
          Washington.

Valee, Frank G., Derek G. Smith, and Joseph D. Cooper

1984   Contemporary Canadian Inuit. In *Handbook of North American Indians,* vol. 5, *Arctic,* edited by David Damas, pp. 662–675. Smithsonian Institution, Washington.

Verano, John W., and Douglas H. Ubelaker

1992   *Disease and Demography in the Americas.* Smithsonian Institution Press, Washington.

Walthall, John A.

1980   *Prehistoric Indians of the Southeast: Archaeology of Alabama and the Middle South.* University of Alabama Press, Tuscaloosa.

Washburn, Wilcomb (editor)

1988   *History of Indian-White Relations.* Vol. 4 of *Handbook of North American Indians,* edited by William C. Sturtevant. Smithsonian Institution, Washington.

Watson, P. J., and M. Fotiadis

1990   The Razor's Edge: Symbolic-Structuralist Archaeology and the Expansion of Archaeological Inference. *American Anthropologist* 92:613–629.

Wauchope, Robert (editor)

1964– *Handbook of Middle American Indians.* 16 vols. plus supplements. Uni-
1976   versity of Texas Press, Austin. [This highly recommended series is complete.]

Webster, David

2002   *The Fall of the Ancient Maya: Solving the Mystery of the Maya Collapse.* Thames & Hudson. New York.

White, Leslie A.

1959   *The Evolution of Culture.* McGraw-Hill, New York.

Wilson, Samuel M.

1990   *Hispaniola: Caribbean Chiefdoms in the Age of Columbus.* University of Alabama Press, Tuscaloosa.

Wilson, Samuel M. (editor)

1997   *The Indigenous People of the Caribbean.* University Press of Florida, Gainesville.

Woodbury, Anthony C.

1984   Eskimo and Aleut Languages. In *Handbook of North American Indians,* vol. 5, *Arctic,* edited by David Damas, pp. 49–63. Smithsonian Institution, Washington.

1973   *The Cultural Geography of the United States.* Prentice-Hall, Englewood Cliffs, New Jersey.

Zorita, Alonso de
  1963   [ca. 1570] *Life and Labor in Ancient Mexico.* Translated by Benjamin
         Keen. Rutgers University Press, New Brunswick, New Jersey.
Zuidema, R. T.
  1990   *Inca Civilization in Cuzco.* University of Texas, Austin.

Index